S0-AJA-371

My Three Lives

My Three Lives

CELIA LIPTON FARRIS

PALM BEACH, FLORIDA

Published by IRC Promotions, Inc.
777 S. Flagler Drive, Suite 500-East
West Palm Beach, FL 33401

First printing February 2008

Copyright © 2008 IRC Promotions, Inc. [and assigns]
All rights reserved

Library of Congress Cataloging-In-Publication Data has been
applied for.
ISBN: 978-0-615-16596-7

Printed in the United States of America by Ellison Graphics
Corporation, Jupiter, Florida

Set in Caslon 540 with Trajan and Cochin Italic

Without limiting the rights under copyright reserved above, no
part of this publication may be reproduced, stored in or introduced
into a retrieval system, or transmitted, in any form, or by any
means (electronic, mechanical, photocopying, recording, or otherwise), without the prior written permission of the copyright owner
and publisher of this book.

The scanning, uploading, and distribution of this book via the
Internet or via any other means without the permission of the
publisher is illegal and punishable by law.

In memory of my husband
Victor W. Farris

and for Ce Ce, Marian,
Stephanie,
and my family

PROLOGUE

As a child growing up in London during World War II, enduring daily bombings, destruction, and death, I never dreamed that someday I would make my home in Palm Beach, Florida—a beautiful island bathed in sunshine with historic homes and residence to some of the most famous people in the world. Nor did I realize during those war-torn years in England, that my life would ultimately shape itself into three phases, three lives, if you will—all different, yet interwoven.

The road to Palm Beach has not been easy. Along the way, paths have led from London to New York, Los Angeles, and Florida.

Early in 2003, I received a long-distance call from a friend in London. We were at war. Allied troops were flying over enemy territory. My friend said, "I wanted to tell you that this morning I turned on the BBC World Service and heard your recording 'Maybe It's Because I'm A Londoner.' It was being played to the troops in Iraq."

As a singer, I was happy to hear my songs were being played. More years ago than I care to remember, I gave up my career in the London theatre and on Broadway. I had also entertained in war zones for the Army, Navy, Air Force, and Marine Corps. I had planned to stay in show business for the rest of my life. However, I gave it all up for love, marriage and family. Yet, now the troops were listening to me in Iraq. It made feel very good. But, also, so sad that the men and women of the armed services were once again in harm's way. Indeed, my life and career had come full circle—a life of extraordinary challenges and many blessings.

Captain Hook: "Who are you Peter Pan?"

Peter Pan: "I'm youth, I'm joy. I'm a little bird that's broken out of an egg."

"Peter Pan" – Sir James Barrie

PALM BEACH, FLORIDA . . . APRIL, 1995

As I prepared for my journey to London in May, where I would perform on stage in Hyde Park to help celebrate the 50th Anniversary of VE-Day, before Queen Elizabeth II and the entire Royal Family, and what turned out to be an audience of more than one-million people, memories were evoked of a Royal visit to Palm Beach 10 years earlier by His Royal Highness Prince Charles and Princess Diana.

The island has played host to a good many members of the Royal Family over the years, and they usually glide through their visits here, unmarred by controversy. But, the visit of Britain's future King, His Royal Highness Prince Charles, and Diana Princess of Wales in November 1985 was different. The guiding hand behind the visit of the Prince and Princess of Wales to Palm Beach was Armand Hammer and his benefit for the United World Colleges.

Mr. Hammer founded the United World Colleges and prevailed on Prince Charles to serve as president of the International Council. Prince Charles was interested by the largesse in Hammer's attempt to promote international understanding and encourage world peace through the United World Colleges' movement. Prince Charles has since stepped down as President.

Unlike the rather formal Palm Beach fundraising events, Armand Hammer's Ball soon became a cause célèbre. The first hint of trouble emerged when a few Palm Beach residents received their invitations in early September, to attend the Ball on November 12 at the Breakers Hotel. I was one of the invitees, having been an early donor to the United World Colleges. I remembered meeting His Royal Highness Prince Charles for the first time in May 1982 at Broadlands, Lord Mountbatten's estate in southern England. I was attending an event for the Mountbatten Memorial Trust. Lord Mountbatten, the last British Viceroy of India, was the Prince of Wales' favorite uncle. He was assassinated by the IRA in 1979.

8

Princess Diana and I at The Breakers, Palm Beach, 1985

The Charity Ball in Palm Beach was intended to benefit the College Armand Hammer had founded, and which His Royal Highness Prince Charles had dedicated in Montezuma, New Mexico, three years earlier. The invitations may have impressed some, but not Town Councilwoman Nancy Douthit, an heiress to the Simmons bedding fortune. She felt that the Town ordinance governing charitable solicitations had been violated because Hammer had not filed for, or received, a permit. Hammer had made many contacts in Soviet Russia, dating from the time of Stalin in the 1930s. These links irked some Palm Beachers.

At a meeting of the Town Council in September 1985, the matter was discussed. Attending were many town residents opposed to Armand Hammer's views at the time, and a representative from Armand Hammer's Occidental Petroleum Company who assured the Council that the Town would be reimbursed for any costs incurred by the Ball and the Royal Couple's visit. A letter to the Council the day before from Ball chairwoman, Patricia Kluge—then married to philanthropist and brilliant businessman John Kluge—promised the Council that organizers of the Ball would donate $75,000 to the Palm Beach Community Chest. The Council—with Councilwoman Nancy Douthit casting a nay—voted to grant the permit.

What started off as dissatisfaction with Hammer's international business dealings and his failure to follow permit rules, gathered even more controversy in Palm Beach. Some town residents, who wanted to attend and did not receive invitations, found that because of limited seating they couldn't even buy tickets priced at $10,000 per couple. Beneficiaries paid $50,000 a pair. Most of the invitations were being sent to Hollywood luminaries, nationally-known politicians, and business tycoons.

To quell the growing unrest, Mary Sanford—known as the "Queen of Palm Beach" at that time—was enlisted to serve on the Ball Committee. And serve she did, until a British magazine called "Knave" revealed that a decade before they had published a controversial picture of Mrs. John Kluge that the family did not like. Mrs. Sanford left town and did not attend the Ball. The Kluges issued a statement saying that they suddenly had to travel abroad so they would be unable to attend the Ball. But, the show did go on. And what a show!

Prince Charles and I at The Breakers, Palm Beach, 1985

Among the 500 guests who attended the event at The Breakers Hotel on November 12, 1995 were Bob Hope, Ted Turner, Gregory Peck, Ross Perot, Eva Gabor, United States Senator Albert and Mrs. Gore (Vice President' Gore's father and mother), Sherry Lansing, Jerry Weintraub, United State Senator Paula Hawkins, United States Congressman Dan Mica, and Victor Borge. Merv Griffin was Master of Ceremonies. One of Hollywood's best known British imports, actress Joan Collins, was there as well, looking absolutely beautiful and wearing a gown that showed off her many charms.

His Royal Highness Prince Charles was not fully aware of the sentiment held by some in Palm Beach—those who wanted to attend the Ball and could not, because so many out-of-towners were given precedence in obtaining tickets. In his after-dinner speech, he sounded a discordant note when he said he was fed up with the criticism that preceded the fundraising event, and extolled Armand Hammer's United World Colleges and its concept. Prince Charles could not have known of the suit filed the previous week in Palm Beach County Probate Court by Armand Hammer against the estate of his brother, Victor. The suit claimed that Victor Hammer was indebted to his brother for three promissory notes. Victor Hammer, whom I had known, was a dear, sweet man, whose life-long passion was art. He founded the Hammer Galleries as a young man.

I had planned to take my eldest daughter, Marian, with me to the gala. My daughter Ce Ce was in Baltimore at that time teaching kindergarten and was unable to join us at the event. By chance, a week before the event, I casually mentioned it to a sweet girl who handled my affairs at the bank, while we were on the telephone.

"Oh, Mrs. Farris, how wonderful," said Lise Dalpé Kenny. I detected the wistfulness in her voice, coupled with a charming and reserved curiosity. I asked whether she had ever been to a ball.

I heard her sigh before she answered, "No!" "Well, Dear, would you like to go with me?" I asked firmly, quickly making up my mind. On the other end of the phone there was silence. "Hello? Lise are you still there?" All I could hear on the telephone was electronic static. Then, a breathless, timid voice asked, "Are you sure? Do you mean it? Oh, Mrs. Farris!"

Then she squealed. The phone went silent again. "Hello? Lise, are you there?" "Yes Mrs. Farris," she responded. Her next question, "But, what will I wear? I don't have a ball gown," she cried. "Don't worry about that. Pop by the house when you get off work and we will rummage through my wardrobe. There should be a gown you would like to wear," I replied. Later, we picked out an exquisite black gown.

At the Ball Lise beamed with excitement and wonder as she peered wide-eyed at the glittering array of sophisticated, gowned women and suave men attending the formal affair. The gathering of society's top-drawer, film and show-business stars, and His Royal Highness Prince Charles and Diana Princess of Wales, against the back-drop of the palatial ballroom at The Breakers, surpassed any image seen on a movie or television screen. Looking back, I recall Lise took the pomp, protocol, and cere-mony in her stride.

I was more concerned with Marian, who got stage fright, and threatened to bolt from the receiving line even before we were to be presented to their Royal Highnesses. "Mother, I'm leaving," she whispered nervously, moving away from me. "I'm going to the ladies room,"–using any excuse she could think of. "No, you're not!" I hissed back at her, firmly grasping her wrist." You're going to meet His Royal Highness Prince Charles and Princess Diana if I have to handcuff you to me with a napkin!"

The butterflies in her stomach seemed to vanish as soon as she stood in front of the Prince. Bobbing a curtsey, Marian nervously blurted out to the Prince, "I'm terrified!" His Royal Highness Prince Charles, his eyes sparkling, gave her a lopsided smile of empathy and advised her, "Get yourself a scotch and water and you'll be fine. That's what I'm going to do in just a few minutes." Marian took his advice and, when Princess Diana stopped by our table later, she was completely at ease.

A bigger shock awaited us all the next morning when "The Palm Beach Post" front-page story said, " 'This is like a Cinderella story for me,' said Lise Dalpé, a 25-year-old Canadian, fortunate enough to have one of the best tickets. She attended her first ball with a warning from her mother. She said, 'Don't touch Princess Diana; Nancy Reagan got in trouble that way.' " Now Lise Kenny is married, a mother, and my valued secretary.

I felt a glow of happiness watching two young women thoroughly enjoying that evening. Perhaps it was the music, or being in the presence of Britain's future King, or the opulence of the room that had me remembering–or comparing–my un-Cinderella-like childhood in Britain.

His Royal Highness Prince Charles is now married to the Duchess of Cornwall. As I recall, the BBC came in to interview me in 2005 and I told them it was ridiculous to make comparisons.

The BBC flew in from Washington to interview me.

Edinburgh, Scotland

THE EARLY YEARS

I was born Celia Lipton in Edinburgh, Scotland.

My very beautiful Scottish mother

Lauder, Scotland

My beautiful Scottish mother, Marian Parker and my father, Sydney Lipton, the renowned British impresario and orchestra leader, both wanted me to receive an excellent education, attend a finishing school in Switzerland, marry an Englishman, and live a life far from the limelight…of show business, that is. But, I had other plans for myself.

An only child, I was born in Edinburgh. We visited our relatives in Scotland, every year, but I spent most of my life living in London. Every time I heard my father, who was an accomplished concert violinist, play, I would either sing or dance in accompaniment. By the time I was three, my mother, a world-champion dancer, took me to ballet classes and later to tap dancing classes—not to mention learning the Highland Fling from the Scottish lady herself!

My earliest recollection of live performances were in Edinburgh and Lauder (20 miles from Edinburgh), at the home of my maternal grandparents. In the evenings, my mother and her sister Esther would sing duets in harmony, while my grandfather played the organ, and Aunt Betty (another of my mother's sisters) danced the traditional Scottish Sword Dance, with two pokers substituting for swords.

By the time I was six I had become a "producer." I loved to imitate the stars I had seen in films. Bette Davis and Katherine Hepburn were my favorite impersonations. When my (London) cousins came for Sunday lunch I'd announce that we were going to put on a play. I had already made up the scenario and directed them on how to perform it. After some short rehearsals, and when I was satisfied with the performance of "my cast," I invited all the grownups to watch.

Marian Parker Lipton

I sang, I danced, I impersonated my favorite stars, I stood on my head, I became Lorna Doone, Tess of d'Ubervilles or Scarlett from "Gone With The Wind" in front of the mirror, and for my parents.

Being an only child often left me with a great deal of time on my own. I would spend those hours reading and then making believe I was the heroine, and I would act out her emotions in front of a mirror. I thought I was a bit of an ugly duckling because I was so thin, and sometimes because I would hear people remarking, "Poor child. Why doesn't she look like her mother?" they would say. And I would think to myself, "But I can sing, and dance, and stand on my head." My mother was blessed with a very curvaceous figure.

My mother was far too busy starring in her own dreams of romance with my father. It's true that horror stories abound about the children of unhappy marriages, but growing up in a blissfully happy marriage also has its drawbacks. My parents were so totally in love, so completely wrapped up in each other, that I never got quite the amount of attention I craved. Adding to that, my father's work took him out all night—every night—and my mother would accompany him. Consequently, they slept all morning.

An early photo of me in London.

Sydney Lipton, orchestra leader and impresario, was featured at the Grosvenor House Hotel for over 30 years, and on the BBC every Saturday.

Celia Lipton, left, and with her Father's Band, below

At that time experts were predicting an outstanding future for my father, as a great classical violinist. So we moved from Edinburgh to London where he could pursue his career. He had started the violin at age seven and had studied with James Matthews, who was a conductor of the Hallé Orchestra in Britain and professor of violin at the Royal Academy of Music in London. My father then went on to study with the Russian violinist, Sasha Lassersohn.

My parents were planning a future where Sydney Lipton would become a world-renowned artist, performing for standing-room-only audiences in all the major capitals of the world. But, all those hopes were dashed when I was about seven. Our little family was taking its customary Saturday summer walk on Clapham Common in London. Parks in London and the Common were always filled with old-fashioned deck chairs provided by the local authority, and available for rent at just a few pennies. The weather that day was sunny and my father rented chairs. One of them, made of old wood and held together on rusty hinges, was stuck. My father wrestled to open it and the deck chair snapped, slicing off the flesh of the top joint (the cushion) on the first (index) finger of his left hand. As the blood streamed down his hand, the pain of his injury and the painful knowledge that he might never become a concert violinist at all overcame my father.

Both of them wept. And, so did I. It was the first time I had seen my parents cry. The injured finger was the one that is of critical importance to a violinist. All the fingers of the left hand are necessary to play the violin. As there are no frets on that instrument, as with a guitar, the index finger is the one used for measurement and accuracy in key and tone–moving from one position to another.

My father was rushed to the hospital where his injured finger was stitched. The once-soft cushion of his first finger was now hard. A classical violinist needs a soft cushion to play well, and his plan to join the newly formed BBC Symphony Orchestra, directed and conducted by Sir Thomas Beecham, was dashed. The prospects for my father's future appeared to be bleak, indeed.

My father lost work in recording sessions and concerts and, although my mother was a great manager, our family of three was broke. My mother's sister helped us temporarily. Meanwhile, I didn't register a change in the lifestyle, or that we were going through times of trouble. As a conductor and musician, work was sporadic for my father, and my mother, in her typically Scottish way, was far too disciplined to let me know what was really going on.

Soon luck came my father's way when he became the Music and Entertainment Director of the Grosvenor House Hotel–then, and now, one of London's most elegant hotels, the equivalent of what was once New York's Plaza Hotel.

His talent combined with good fortune then led to his conducting the Grosvenor House Hotel Orchestra for more than 30 years, which began broadcasting every Tuesday and some select Saturday evenings on BBC Radio. England tuned in to hear the words, "You are listening to Sydney Lipton's Orchestra broadcasting from the Silver Room at the Grosvenor House Hotel."

This was the heyday of big bands; such as, Glenn Miller, Artie Shaw, Benny Goodman, Harry James, Tommy Dorsey, and Count Basie. All over Britain and America, every age group danced to the sound of Swing. The big bands were spectacular in those days, and so popular.

My father's band was one of the most popular in England, and, even today, some people nostalgically remember dancing to the music of Sydney Lipton and his Orchestra. They played for eight consecutive annual household parties at

Buckingham Palace and for special events at Windsor Castle, attended by Her Majesty Queen Elizabeth II and other members of the Royal Family in the 1950s.

During one of the appearances at Buckingham Palace, my mother was invited to attend. Her gown that night was à la Scarlett O'Hara–tight bodice, and ultra-bouffant from the waist down. The "bouffant" effect was achieved by the very full crinoline petticoat she wore underneath. Once the dancing began, my mother never missed a turn. One of the gentlemen she danced with was Peter Townsend. He was attending the event with Princess Margaret.

Around midnight, my father's orchestra played "God Save the Queen," and the dancing was over. The orchestra packed up, and my parents proceeded out of Buckingham Palace, across the parade ground, when the elastic on my mother's crinoline gave way, and her petticoat sank to the ground. Looking neither to the left, nor to right, as if nothing had happened, my mother stepped out of the petticoat and the crinoline, then kept on walking.

My father and his band also played for Sophie Tucker and Edgar Bergen–Bergen and my father became close friends–and, for Edward, Prince of Wales, who abdicated the throne and married Mrs. Simpson. He was very amused when Prince Edward would get on the drums and played with the orchestra. My father also played for Humphrey Bogart, Charlie Chaplin, Barbara Hutton, the Duke and Duchess of Westminster, Sir Thomas Lipton (who enjoyed his music), and Margaret Sweeney (who later became the Duchess of Argyll).

I don't know if all that glory compensated my father for his dream of a career as a concert violinist. But, he threw himself into his new career and was successful as an orchestra leader, although this vocation never seemed to take the place of his original ambition. So once in a while, he played the violin.

While my father was launching his career at the Grosvenor House Hotel, my mother was busy deciding on the best schooling for me. My Godmother convinced my parents that a Catholic education was the best in the world. Although I was baptized Episcopalian, I was dispatched to St. Joseph's Convent boarding school in Hendon, North London. At that time, British boarding schools were strict and very regimented institutions that were supposed to build character. Thank God things have changed over the years. No doubt the good nuns at St. Joseph's were only putting into practice the words of Mr. Squeer, a character in the Charles Dickens novel, "Nicholas Nickleby": "Curb your appetites my dears, and you've conquered human nature."

We were always hungry and never seemed to get enough sleep, certainly not with a wake-up call at six a.m. In the vast dormitory we would rise from our hard cots, separated from each other by curtains. Beside our cots was a small table on which sat a large jug of cold water and a washbasin, a towel, soap, toothpaste, a toothbrush, a brush, and a comb. Behind the curtains we would perform our morning ritual of washing with cold water, which dipped to freezing when winter set-in. We then dressed and assembled for prayers, which were followed by rigorous inspection of uniform, hair, nails, and teeth.

My grades were dreadful, I was unhappy and frightened. I was still only interested in dancing, singing and impersonation. The one teacher I liked at the Convent was the piano teacher, and I wanted to be her student. But my father had other plans. He wanted me to follow in his footsteps. Some weekends I was allowed to go home, where my father arranged for James Matthews to come down from Manchester to give me lessons. For hours on end I would play the violin, but my fingers hurt so badly, and I was so unhappy, that my parents finally gave in to my pleas and allowed me to give it up in favor of the piano. I returned to school and began my lessons with the angelic nun who was the piano teacher.

I did very well studying the piano and was also becoming fascinated by Catholicism. When I came home one weekend, I informed my parents that I wanted to convert to Catholicism. That wish never materialized, because we moved to Surrey and that meant I would have to leave St. Joseph's.

I was enrolled in a day school, the Miss Fordham's School for Young Ladies, in Surbiton, Surrey—a suburb of London. Although the school's atmosphere was vastly different from what I had become accustomed to at St. Joseph's, I quickly adapted. I liked my brown school uniform and made new friends.

My friends and I were often taken to the movies. And, after every movie we saw, in my imagination I became one of the stars in the film. Once, after watching Katherine Hepburn perform in a part that required masses of curls on the forehead, I appeared at school with a hairstyle à la Hepburn's. It wasn't long before Miss Fordham, the head mistress (an awesome figure), sent for me in her study. Trembling with fear, I stood before her as she demanded to know what I had done to my hair.

I always loved sports.

After I explained, she produced a hairbrush and a bucket full of cold water, and swiftly put an end to my day as Miss Katherine Hepburn.

Recognition was what I sought, and it finally came my way after we had moved to an area called Berrylands, a short train ride from Surbiton. At that time I was going through a tomboy phase (probably inspired by Katherine Hepburn's performance as Jo March in "Little Women"). And, although I practically lived on chocolate bars, chocolate being one of my passions, I was painfully thin like a streak of lightening going across the field. I seemed to have incredible energy for sports like netball (basketball in America). I also loved climbing trees, and spent many hours clambering up the branches that overlooked a mud-filled, rat-infested stream that ran parallel with the railroad tracks.

On one such tree-climbing expedition, I lost my footing and began to fall. Saving myself by catching on to a branch, I screamed for help, petrified at the thought of plunging into the stream and being attacked by the water rats.

Suddenly, what seemed like hundreds of people (most of them on their way home from the railroad station) rushed in my direction just before my would-be rescuer reached me. I fell into the stream, and was pulled to safety by a kindly man who waded in to help. I rushed home covered in mud, slipped into the back door of the

Photo: November Books Ltd.

Sydney Lipton and his orchestra at the Grosvenor House Hotel.

house, determined to scrub myself clean before my mother and father could see me and call a halt to my tree-climbing adventures.

My mission was almost accomplished when the phone rang. My father answered. He was informed by a newspaper reporter that his daughter had almost drowned in a river. The shock and incredulity was palpable in my father's voice. Realizing I had better show myself, because my parents were not aware that I was in the house safe and sound, I came to the phone and told the reporter the whole story. The end result was my first press mention. The story headlined: "Sydney Lipton's Daughter in Near Fatal Drowning Accident."

Right after this "near fatal accident," my mother began taking me to the Grosvenor House Hotel, where, still dressed in my school uniform, I watched my father rehearse with the orchestra. I got to know all the musicians, and they took on the semblance of being my father's family.

Then MCA Corporation began flying in American shows with stars. The show-girls were a popular draw at the Grosvenor House Hotel. I was completely fascinated by those almost-six-foot-tall beauties with their masses of platinum-blonde hair. To me, a little English schoolgirl, watching them parade across the stage, was the epitome of glamour.

American show girls rehearsing at the Silver Room, MCA shows, Grosvenor House Hotel.

For my mother, however, the showgirls represented a threat. Always violently jealous of my father, my mother guarded him fiercely. My father was the famous Sydney Lipton of the Grosvenor House Hotel. It seemed to her that every woman in the universe (as well she might) found my father attractive. She started out sitting with me in rehearsals, quite content to watch my father conduct. Suddenly, her eyes would narrow, and she'd grip my arm and whisper in outrage about some blonde, the third on the left, the one in the purple organza, who had her eye on my father. She could be quite insistent. I would look at her in astonishment for imagining something that simply wasn't so.

My mother's jealousy would often erupt into a blazing rage, and my father would end up sleeping on the couch. Since my mother was living in an era when it was legendary for showgirls to snare English Lords or multi-millionaires, she felt her concerns were justifiable.

While my mother was jealously guarding my father, I was living in two worlds. One world – the duller one – was a world in which I played with my little dog Scottie (who kept running away, even though my father built higher and higher fences).

Another world was going to school where I devoured the classics, and landed the part of Puck in a school play of Shakespeare's, "A Midsummer Night's Dream."

We were studying Shakespeare heavily at the time. I fantasized about one day becoming a great actress, especially after my performance impressed enough people in the audience who approached my mother and told her that I was talented.

It was full of stars – "My Grosvenor House world." The Silver Room of the Hotel was the center of my exciting world, and I was delighted when I was allowed to celebrate my birthdays there on Christmas night. The hotel's entire staff celebrated with me, which included the Maitre d', headwaiters, waiters, senior waitresses, waitresses, chefs, bus boys and the ladies who supervised the powder rooms. Then as the orchestra played "Happy Birthday," it seemed as if the whole world, my "Grosvenor House Hotel world" was celebrating.

The Hotel world was a sophisticated universe through which I roamed (very much like Eloise at the Plaza – from the American book), a little English school-girl enthralled with the leggy showgirls smelling of Chanel No. 5, sipping champagne, and passing me sugary pink-and-white petite fours. I loved their American accents, their masses of platinum-blonde hair, jewel-encrusted false eyelashes, long carmine-colored fingernails, and the diamond bracelets wrapped around their elegant wrists. Growing up around that hotel, I highly recommended it!

Sometimes, the showgirls let me play with their vast make-up cases, complete with multicolored eye shadow and pancake. They laughed indulgently as they carefully painted my lips with an array of reds. I listened to their every word as they discussed Lords, Ladies, satin gowns, diamonds, and furs. They looked like goddesses. I remember thinking that I wanted to be just like them when I grew up. Prior to meeting them I had wanted to be a nun, quite a change for a young girl.

When I wasn't at the Grosvenor House Hotel on the weekends, I would go skating with my school friend Marjorie at the Silver Blades Rink in Richmond, near our home. At that stage of my life, I was still very naïve about the facts of life because no one had enlightened me. When I met Tony, a schoolboy on whom I had developed a crush, on the roof of the Silver Blades Rink, I began to get my first sense of the battle of the sexes. After a few moments of conversation, Tony inexplicably stuck his hand down the top of my dress. I remember thinking, "Why is he doing that? He isn't going to find anything!"

Deciding that I was obviously not cut out for romance, at least not at that moment, I turned my attention to my consuming passion – show business. One day, when I was about 14, I read in the paper that a search was underway for a young girl who could sing and talk like Judy Garland. She would appear with the BBC Symphony Orchestra and Chorus on a radio broadcast of the sound track from the MGM film, "Babes in Arms." The live broadcast was scheduled to be repeated three times. Without telling my parents what I planned to do, I resolved to audition.

I didn't tell them because I was reasonably sure they would stop me. But I thought that if I succeeded in winning the role, my parents would finally take my talent seriously. From the time I was three years old, I had a deep-rooted feeling that I not only wanted to perform, but I had to perform. Alone, I took the bus to the BBC studios and arrived at the audition, not at all nervous, but extremely surprised to find 400 other "would-be Judy's" accompanied by their mothers and fathers, all auditioning for the Garland role in "MGM's Babes in Arms." Somehow it never occurred to me that there would be any competition. I was just so sure that I was destined to fill the role. To me Judy Garland was a great talent and I had taught myself to sing and talk like her, and to emulate her every gesture.

When it came my turn to audition, I was in my element. I was no longer Celia Lipton. I was Judy Garland right down to her American accent and her slight lisp. After my performance, the hall that had been full of noise suddenly fell silent. A booming voice that seemed to come from heaven said, "Little girl, don't leave. I want to talk to you." The voice turned out to be that of Douglas Moody, the producer, who had been watching the auditions from a viewing-box.

While I was waiting for him to come down from his lofty perch, it suddenly dawned on me that I would have some explaining to do to my parents. I was also worrying about how I was going to explain to the producer that I was not only unaccompanied by either of my parents, but also that I was there auditioning without their permission.

But all apprehension was cast aside when the producer arrived and told me I was "terrific." Then he asked, "Where is your agent?" "He's sick," I replied. "Where is your mother?" he inquired. "She could not make it," I said. He told me he had to talk to someone because I was underage. "Where is your father?" he sighed. I shook my head again and hesitantly said, " I don't know."

Finally, I gave Douglas Moody my father's name, he exclaimed with excitement and enthusiasm, "Oh, yes, your father is a friend of mine." He asked me to wait while he went off to telephone my father. I imagined my father would be extremely upset and demand that I be sent home immediately. The telephone call seemed to take an eternity. Now, I was scared.

It was a perplexed, but smiling Douglas Moody who told me that my father was "in shock." Mr. Moody had got an earful. "I was far too young and inexperienced," but he had managed to persuade my father that I was the one and he wanted me. This would be tremendous publicity for the show, "MGM's Babes In Arms."

Sensing a good story that would appeal to any journalist worth his salt, Moody made another call. The next thing I knew, I was in a taxi and on my way to my first ever newspaper interview—with Jonah Barrington of the British national newspaper, "The Daily Express." Jonah, a charming man, put me at ease at once, asked me to impersonate Judy Garland, and then applauded enthusiastically as I did my Garbo and Hepburn imitations for him.

He wrote in the paper: "Biggest radio role of the War—Judy Garland in the "Babes In Arms" broadcast went yesterday, by unanimous vote, to 14-year-old Celia Lipton, daughter of band leader Sydney Lipton. It was a triumph because if there hadn't been a Celia Lipton there probably would be no broadcast, since the BBC does not consider that anyone else could carry the part. She is on, talking and singing in the Garland style throughout the show. She's done it all off her own bat without any help from dad, who has resolutely opposed her going into show business since she was a child. Slim, fresh, sparkling and hazel-eyed. Totally unspoiled. Ambitious (she means to be a film star or bust) and a non-swollen headed. A genius for impersonation."

Reluctantly, my father gave his blessing to my show business career, warning me, "Be in show business if you want, but don't ever let me hear that you were late for musicians and rehearsals." I always remembered that. I was so thrilled to be performing at last, that I planned to be early for every single rehearsal, and to work very hard.

The first of the three proposed broadcasts was "Babes In Arms," in which I would sing, "I'm Just Wild About Harry," "I Cried for You," and "Good Morning, Good Morning." Mickey was played by a child actor named John Singer, and he, the cast of other children, and I, rehearsed endlessly.

I also studied with a teacher, Miss O'Brian from the Royal Academy of Dramatic Art. Insisting that I wanted to make the most of my big opportunity, I convinced my parents to let me leave school and finish my education with a succession of tutors.

When "Babes In Arms" was broadcast, I was described as "Britain's Judy Garland." Today, everyone forgets how vital radio used to be in the lives of people. Whole families used to plan their weekly schedules around their favorite radio programs they would cluster around the radio and visualize a whole other world.

Soon after the "Babes In Arms" broadcast, my parents and I went up to Lauder, Scotland, for our annual visit. When we arrived and walked down the village street, the villagers peeked out from behind their curtains and some, having seen my picture in newspapers, waved and shouted things like, "Lassie, we heard you on the radio." It was great fun! At my grandfather's home, we had musical evenings of fun and warmth, with all of us singing, while my father played the violin, and my mother led the singing.

Back in London, time seemed to fly by. The BBC hired me to broadcast two more Garland soundtracks, "The Wizard of Oz" and "Strike Up the Band," each three times. Jules Stein and the MCA Corporation wanted me to come to America, but my father put his foot down saying, "She's too young." Thanks Dad! When the broadcasts with the BBC were over, I knew I would never give up show business. Not now. I also knew that, as much as I had been initially gratified by it, I had to change my title of "Britain's Judy Garland." I needed to be recognized "as Celia Lipton," but that was to happen a few years later.

I hadn't fully realized, until I started touring, that I was quite well-known throughout the land. I had recorded, "Good Morning, Good Morning" for Columbia Records when I was 15 and the record was a hit. As a result of this record and my BBC broadcasts, I had become something of a household name in England. In 1940, the trade newspaper "Melody Maker" voted me, together with Vera Lynn and Anne Shelton, the top three vocalists in the country. I had only been singing for a year professionally. The appreciative audiences, for whom I performed while on tour, never let me forget that they knew exactly who I was and how they felt about me. They never made me feel like a child, or that I was something on the order of a child prodigy. They made me feel like a star.

Several years after, I was appearing in Plymouth and through Judy's agent, Harry Foster, who was also representing me, I found out that he had booked her into the London Palladium. Judy was due to arrive in Plymouth aboard a ship, and Harry had calculated docking time down to the minute. He had also found out how long the ship would be at anchor waiting for a berth. So he arranged to have a group of reporters join him aboard a tender that would go out to the ship and get Judy off before the vessel docked. The rationale behind this maneuver, according to Harry, was to avoid the fans.

I asked Harry if I could join him on the tender to meet Judy. Gently, Harry explained that the tender was being used solely for the press and himself, and it wouldn't be appropriate for me to tag along. Undaunted, I decided that I was going to see Judy anyway! If I couldn't be on the tender, I'd hire my own boat, which is precisely what I did. I found an old fisherman, who was willing to take me out aboard his motorboat, and "intercept" the tender once it was underway.

We set out on choppy waters and soon saw the tender heading in our direction. Realizing that it was progressing at a speed that would pass us quickly, the fisherman maneuvered his boat into the lane of the oncoming vessel. This forced the tender to slow to a snail's pace. Once it was abeam, the fisherman told me to "hold fast," because he was going to get his boat ready to start circling the other vessel. I "held fast," until I caught sight of Judy and Harry, and then all caution was thrown to the wind.

I stood up waving and shouting, "Welcome to Plymouth, Judy!" Judy waved back and blew me a kiss and Harry, apparently impressed by my ingenuity, held his hands up displaying the "V-for-Victory" sign.

When Judy's show opened at the Palladium, I sent her flowers in the shape of a boat with a card inscribed, "From the girl on the boat." My mother and I attended the opening. I just adored her. After the show, we went backstage and met her. When we were introduced, she smiled her winning smile and told us that we were the prettiest mother and daughter she had ever seen. She said that she could sense how close we were, and admitted that she wished it could have been that way for her. From that moment on, I felt strangely protective towards Judy. She was so vulnerable; it almost broke one's heart. I saw her again, many years later, in Nassau, where we were staying at the same hotel.

One day, after we had lunch together, we visited the ladies room to primp before we sallied forth, and Judy, always witty, sighed with relief that we were alone, confiding, "Usually, when I go to the 'Ladies,' I can't even pee because people keep sliding autograph books under the door for me to sign."

My Judy Garland broadcasts were over. Once again, the newspaper came to my rescue. I read that one of my father's rivals, Jack Harris, an American orchestra leader, was auditioning a replacement for his singer, Pat Taylor. Using the example of the Grosvenor House Hotel showgirls as what someone in American show business would appreciate, I applied heavy make-up, put on a pair of outrageously high heels and, under the name of "Celia," I auditioned for Jack Harris, who was looking to replace Dinah Miller in a show. When he told me that he intended to hire me, I confessed whose daughter I was. Highly amused, he picked up the phone and, said to my father, "Syd, I've got your kid here—she just auditioned for me."

Jack Harris, holding the phone away from his ear, let me hear my father's exasperated response, "Oh no, not again!" Un-phased, my father's rival added that he wanted to pay me £7 a week. My father recalled the incident in a radio interview many years later, in 1993: "Jack Harris came back to me on the telephone and said that he wanted to engage Celia as a singer and I thought, to hell with it. If she's going to sing with a band, she'll sing with my band and I can keep an eye on her."

I didn't know it at the time, but in the National Jazz Archives, Jack was quoted as saying, "We all feel she has possibilities of (being) the best girl vocalist the country's ever had." My father's conditions were that I would pass my school exams and keep up my piano practice. Sam Browne, a good friend and well-known singer, had coached me on microphone technique.

By auditioning for Jack Harris, I had forced my father's hand. And perhaps that was the way I had subconsciously planned it. Apart from the childhood performances for my London relatives, and the impromptu family performances in Scotland, what followed was my first performance before a live, paying audience. I appeared with my father's orchestra at the London Palladium where he gave a Sunday concert. I was nervous. Not because of the concert attendees who filled the Theatre, and not because my father was there. I knew instinctively that my future would depend a great deal on how I was received by this audience.

My father introduced me with the words, "A little girl is coming out to sing for you, and her name is Celia." With that, I came out on stage, my nervousness suddenly dissolving, and I sang, "I'm Just In-Between." Then with the applause still resounding in my ears, I sang an encore, "You're As Pretty As a Picture." When the applause subsided, my father took my hand, and alternated at looking out at the audience and smiling down at me. He paused and said: "I'll let you into a secret: this little girl is my daughter." The crowd went wild.

I made my first radio debut less than a week later with my father's orchestra, and within a few months I sang at the "Jazz Jamboree" in aid of the Musician's Union. Our orchestra regularly appeared alongside those of Joe Loss, Ambrose, Geraldo, Al Collins, Jack Jackson. In his review for the "Melody Maker," in April 1939, Mathison Brooks wrote, "If she [Celia] isn't destined for high musical comedy honors I will eat my editorial hat... Daddy looked very proud of her, as well he might, when the audience, cheering the child wildly, showed that it knew a good thing when it saw one."

Soon after this, my father signed a contract with Decca and I cut my first recording in October 1939–just after the outbreak of World War II. I sang "We're Going To Hang Out The Washing On The Siegfried Line"–an allusion to the defensive guns, pillboxes, and tank traps on the Nazi-German side of the border with France. I shared the vocal chorus with Ivor Davies, and other members of the Grosvenor House Dance Orchestra.

Lew Stone engaged me in January 1940 for his recording on the Decca label of "My Wubba Dolly." A couple of days later, Jack Hylton–who was to become one of the leading British impresarios, orchestra leaders, and television producer after the war–recorded with me on the HMV label, "There'll Never Be Another You" and "Let The People Sing."

Columbia Records put me under contract, and I recorded at Abbey Road Studios where the Beatles would eventually record. Some of the songs I recorded included, "How About You," "For Me And My Gal," "Good Morning, Good Morning," "Where Or When," "Wrap Yourself In Cotton Wool," "Tangerine," "Blues In The Night," "It's A Hap-Hap-Happy Day," "Over The Rainbow," "Kiss The Boys Goodbye," and "Dearly Beloved." The company's recording of me singing Charles Trenet's, "Boom!" in November 1940, caused some surprise in the business since the song required me to perform in French, as well as in English, which was quite different at the time.

The first year of the war was a hectic time for me. All performers were expected to support the war effort, and I was no exception. Indeed, I wanted to do everything I could to support the war effort, as everyone did.

JANUARY, 1942   NINEPENCE

THEATRE WORLD

Celia Lipton performing her own act,"Applesauce," at the London Palladium. In the early days of her theatrical career she sang with her father's Orchestra, The Sydney Lipton Orchestra.

The cover of "Theatre World" magazine featured my performance at the London Palladium at age 15.

I was often on the BBC Forces Program. In February 1941, I was obviously the right actress to do the "Judy Garland Story." (Judy remained immensely popular in Britain right up to her death in 1969. I was devastated. So, I painted Judy with a bouquet of yellow roses. She would be so proud of her daughter Liza Minnelli, who has carried on the great family tradition in the theatre and films.)

Of course, at that age particularly, I did not neglect the social scene that London had to offer. On the declaration of war on September 3, 1939, the government closed all the theatres, dance halls and cinemas—a knee-jerk reaction to the crisis. They were reopened in two weeks and, although no longer lit up because of blackout, were as boisterous as ever. I was dying of curiosity about what went on in the nightclubs of London. After a great deal of beseeching, my father took me to a club called the Suivi. I remember him cautioning me beforehand, saying that I was going to be very disappointed; there was nothing to nightclubs. They were very dark, everybody drank, and I wouldn't like it. But he was wrong—I loved it!

I danced with David Niven, and the well-known, British photographer, Anthony Beauchamp. After that I wanted to dance, dance my head off. Acting as my chaperone, my father allowed me to dance with others—when he was sitting one out. One night, my visits with my father to the clubs came to a screeching halt. Baron, the Society photographer, decided that he wanted to dance with me. Instead of waiting for my father's permission, he kept cutting in while my father and I were dancing. Baron kept insisting that my father had danced enough with his beautiful girlfriend, now he wanted to dance with me. My father refused. After about half-a-dozen attempts by Baron to cut in, my father decided that we should leave. On the way home he told me sternly that he was no longer going to escort me to clubs because he was not prepared to encounter any more of these type of gentlemen. "Now you know what nightclubs are all about," he remarked. But, I was still fascinated!

I was now without an escort, which was serious. No escort, no clubs, but, it wasn't too long before I resolved the problem. At a friend's tea I met two young brothers, university students, who happened to be my neighbors. The brothers, George and Dick, loved to spend time with me. I told them I knew that most of the stars went to the Club Les Ambassadeurs, and among the glitterati were the likes of Rex Harrison, Patricia Medina, Laurence Olivier, Vivien Leigh, Kay Kendall, Deborah Kerr, Joseph Cotton, and many more.

When I confided to my two new friends my desire to go to Les Ambassadeurs, so I could dance and study the beautiful actresses glittering in the lights of the nightclub, they responded in unison that they would take me. I was elated. It was George who helped me with my earliest "gilding." He introduced me to my first pair of spike heels, and showed me how to apply make-up that would make me look older, so he could secretly take me out dancing at nightclubs.

One of the "in" places, particularly for university students, was a club at the Cavendish Hotel, owned by Rosa Lewis, who has been the subject of several television documentaries, and was the mistress of King Edward VII. The King's death must have left a lasting void in her life, or so it seemed to me judging by her attire. Rosa Lewis would appear from behind black, filmy curtains swathed in widow's weeds, her face totally hidden by her black veil. I was mesmerized by her mystery and theatricality. And enthralled enough, to want to go back to her club, more than once, after George took me.

Another, less bizarre encounter took place when Dick and George took me to a party being hosted by a star in the theatrical world—Hermione Gingold. She used to hold court, not in the usual quarters for entertaining, but in her bedroom—in her bed, no less, surrounded by friends. When I was introduced to her, she recognized me from the publicity as Sydney Lipton's daughter and declared henceforth that I was to be called "Baby Cel."

But, the war clouds over Europe ended all those carefree adventures. Just before my whole world changed, I was to be taken to the Royal Ascot races, near Windsor Castle—my first visit there—by Edward Rayne, the Rayne-Delman shoe heir, and the son of my parent's close friends. Edward Rayne was to later receive the OBE and eventually become a member of the British House of Lords.

I shall never forget the outfit I wore to Ascot that day—it was a white eyelet gown, with a huge eyelet hat to match. Unfortunately, the color white was not the perfect choice. Following the races my outfit was closer to a grayish-black after picking up the dirt and dust floating around. I didn't care—I had been to Ascot. There I had munched away to my heart's delight on strawberries and quail eggs.

(Years later, when I was living my third life—in Palm Beach—and decided to recapture that exciting day at Ascot by making arrangements to attend the races there in the summer of 1992, I found I needed the intervention of an American Congressman to gain admittance! But, more about that later.)

Captain Lipton on leave from the Army.

London under siege during the blitz.

My career with my father's orchestra skidded to a halt when he decided to join the army during World War II. Always a man of principle, his conscience was continually disturbed by the ever-increasing parade of fighting men who spent their leave dancing at the Grosvenor House Hotel. When American bandleader Glenn Miller enlisted in the army, he took his orchestra with him, but my father didn't follow suit. He enlisted with Her Majesty's Royal Corps of Signals as Signalman Lipton and trained in Wales. Later, he was commissioned as Second Lieutenant in the Royal Artillery, and then promoted to Captain.

My father was away for seven years. My mother and I had to learn to get along without him. Apart from writing him 22 letters every week, my mother spent much of her time waiting on tables for the American Red Cross.

At night she was a firewatcher, assigned to help put out any fires on the roof of our building, caused by incendiary bombs. I recall my mother on her first night running up and down our hallway with a tin helmet on her head, she was almost weeping and trembling, and did not want to go on the roof. "I don't like being the chief firewatcher," she said.

"Look out the window mummy," I said. "They won't miss you...the whole of London is on fire!" In the end, she went to the roof, and I went down into the shelter alone.

But more often than not, she was on tour with me as I developed my stage career. My father's departure meant that there were no more nights singing with the orchestra at the Grosvenor House Hotel. But, as usually happens, as one door closed another door opened. Jack Hylton, a famous orchestra leader who was also an acclaimed producer, and one of England's top talent agents, offered to manage me. Naturally, I accepted and soon was touring in Vaudeville all over England. It was the best training any performer could have.

I was being paid what was then a princely sum of £100 a week. I had become a star. Even so, life was fairly short on glamour. My mother and I would travel all over Great Britain from one performance stop to the next. I performed in Bradford in England; then to Scotland, where I performed in Edinburgh, Glasgow, and Aberdeen; then to Ireland, where I performed in Dublin; then to Wales where I performed in Cardiff. Each Sunday, it was another town, another city–Liverpool, Leeds, Hull, Coventry, Bristol, Manchester, Plymouth, Southampton, Oxford, Cambridge,

Brighton, and many more that I cannot remember. Being "on the road" was not easy and, in fact, most of our traveling was done by rail because gasoline was rationed.

In Edinburgh, Scotland—where I was born—I played in "Skylarks," by Gordon Courtney, at the Empire Theatre. It was a variation on the theme of the return of the prodigal son, only I was the "prodigal daughter." With England at war, the trains, when they were running, were packed with soldiers, sailors, and airmen. If you were able to get aboard, it often meant standing all the way to your destination. Somehow the interminable standing never bothered me, because I was on my way to do what mattered the most to me—to perform.

Once we finally arrived at our destination, we'd be full of trepidation about what the "digs"—as we'd call the hotels and boarding houses in which we stayed—would be like. Many of places we stayed in were lovely, especially some of the hotels. It all depended on the town. When we returned from the theatre at midnight to a place that was dimly lit, on a grimy back street, and the dinner provided was frozen cod or beans on toast, we'd all fall into bed feeling exhausted and hungry.

In the morning, I would be up bright and early and go directly to the theatre, where I would rehearse with orchestras that were not always up to par. Many of the orchestra's regulars were in the armed services, and those who filled in for them did the best they could. But, less-than-perfect accompaniment can result in a less-than-perfect performance for an artist. So I began bringing my own pianist with me for all my performances. Before leaving the theatre, I'd check the lights, test that the curtain didn't stick, find out what the backdrop was (so I could decide what to wear), and make sure the piano was properly tuned. Usually I had my own dressing room, but sometimes conditions were dusty, dirty, dank, and not good for the voice at all. Some theatres were better than others.

I worked with child acrobats, accordionists, dog acts, and British stars like Max Miller (known as the "Cheeky Chappie," because his jokes were somewhat off-color), Arthur Askey, and Tommy Trinder (British household names until their deaths in the 1970s and 1980s). Also on the road in this time frame was Julie Andrews, traveling with her parents. Although we never worked together, we often stayed at the same lodgings, but kept missing each other.

Celia Lipton has just been introduced to London by Mr. Black as the singing star of " Get a Load of This." Celia is also a brilliant mimic, and her radio impression of Judy Garland could hardly be distinguished from the " real thing."

My early act, which included singing and imitating Katherine Hepburn (photo right) and others, prompted George Black to sign me up at the age of 17 in "Get A Load of This."

Two young comedians that I worked with in those days were Eric Morecambe and Ernie Wise, who were gaining enormous popularity doing separate acts in a Bryan Michie production called "Discoveries." They decided to team up this time and do an act together. Before one of their rehearsals, they asked me to watch them and to tell them what I thought. It was the prototype of the future "Morecambe and Wise Show," which I was the first to see. I was flattered to be told that my approval was important because I was top of the bill. At the time they were 15 years old, and eventually became famous, on both sides of the Atlantic, as Morecambe and Wise.

I sat in on many of their rehearsals. They were so screamingly funny that I found myself encouraging them. I am proud to have been among the first to see their work. I sometimes look back on my Vaudeville years from the perspective of my life today in Palm Beach, and wonder just how I endured the cold, damp, dingy boarding houses, the dirty railway stations, the bombs falling, and the sheer hard work.

I appeared in old Victorian theatres, whose once-grand façades were crumbling, on stages that had seen better days. I recall working with an extremely enterprising husband-and-wife team known as the "Great Garcias." The wife walked a tight-rope from the stage right up into the gallery and then–hanging onto an umbrella–slid back again (over the audience's heads) to the stage, where her husband was waiting for her.

Life on the road during the Blitz was grim. Once, I arrived in Bristol to record a show for the BBC after the night's heavy bombing. We couldn't find the studio because the BBC had gone underground. Nothing was left except bombed-out streets and water hoses. We were horrified. But, eventually we became used to all the devastation around us–we had to, to survive. Although I was scared that a bomb would fall during one of my performances, the minute I went on stage I forgot about that, and sang my heart out. I loved being in Vaudeville because I was in control of my own act. I could choose the songs to sing.

Normally, I did two shows a night, and on days off I sang at benefits for the troops. I sang on warships in Portsmouth, and at every Red Cross Club in London for American servicemen (who loved my impersonations of American stars), and I performed my own act at the Palladium. On that occasion, my entrance was unique, coming up from underneath the stage in a life-size radio, while singing "Over the Rainbow." It was tremendously effective at the Palladium. In one performance

Performing for the American Armed Forces at the Red Cross Club, London.
This photo was taken by a soldier and given to me many years later.

I tripped walking across the stage—almost falling on my face. But, in show business when you trip it's called a "a return date." The audience was sympathetic.

I also entertained for the USO and its British counterpart, Entertainment National Services Association (ENSA), and sang to airmen in hangars all over Britain. Once I had to change in the men's room (facilities were limited), and ended up with my foot holding the door shut because there was no lock. As I was going through the contortions of trying to get into an evening gown, with my foot wedged up against the door, there was a constant banging on the door accompanied by an irritated male voice demanding, "Hurry up in there!" When he heard my voice asking him to wait, his manner changed completely. He wanted to come in and help me—an offer I politely declined.

I learned to change clothes in the most extraordinary situations…Inside a car or truck (when my mother and I could get a ride), in train station restrooms and in the restrooms on trains. On another occasion, when a line outside the men's room in an aircraft hangar snaked around the building, I decided to use an American Military Police truck as my "dressing room." There was no one in sight, and the darkness seemed to offer added privacy. I was rather pleased with myself in finding what I thought would be a chance to change clothes without the usual hurry. I was always careful not to hold up lines of people outside restrooms. I had to go from daytime clothes to glamorous stage clothes, and usually in a matter of minutes.

As I was zipping up my evening dress, two burly military policemen rounded the corner of a building and began approaching the truck. Suddenly they stopped, and holding a flashlight to a sheaf of papers, started scanning the pages. I thought they were going to arrest me for using a military vehicle, and that my career would be over. The taller of the two military policemen shook his head, muttered something inaudible, and the two turned around, disappearing into the night. I bolted out of the truck like a streak of lightning, arriving disheveled and out of breath at the hangar where my mother was waiting for me. I told my mother and was overheard by a group of airmen within earshot. One of them, an East London Cockney, from his accent, declared, "What a missed opportunity, to walk away when they could have seen a bloomin' English beauty without her clothes on."

I sang, day in and day out. I was now being asked to sing not only on British warships in Portsmouth, but on American ships as well. I sang wherever I was asked to perform. Even when stricken with rubella, I still turned up at the studio, as planned, to cut a record. Another time I sang with sinus trouble so serious that I became deaf in one ear, and had to have my sinuses punctured. Somehow my ailments seemed minuscule compared with what the fighting-men and women were facing. I would not allow myself to succumb. Like everyone else, I carried on.

The only time I found it impossible to carry on, and put up a brave front, was the time I entertained at a soldiers' burns hospital in East Grinstead, located south of London. Many of these men had been severely burned, some almost beyond recognition. I wanted so very much to make them happy, to make them forget. Instead of weeping and showing the anguish I felt, I sang "You Made Me Love You," trying to make it seem as if, it had been written especially for them.

My heart was breaking for those men, and I just could not compose myself enough to sing another song. Instead, I went around the ward and shook hands with each and every one of them. Some of the soldiers didn't really have hands, just bones— all the flesh had been burned off. I left the ward and cried for days. I was still a child when I visited the burns hospital. And, up to that point, I had never experienced anything before that left me feeling so emotionally distraught and completely bereft. These men were there to be treated by one of the great plastic surgeons in England.

Soon I was on the road again, appearing in Edinburgh, where I was approached by George Black, who offered me a leading role in "Get A Load Of This" at the London Hippodrome. This was a tremendous honor because, in terms of power, George Black was not only England's answer to Florenz Ziegfeld, but also he owned the London Palladium, and other important theatres throughout the country.

When I received the script, I found that "Get A Load Of This" was a musical in which I was to play a nightclub singer with Vic Oliver as the leading man. At that time, Vic Oliver was married to Sarah Churchill (Winston Churchill's daughter). While she and I became very good friends, Vic Oliver—who was regarded as the British Jack Benny—taught me comedy timing. I was a leading lady at 17, and Vic was a true professional to work alongside.

GET A LOAD OF THIS

CAST :

Vic Vandyke	...	...	VIC OLIVER
His Stooge	...	...	JACK ALLAN
Celia	...	...	CELIA LIPTON
A Table Entertainer			ERIC MASON
Cigarette Girl			DORCAS WHITE
Rabener	...		ALBERT LIEVEN
Borg	...		CHARLES FARRELL
Willy	...		PETER BERNARD
Fanquist	...		VALERIE WHITE
Lacey	...		JOHN LOTHAR
The Raven	...		GAYLORD BRIAN
Maitre d'Hotel			GEORGE HAMILTON
The Model	...		IRIS LOCKWOOD
Mrs. Stuyvesant Smith :			
			GEORGIA MacKINNON
Professor Gilbert			ARNOLD ROOKE
Ben Slade	...		PAT CLAIRE
Chas. Overton		HAROLD WILKINSON
Secretary			PAXIE MONTAYE
	...		JACK BARKER
Commissioner			DAPHNE BARKER
O'Ryan			VERNON JON
Sergeant	...		CHARLES ROLFE
Cop	...		LYN WILLIAMS
	...		MARGO KING
			CHICK ALEXANDER
Bandleader : BRETTON BYRD			

MUSICAL NUMBERS

Lyrics by MANNING SHERWIN & VAL GUEST

"THE FALL"

"SELF IN COTTON WOOL"

"Y IN ME"

"DE"

"E CARROUSEL"

"ZVOUS"

"BROADWAY"

TIONAL NUMBERS

"MS" (Michael Carr and Jack Popplewell)

(Al Lewis, Larry Stock and Vincent Rose)

"HERE'S YOUR WREATH" BALLET

led by Arthur Young

The Management reserve the right to Substitute any Artistes

In accordance with the requirements of the Lord Chamberlain—
1.—The public may leave at the end of the performance by all exit doors and such doors must at that time be open.
2.—All gangways, passages and staircases must be kept entirely free from chairs or any other obstructions.
3.—Persons shall not in any circumstances be permitted to stand or sit in any of the gangways intersecting the seating, or to sit in any of the other gangways. If standing be permitted in the gangways at the sides and rear of the seating, it shall be strictly limited to the number indicated in the notices exhibited in those positions.
4.—The safety curtain must be lowered and raised in the presence of each audience.

I starred with Vic Oliver in "Get A Load of This" when I was 17.

Another professional who worked on the show was Norman Hartnell, Her Majesty Queen Elizabeth II's dress designer. He was able to design clothes that combined sheer beauty and disguised my painfully, thin figure. He fashioned endless yards of rose-colored, pink tulle into an illusion that made me appear to be quite amply endowed. Those were the days, unlike today, when a female who possessed a reed-slim body was considered out of vogue.

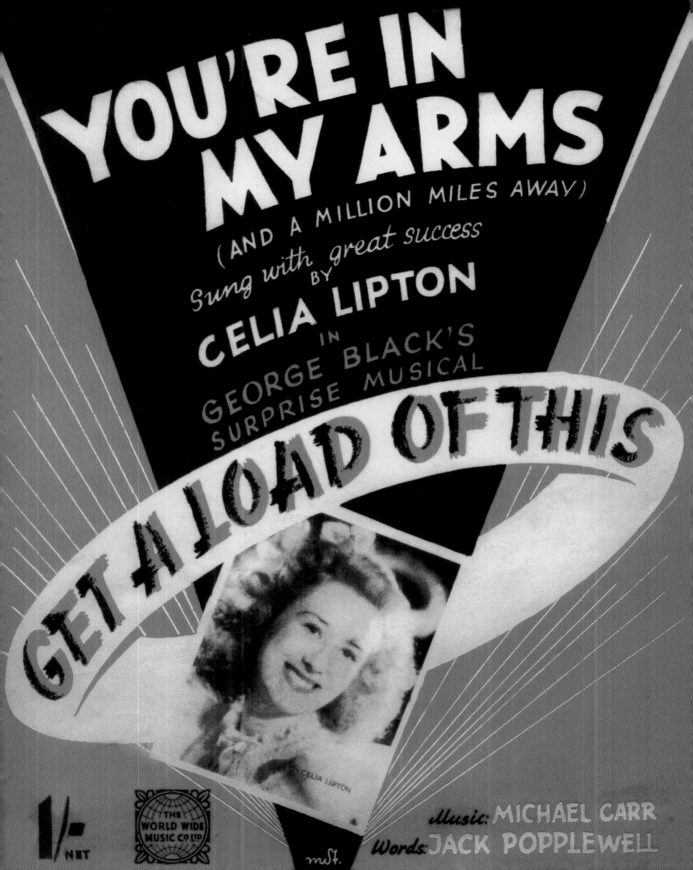

GRID LEAK
RECORDS CIRCLE

CONCERT SELECTION

Mantovani and Orch. Serenade from Student Prince. Decca F8179.

Paul Robeson and Orch. Love at my Heart, and Now Sleeps the Crimson Petal. H.M.V. B9281.

Alec Templeton (Piano). Concerto in A Minor (Grieg); Pathetique Symphony (Tchaikovsky). Bruns. 03351.

Ida Haendel (Violin). Schon Rosmarin (Kreisler); Tambourin Chinois (Kreisler). Decca M520.

Kentucky Minstrels (Choir). O, Dry Those Tears; Church Bells of England. H.M.V. C3298.

I. M. Sauroma (Piano). Tchaikovsky's Concerto No. I B Flat Minor; Grieg's Concerto in A Minor. H.M.V. C3297.

Maggie Teyte (Soprano). Offrande; L'Heure Exquise. H.M.V. DA1821.

Watson Forbes (Viola). Sussex Lullaby; Intrada. Decca M515.

Hallé Orchestra. The Wasps (Vaughan Williams). Col. DX1088.

Linda Gray (Contralto). Johnny, My Dear; Hills of Donegal. Decca M518.

Rawicz and Landauer (Pianos). Knightsbridge March; Scene Du Bal. Col. DB2088.

Symphony Orch. Reminiscences of Tchaikovsky. H.M.V. C3299.

LIGHT MUSIC

Ambrose. I Threw a Kiss in the Ocean; Everything I Love. Decca F8182.

Turner Layton. Lamplighter Serenade; Somebody Else is Taking My Place. Col. FB2833.

Duke Ellington (Solo Piano). Solitude; Dear Old Southland. H.M.V. B9285.

George Formby. Andy the Handy Man; They Laughed When I Started to Play. Regal MR3648.

Tauber. Jealousy; Love's Last Word is Spoken. Parlo. RO20513.

Celia Lipton. Blues in the Night; Tangerine. Col. FB2832.

Billy Cotton. Hold Your Hats On; Somebody Cares for You. Rex 10146.

New Organoleans. Basin Street Ball; Desert Patrol. Col. FB2837.

Sandy Macpherson. Sandy Forges Signatures. Col. FB2848.

Vera Lynn. Jealousy; Where in the World. Decca F8185.

Hutch. This is Worth Fighting For; Where in the World. H.M.V. BD1013.

Artie Shaw. Stardust; Georgia on My Mind. H.M.V. B9288.

Vocal

From the latest Judy Garland-Micky Rooney film " Babes on Broadway " comes a new hit-tune, *How About You?* recorded by most bands and several of our most popular singers, including Judy Garland herself, who, as one might expect, makes a very good version and backs it with *F. D. R. Jones.* also featured in the film (Brunswick 03305)

Celia Lipton, who is still thrilling her audiences in " Get a Load of This," has some able support from John Singer in her setting of *How About You?* which is noteworthy for the second chorus which is given a new twist by substituting Mayfair for New York, and Coward for Gershwin. For her second number Celia chooses another film tune, this time from " Sweater Girl "—*I Don't Want to Walk Without You,* another very popular number which is enjoying much success—a fine pair on Columbia FB2797.

If neither of these strike the right note, perhaps Dorothy Carless' record of the same " Babes on Broadway " melody will. She sings the straight version with her usual charm and backs it with *I'll Always Remember* on Decca F8120.

Celia Lipton, the bright young star of " Get a Load of This," is grand on **Columbia FB2797,** " How About You " and " I don't Want to Walk Without You."

THIS MONTH'S CHOICE

How About You? ; *I Don't Want to Walk Without You,* Celia Lipton (Columbia FB2797).

Someone's Rocking My Dreamboat ; *Absent-minded Moon,* Leslie Hutchinson (H.M.V. BD1006).

Cancel the Flowers ; *'Tis Autumn,* Tony Martin (Decca F8119).

Medley of British Patriotic Songs ; *Medley of Soviet Patriotic Songs,* Reginald Dixon (Regal MR3630).

Someone's Rocking My Dreamboat ; *I Don't Want to Walk Without You,* Eric Winstone's Accordeon Band (Regal MR3633).

Humpty Dumpty Heart ; *This is no Laughing Matter,* Glen Miller and His Orchestra (H.M.V. BD5749).

How Green was My Valley ; *I Don't Want to Walk Without You,* Carroll Gibbons and the Savoy Hotel Orpheans (Columbia FB2799).

Deep in the Heart of Texas ; *How Green Was My Valley,* Joe Loss and His Band (H.M.V. BD5746).

"Get A Load Of This" was a huge success. It played for a year and a half at the London Hippodrome (which became known as The Talk of the Town Theatre), then moved on to the Prince of Wales Theatre, and just kept going. Although I enjoyed what I was doing, I preferred the musical hall act routine, as opposed to the formal structure of a show, where one came on and off stage during the acts. I felt closer to the audience doing the music hall routine. There, when I came out on stage to do my act, I had an allocated amount of time to perform. It was incumbent on me, and only me, to work the audience's response up to the kind of crescendo, where they would respond to me, I hoped, with appreciation and warmth. It was very much like a love affair.

While I was missing my "love-affairs" with audiences, "Stage Door Johnnies" were avidly pursuing me. After every performance of "Get A Load Of This" those Romeos waited for me at the stage door. They sent me flowers, buckets of chocolates, and love notes. My mother warned me to be cautious. I heeded her advice and turned down most of the invitations.

A more formal invitation arrived one day, and I had no hesitation in accepting it. I was invited to lunch with the Royal Household Guards. It was a custom at the time that all leading ladies of the current shows in London be invited to lunch with the Guards. Mary Martin and the actress Gertrude Lawrence were starring in London shows, and they were also invited to attend the luncheon. We were seated together, and I found myself so awestruck in their presence that I became overwhelmed with shyness, and never uttered a word, until it was time to leave. I plucked up enough courage to ask Mary Martin to have tea with me. She accepted.

I asked her to meet me at the Claridges Hotel. Claridges, long regarded as the "annex of Buckingham Palace," was to me the epitome of grandeur befitting Mary Martin—one of theatre's grand ladies. Mary arrived on time, and thanked me for extending such a kind invitation to her. When I tried to talk to her about the Noel Coward play she was appearing in at the Drury Theatre, she brushed it aside and concentrated the conversation on my career. She gave me many insights into her years of experience, and ideas on how to reach the goals I had set for myself. When we were bidding each other goodbye, she called me "little girl." She said she was very impressed that someone as young as I had come this far; I had a tremendous talent and would go far.

Years later, all shyness by now overcome in the presence of movie idols, I invited Mary Martin and Carol Channing to a party for the show "Legends" at my home in Palm Beach. Perhaps Mary Martin was told beforehand that Consuelo Vanderbilt, the Duchess of Marlborough, had lived in my home. From the moment she came through the door, Mary immediately began looking around. At times she almost resembled a museum curator as she inspected the antiques and paintings. I don't think she missed a single object as she meandered through the rooms. Everything must have passed muster because, finally, she came up to me and, because I had probably become frozen in her memory as the little girl she had met in England, Mary quipped, "That little girl did all this?"

I missed my father very much after he joined the armed services. Although we wrote to each other often, the war interrupted the usual, prompt delivery of mail, and some of his letters took months to reach me. In my letters to him, I tried to fill him in on every aspect of what I was doing in "Get A Load Of This," but the letters could never compensate for having my father in the audience watching me.

I especially missed him when, during the run of the show, I filled in for Bebe Daniels at the Palladium—appearing opposite Ben Lyons—singing a few songs, and then dashing back to the theatre on time for my entrance in "Get A Load Of This." I was appearing in two shows at separate theatres in one night. My father would have been proud of me, I thought, because I was living up to one of his earliest admonitions, "Be in show business if you want, but never be late for musicians or rehearsals."

A critic of "Get A Load Of This" complained that I used a microphone. Determined to sing without a microphone I searched for the best singing teacher in London. Maestro Georges Cunelli quickly became the most important part of my life. He was tiny, wizened, with one kidney, but to me he loomed larger than life. He had a studio at Wigmore Hall in London, and I found myself almost living there. With my father away at war, the Maestro became like a father to me.

Maestro Georges was a strict disciplinarian, and I was fortunate to learn from him that there wasn't anything you couldn't give up to become a good artist. I learned the meaning of discipline from him to reach purity and clarity of tone in my voice. In a very rich, Italian accent he said he would train me to sing without a microphone. But, I was to have no boyfriends, no cigarettes...and no drink. "If you smoke cigarettes, I make you eat cigarettes."

His training was with the same intensity as that of a prizefighter. When I had a show coming up, he would find me, get me on the telephone, and talk to me for a minute. Sometimes, it was to warn me against overusing my speaking voice on the phone. At other times, he reminded me not to argue with my mother. He took no nonsense from me, and was not above telling me to shut my mouth and "save voice." When he was making a point, he called me his "skinny lobster." Sometimes I was "all arms and legs, with no balcony" (a "balcony" to him was a very large bosom), again, in his heavy accent he said, "You have no balcony." I, his skinny little lobster responded, "I will sing just like a diva with a big balcony!"

The Maestro kept his promise, and together we did it. I was soon singing without a microphone, with a voice so strong that I was heard clearly and distinctly all the way to the back of the theatre. He left me with a profound awareness that discipline and sacrifice, once learned, remain ingrained for the rest of your life.

His teaching and my own dedication soon paid off. I was offered a leading role in the pantomime "Jack and Jill" at the London Casino, playing the principle boy. It is the tradition in English pantomime for the leading boy to be played by a girl.

According to tradition, the principle boy's costume consists of pantyhose and a doublet. Since my legs were so thin, I ended up wearing several pairs of pantyhose so my legs would look strong enough to carry the rest of my body! Although, the reviews were great, and I really enjoyed appearing with Stanley Holloway, who was later to star in the movie "My Fair Lady."

Next, Jack Hylton asked me to play Peter in the theatrical production of "Peter Pan" in a nine-week tour of the United Kingdom. To play the part of Peter in the English theatre is one of the highest accolades a young actress can receive. Sir James Barrie, a British playwright and novelist born in Scotland, wrote "Peter Pan" (The Boy Who Wouldn't Grow Up) in 1904. Sixteen years later, in 1920, Barrie's play was first staged, and its success is legendary. Soon after, the play was turned into a musical. England's greatest actresses had played the part of Peter in "Peter Pan."

I not only felt privileged and tremendously honored to have been chosen to play the part of Peter Pan, but also I felt deep gratitude toward those who had faith in my ability to give a stellar performance. I was the youngest actress at that time to ever be awarded the role. "Daily Express" critic, Jonah Barrington, wrote, "When I told this girl she will be a star, she never let me down."

I loved playing the part of Peter—flying across the stage, entertaining children—and was pleased, of course, when the local papers praised my performance. A London critic wrote, "One thought her Peter to be one of the best for some years past." A Manchester critic raved, "To be able to bring something fresh and slightly different to the immortal part of the boy who wouldn't grow up is no mean achievement. Celia Lipton, playing 'Peter Pan' with an extra hint of precocity at Manchester Opera House last night, achieved it. She emphasized the pathos and age-old wisdom."

On December 15, 1945, I played Peter at London's Scala Theatre with George Curzon doubling as Captain Hook and Mr. Darling. It was one thing to play the provinces, like Manchester, but to play London in such a role, fulfilled one of my greatest ambitions at the time.

The then highly-respected magazine "Punch" called my performance "attractively faun-like," and the weekly "Spectator Magazine" said I had "an indubitable charm all my own." Other critics wrote, "Celia Lipton is a magnificent Peter...graceful, ebullient, capable of great histrionic effort..." "I've never seen a better Peter than Celia Lipton." "She slips effortlessly into the role of Peter." I was an actress at last!

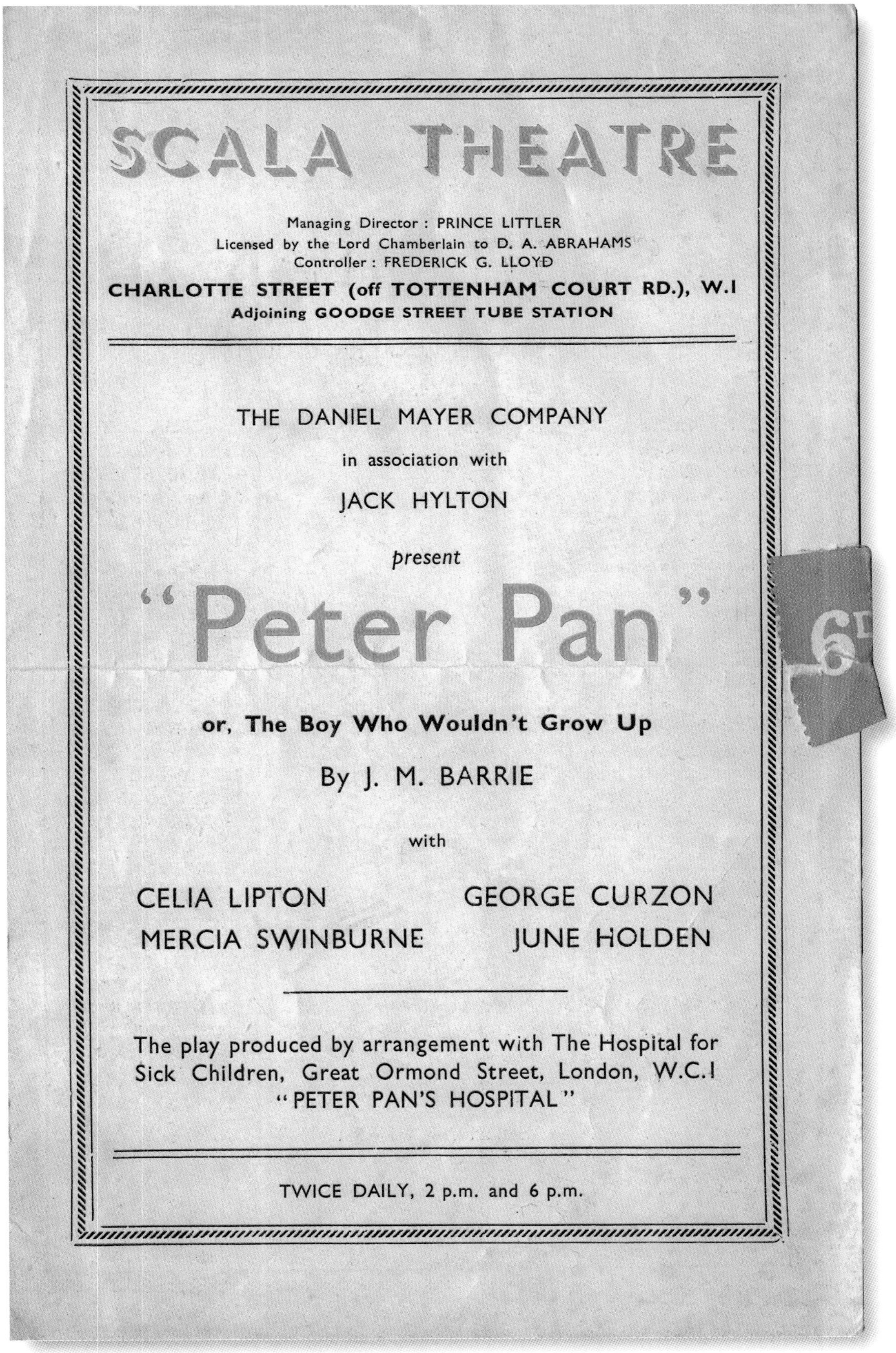

SCALA THEATRE

Managing Director : PRINCE LITTLER
Licensed by the Lord Chamberlain to D. A. ABRAHAMS
Controller : FREDERICK G. LLOYD

CHARLOTTE STREET (off TOTTENHAM COURT RD.), W.I
Adjoining GOODGE STREET TUBE STATION

THE DANIEL MAYER COMPANY

in association with

JACK HYLTON

present

"Peter Pan"

or, The Boy Who Wouldn't Grow Up

By J. M. BARRIE

with

| CELIA LIPTON | GEORGE CURZON |
| MERCIA SWINBURNE | JUNE HOLDEN |

The play produced by arrangement with The Hospital for Sick Children, Great Ormond Street, London, W.C.I
"PETER PAN'S HOSPITAL"

TWICE DAILY, 2 p.m. and 6 p.m.

6D

This year's " Peter Pan " (Scala) is CELIA
LIPTON, an elfin Peter who trips about the
stage light-footed, imparting to the character
a spirit wholly in keeping with J. M. Barrie's
fantasy. Her rendering of the part is said
to be the best ever seen in a London
theatre.

CELIA LIPTON AS PETER PAN
Delightful New Theatre Revival

Modern children do believe in fairies—and if you doubt my word go to the **New Theatre** this week and hear their immediate response to Peter Pan's appeal to them to save Tinker Bell. Barrie's whimsical fantasy has established its claim to immortality, and it was a packed company of children and grown-ups who last night gave a fine send-off to the week

The little boy who wouldn't grow up finds a charming interpreter in Miss Celia Lipton, who is in truth, as Peter declares, youth and joy, and from the first thrilling entrance when she flies through the window dressed in "autumn leaves and cobwebs" endears herself to the audience.

Diana Calderwood is a sweetly pretty Wendy, bringing a quaintly childish dignity to her role of "mother."

What excitement there is when Michael shrieks "I flewed," and the crustiest adult heart must melt at the delighted roars of laughter which greet the pranks of the lost boys, the gambols of the redskins, and the fearsome threats of the pirates and their chief. Captain James Hook, that same blackavised chief with the menacing hook and fitted snuff-box is played with a grand sense of fun by George Curzon, whose superiority is undoubtedly due to his avowed allegiance to Eton and Balliol. The spirit of Italia Conti hovers over many in the big cast of talented child players, of whom we remember particularly Malcolm Somers as Michael and Keith Noble (Slightly).

John Derrick, one-time Little Theatre favourite, demobilised last October from the Army, presents a lovable study of the children's father, George Darling, and Mercia Swinburne is the attractive Mrs Darling.

For the finale, Liza (Diana Kennedy) flies home on the broomstick, so that Peter and Wendy may wave us goodbye from the little house in the star-filled heavens. It is a graceful, forgivable divergence.—M.W.

LEARNING TO FLY.—Celia Lipton, who will be Peter Pan this year, gets used to the feel of that harness for the flying scenes at rehearsal.

CELIA LIPTON, who takes the title rôle in "Peter Pan," presented at the Scala Theatre, London.

VISIT BY PETER PAN.—Miss Celia Lipton, this year's Peter in the production of *Peter Pan* at the Scala Theatre, yesterday paid a visit to the Hospital for Sick Children, Great Ormond Street, where there is a "Peter Pan" cot endowed by Sir James Barrie. She is seen with some of the children.

World's Press News
20 Tudor Street, London, E.C.4.

Cutting from issue dated.............. 1 0 JAN 1946

WORLD'S PRESS NEWS, January 10. 1946

First Post-war Kiddies Party at the Press Club

More than 250 children and half as many parents were at the first Children's Party held at the Press Club since 1939. It was a hilarious success. For four hours the youngsters, between the ages of four and fourteen, were entertained with conjuring, Punch and Judy, community singing and games. Will Hay came along to auction a child's pram and other gifts. A telegram of greetings was received from the King and Queen.

Father Christmas was Morley Richards, the Club chairman, and a committee, headed by H. C. Vickery, appeared as pierrots. Fred Pignon was Harlequin.

Before the children left, they were paraded in age groups before the Christmas tree. Each was given a carrier full of presents and oranges. The Club staff, led by A. Lazenby, the secretary-manager, worked like Trojans to make the party a success.

Cutting from

.... News paper World

Dated .... 1 2 JAN 1946

Address of Journal........................

Press Club's Children's Party

More than 250 children, and half as many parents, were at the first Press Club children's party held since 1939. It was a hilarious success.

For four hours the youngsters, between the ages of four and fourteen, were entertained with conjuring, Punch and Judy, community singing and games. Will Hay came along to auction a child's pram and other gifts. Peter Pan (Miss Celia Lipton) told the children the story of Barrie's immortal character, and Frank Foster brought along his troupe of jugglers and clowns.

Alderman Wells, one of the Lord Mayor's Sheriffs, brought greetings from the Mansion House. There was, in addition, a telegram from the King and Queen.

Father Christmas was Mr. Morley Richards, the Club chairman, and a committee, headed by Mr. H. C. Vickery, appeared as pierrots. Mr. Fred Pignon was Harlequin.

Before the children left, they were paraded in age groups before the Christmas tree. Each of them was given a carrier full of presents and oranges to take home.

The Club staff, led by Mr. A. Lazenby, the secretary-manager, did much to make the party a success.

Queen
188/189 Strand, W.C.2.

Cutting from issue dated.... 1 0 JAN 1946.

THE THEATRE
"Peter Pan"
Scala Theatre

It is always hard to say whether Barrie wrote *Peter Pan* for children or for grown-ups. In any event it was produced as a play for children at the Scala Theatre. Miss Celia Lipton plays Peter Pan and certainly captures the imagination of all the children present. We grown-ups might have been a little critical due to the introduction of much sentiment into a part which the book paints more boyishly. June Holden plays Wendy with much feeling, and it is very hard to determine her age without reference. Perhaps she could have played a trifle younger. Mr. George Curzon is first class both as Mr. Darling and as Captain Hook. Mrs. Darling is played by Mercia Swinburne; she could not be improved upon. I can see packed houses for the whole length of its run. It is, and always will be, the greatest show for children.
H. C.

The London run of "Peter Pan" lasted about five months, then, it was back to touring with the show, playing theaters in the United Kingdom; The Glasgow Royal, The New Theatre in Northampton, and the Grand Theatre in Leeds. During short breaks I went back to London and recorded some popular BBC shows that included, "In Town Tonight," "Worker's Playtime," "Monday Night at Eight," and a show called "Barnstormers."

After the tour of "Peter Pan," I was booked to do a George Doonan show, "Skylarks" in Coventry. Part of the show required the entire cast to walk on stilts. Aside from the danger of being on stilts, there was often the added burden on the players of having to rehearse until three in the morning.

The toll of late hours and stilt-walking prompted the producer to give the entire cast a weekend off to rest up. I took the opportunity to visit my mother in London. Returning to Coventry on Monday, I couldn't believe my luck in finding a compartment on a train that was not only running, but also on time. Having grown accustomed to no food at the stops along the way, I boarded the train with a sandwich, cookies, and a thermos flask of tea. The only other person in the compartment with me was a charming man, with whom I shared my sandwich.

During the course of conversation, I told him of my ambition to appear in a musical comedy. As the train pulled into Coventry station, his last words were, "I'm sure you will get your wish." With typical British reticence, he didn't say who he was and I didn't ask. Months later, my traveling companion contacted my manager, Jack Hylton, and offered me the leading part in the musical comedy "The Quaker Girl," due to open in London. The man with whom I'd shared my sandwich was none other than Sir Emile Littler, one of the most famous producers in British theatre, and also a famous theatre owner with his brother, Prince.

The leading part of Prudence Pym, "The Quaker Girl," originally created by Gertie Millar, was to have been played in this production by Jessie Matthews, a star with a great following in England. For some reason, Jessie had dropped out of the show and Sir Emile (who remembered me from the train and, unbeknownst to me, knew my work) had thought of me as a replacement. I was honored and overwhelmed because I had only one week in which to learn the part, and step into Miss Matthews' distinguished shoes.

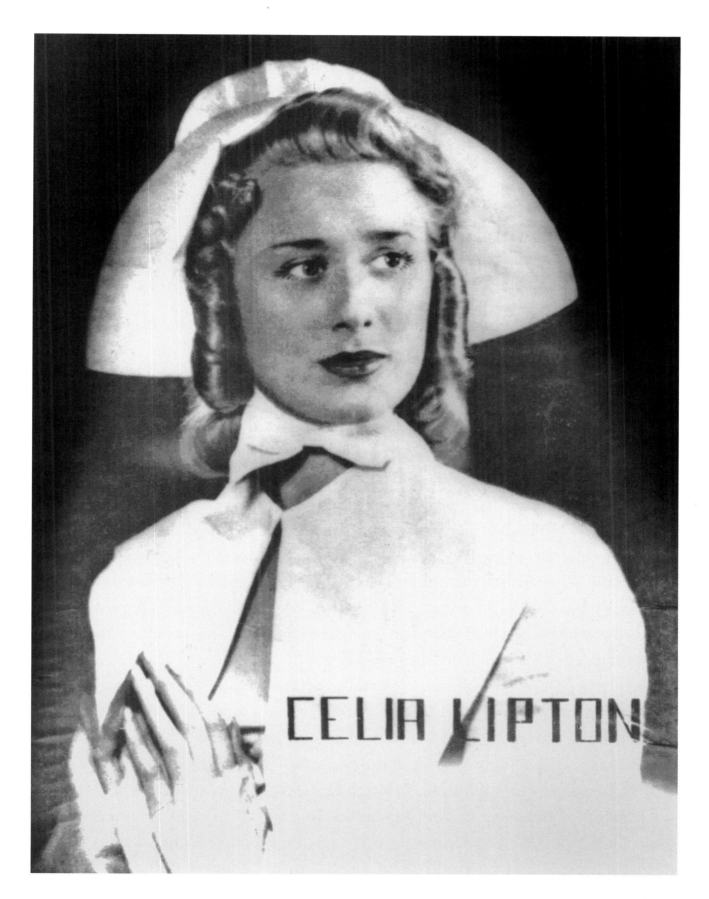

CELIA LIPTON

After only four days of rehearsal I managed to make it to opening night, all the while thanking my lucky stars that I had started singing lessons before now, so that my voice would be equal to the demanding role of Prudence. The director was very gentle, helping me to master the nine songs I had to sing in the musical comedy. The entire cast was very supportive – including Billy Milton, who played my romantic interest ("Tony from America"), Ivy St. Helier, and Hal Bryan.

Nonetheless, I still had to achieve the transition from my own act to musical comedy. When moving about the stage in musical comedy, a performer is on and off stage for three hours – singing, dancing, and acting. Many years later, in my "One-Woman Show" the production was shorter in duration, and I had the use of a microphone.

Before opening night of the "The Quaker Girl" in Coventry, many patrons demanded their money back, having paid to see Jessie Matthews, and not 18-year-old Celia Lipton. So, it was a surprise by the time the curtain rose on that first performance of "The Quaker Girl" at the London Coliseum, the entire theatre was sold out. And, the rest of the week the theatre was packed. This was the moment I had longed for. I began the opening number, all nerves submerged in sheer concentration. At the end of the show, the audience gave me a standing ovation.

After 16 curtain calls, the crowds still clamored for more. As instructed by the director, the two leading men brought me to the front of the stage and left me. I took a last, lone bow in front of the cast and, still in the character of Prudence the Quaker Girl, said, "Dear friends, thou art very kind! Thank you for this welcome to London. Good night and God bless you." I made a final low curtsey. Then, I stepped back into line with the rest of the cast. Pandemonium broke out. The audience screamed and cheered. My future in musical comedy was assured. I was 18 years of age and had just lived through one of the greatest nights of my life.

The reviews were stupendous, "The Stage" newspaper wrote, "Rarely has a young musical comedy actress made such a success as she did." "The Evening Telegraph" critic observed, "The House rose to her." The critic, A.E. Wilson wrote, "In playing the part of Prudence in which Gertie Millar appeared thirty years ago, Celia Lipton became a musical comedy star in a night." "The Daily Telegraph" reviewer wrote, "Lovely to look at, lovely to watch and listen to, Celia Lipton, a great success at 18." "The Sunday Express" review wrote, "Triumph, old-style musical

Coliseum *Charing Cross*

| Managing Director : | PRINCE LITTLER |
| General Manager : | SAMUEL HARBOUR |

EMILE LITTLER

Submits a New Presentation of

THE QUAKER GIRL

Music by LIONEL MONCKTON
Lyrics by PERCY GREENBANK and ADRIAN ROSS.
Book by JAMES W. TANNER

Jarge	DIMITRI VETTER
Mrs. Lukyn	MARCELLE TURNER
William	WILL HENRY
Nathaniel Pym	DEWEY GIBSON
Rachel, his Sister	LUCILLE DALE
Phoebe, English Maid to Princess Mathilde	APRIL ROSS
Princess Mathilde, an Exiled Bonapartist	JOY HAYDEN
Brian Charteris, a King's Messenger	PAT McGRATH
Madame Blum	IVY ST. HELIER
Tony Chute	BILLY MILTON
Jeremiah	HAL BRYAN
Prudence Pym, Niece to Nathaniel	CELIA LIPTON
Mary	ENID MEREDITH
1st Page	SHEILA POET
2nd Page	GLADYS COWPER
Toinette	JASMINE DEE
Monsieur Larose	DIMITRI VETTER
1st Gendarme	JOHN STOCK
2nd Gendarme	HAROLD FARRAR
Diane	PEGGY LIVESEY
Prince Carlo	GEOFFREY DUNN
Monsieur Duhamel, a Minister of State	STANLEY DREWITT
Prinicipal Dancer	PAMELA FOSTER

The Play Revised and Produced by EMILE LITTLER.

ACT I	A Village in England
ACT II	"La Maison Blum," Paris
ACT III	Prince Carlo's Masque Ball
Time	Not the Present

Scenery and Costumes Designed by DORIS ZINKEISEN
Dances and Ensembles arranged by PHYLLIS BLAKSTON
Orchestra under the Direction of MICHAEL COLLINS

Scenery painted by Alick Johnstone. Costumes executed by Jacqmar, Hartnell, Kelly, Hume, Dix, and C. L. Trobridge. Mens' Suits by Hawes & Curtis, Kilgour & French, Morris Angel and Moss Bros. Hats by Sheeta. Masks by C. L. Trobridge. Wigs by Gustave and Nathanwigs. Shoes by Gamba and Anello & Davide. Furniture in Act II by Peter Jones, Ltd. Madame Blum Number in Act II, by Ivy St. Helier, Lyric by Barbara Gordon and Basil Thomas. Opening Act III, Lyric by Heath Joyce and Music by Michael Collins. Emile Littler thanks Major Frederick Lloyd for help at Rehearsal. The Play presented by Emlit Ltd., by arrangement with Associated Playwrights Ltd. Telephone by G.P.O. Make-up by Max Factor. Lighting Eqipment by Strand Electric Co. Dyeing and Cleaning by Zernys. Stockings by Kayser Bondor.

MUSIC FOR "THE QUAKER GIRL" MAY BE OBTAINED FROM THE ATTENDANTS

Stage Director				JOHN REDMOND
Stage Manager	For			HAROLD FARRAR
Wardrobe Mistress	EMILE			ROWENA WEBB
General Manager	LITTLER			IAN PAUL

FULLY LICENSED SALOONS IN ALL PARTS OF THEATRE

BOX OFFICE OPEN from 10 a.m. Please Post Remittance with letter
Telephone : BOOKING OFFICE, TEMPLE BAR 3161 (7 lines)
The Management reserve to themselves the right to make any change, vary or omit any part of the Programme without previous notice.

PRICES : 15/-, 12/-, 9/-, 6/9. BALCONY (Unreserved) 3/- All Children must be paid for

In accordance with the requirements of the London County Council :—
1.—The public may leave at the end of the performance by all exit doors, and such doors must at that time be open.
2.—All gangways, corridors, staircases and external passageways intended for exit shall be kept entirely free from obstruction, whether permanent or temporary.
3.—Persons shall not be permitted to stand or sit in any of the gangways. If standing be permitted in the gangways at the sides and rear of the seating, it shall be limited to the numbers indicated in the notices exhibited in those positions.
4.—The safety curtain must be lowered and raised in the presence of each audience.

STOLL THEATRE KINGSWAY	ALDWYCH THEATRE
BERNARD DELFONT presents	ALFRED LUNT LYNN FONTANNE in
THE **STUDENT PRINCE**	**THERE SHALL BE NO NIGHT**
Music by SIGMUND ROMBERG	By ROBERT E. SHERWOOD
For Times See Daily Press	

comedy which establishes Celia Lipton as the brightest of new stars. Her prim, delicate air, her bird-like singing, her personality and rare charm, you must see her...one of the best voices heard in musical comedy in many a year."

The "Sunday Times" noted that many in the audience went back a second time to see me in the musical comedy. I recorded two numbers from the show for Columbia Records, "A Quaker Girl" and "Tony from America." In his autobiography, in 1976, Billy Milton recorded that "Celia Lipton and I made a perfect team. We never had a cross word the whole time we worked together." Shortly after "The Quaker Girl" came off, Jack Payne remembered in his book, "Signature Tune," "only a couple of years ago (Celia Lipton) was a crooner with a West End band, but she rose to play the Quaker Girl and has taken a prominent part in show business; good luck to her, she is a grand little artiste."

I was indeed now an actress and a singer. "The Quaker Girl" ran for 670 performances to packed houses. The theatre was in the center of London and, night after night, the bombs continued to fall–lethal V1s, which stout-hearted Londoners called

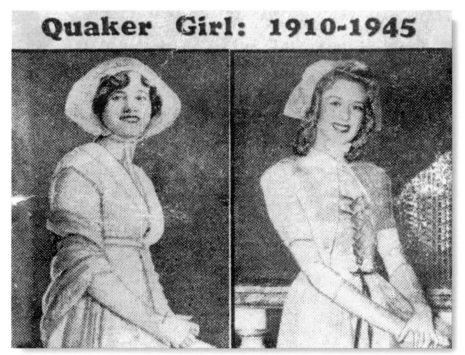

Gertie Millar, the original Quaker Girl, came to see me at the London Coliseum.

"Doodlebugs." Then, V2s—pilotless planes—would crash without any warning.

On some nights the bombing was so heavy that I couldn't get home after the performance, and was forced to sleep at the theatre. But we kept going, even though the bombing raids became more and more destructive. Finally, despite our willingness to carry on, Sir Emile Littler, our producer, decided that the bombings were too dangerous for the theatre audiences and the cast. We left London and began touring the show in the provinces.

We began the tour in Edinburgh and played there for a month. It was one of the happiest months of my life, primarily because my father came home on leave from North Africa, where he had landed in 1942 with the American First Army.

One of my deepest wishes was finally realized—my father was in the audience. He saw me perform, as never before—as a musical comedy star and leading lady. I hoped he would approve of my performance, but he did not say much except, "I am too close to you, so I can't really judge how good your performance was." His reaction was typically British. I sensed my father was proud of me beyond words, yet, always mindful that loving parents might give children swollen heads with too much praise, he maintained his inherent British reserve. If I have observed anything of British and American attitudes in life—having lived in both countries—is the difference between the way British and Americans raise their children. In England, parents are very reluctant to praise their children when it's deserved. I think all parents should encourage their children as much as possible. This instills confidence.

My father was with us at Christmas in Edinburgh, which was my birthday. I invited the entire Quaker Girl cast and all my Scottish relatives to join in the birthday festivities. When my father played the violin, it brought back joyful childhood memories of those happy, impromptu, family musicals. But, it also brought tears to my mother, my relatives, and to me, because we knew that very soon my father would be returning to his regiment.

There wasn't an empty seat in the theatre during "The Quaker Girl's" month-long run in Edinburgh. While my father may have been reluctant to shower me with praise, the "Edinburgh Evening News" let everyone know that a girl born in Edinburgh had become successful, "And as we can claim her in great measure 'oor ain bairn' (our own child), delight is mixed with pride that Auld Reekie (Scottish words for Edinburgh) should have produced such a charming and attractive actress." The "Edinburgh Evening Dispatch" critic wrote, "The modest puritanical Quakeress Prudence, is presented to perfection by Celia Lipton, who fits into the part at all points. Her singing, dancing, and charming demeanor combine to make her performance a memorable one."

Next, we moved on to the King's Theatre in Glasgow. The musical comedy star Evelyn Laye had just played there, and I was assigned to her dressing room. To my surprise, when I opened a drawer I found it was full of cloves of garlic. But, then I remembered that all singers said that garlic was wonderful for a cold. In fact, even today, if I ever have a cold, I eat raw garlic and have discovered it is of great help in fighting that cold. Unfortunately, so did one of my leading men. Whenever he caught a cold which, given the ferocity of the British winter, was frequent, this particular actor took a Turkish bath, and afterwards ate garlic and onions. Then, during the show he would kiss me, not once, but twice on the matinee days.

The tour was fun, but the theatres were often damp and I had a constant pain in my side. I attributed it to not eating. Because of wartime rationing, food was extremely limited and we never had much to eat. But sometimes, loyal fans from nearby farms generously supplemented our ration allowance with eggs and other produce. On tour, I ate nutritious, hearty food only when it was available.

EMILE LITTLER
submits an entirely new presentation of the
WORLD FAMOUS MUSICAL COMEDY

The Quaker Girl

BOOK BY JAMES
LYRICS BY PERCY
MUSIC BY LION
PRODUCED BY
DÉCOR BY DO
DANCES ARRAN

THEATRE ROYAL
GLASGOW
WEEK COMMENCING MONDAY 16th, JULY 1945.
EVENINGS AT 7
MATINEES WEDS. & SATS. at 2
Telephone : DOUGLAS 6822

TRANSFERRED IN ITS ENTIRETY DIRECT
FROM THE LONDON COLISEUM

EMILE LITTLER
PRESENTS

CELIA LIPTON

BILLY MILTON

HAL BRYAN

CELIA LIPTON
BILLY MILTON
HAL BRYAN
JACK MAYER

IN AN ENTIRELY NEW PRODUCTION OF
THE WORLD FAMOUS MUSICAL COMEDY

THE QUAKER
GIRL

WITH

ELAINE GARREAU
ELLA DRURY
DIMITRI VETTER
BUNTY BARNETT

ROSAMUND BELMORE
ELIZABETH STEWART
RICHARD LAWRENCE
FRANK WIGNALL

Company of 60 Artistes
Special Augmented Orchestra under direction of Tom Lewis

After our six month tour was over—and we had played "The Quaker Girl" at the King's Theatre in Glasgow; The Royal Court, Liverpool; The New Theatre, Northampton; The New Theatre, Oxford; The Lyceum, Sheffield; The King's Theatre, Portsmouth; and the Wimbledon Theatre—Sir Emile brought us back to the Stoll Theatre in London.

The Stoll Theatre, enormous in size, was packed at every performance and the show did tremendously well. Sir Emile wanted me to sign a contract that would virtually bind me for life, but my mother said, "I don't think you should do that," so, I did not. The first part of my contractual obligation would begin with me playing the lead in "The Song of Norway." But, my voice teacher advised me against it because the part demanded a coloratura soprano, which I was not.

During the run of "The Quaker Girl," the war in Europe ended. I sang to over 5,000 American troops at the Royal Albert Hall in London, in front of such a vast audience that my stomach began to hit the floor with nerves. Yet, I managed to rally round and give a great performance. After the Royal Albert Hall performance, the American USO asked me and comedian Dickie Henderson, later a TV personality in England, to entertain the troops in Germany. We also performed for thousands of troops in Munich, Wiesbaden, and Berlin.

After my traveling overseas with the USO and E.N.S.A, entertaining the troops, we encountered Russian troops during our travels, mostly in East Berlin. I was afraid of their serious demeanor while I was flying around, constantly entertaining the troops.

After the North African campaign, my father's regiment landed at Tarino, in Southern Italy, as part of the British 8th Army under Field Marshal Harold Alexander. During his seven years of service as an army officer, he was awarded three bronze oak-leaf emblems, issued to members of His Majesty's Force who had been mentioned in dispatches, or had received a military or civil commendation for brave conduct during the war. On July 1, 1945, my father's name was published in the "London Gazette" in dispatches for distinguished service, with a record of His Majesty's High Appreciation and signed by the Secretary of War.

The Colonel of my father's regiment gave him a testimonial that exemplifies the character of the man so dear to my mother and me, our Sidney; "Seldom can there have been a greater transition from the eminence of your pre-war position to the responsibility and loyalty which you so ably carried as regimental signals officer.

Celia Lipton's Great Triumph as the Quaker Girl

WHEN "The Quaker Girl" first caught the fancy of the theatre world over 30 years ago it had a lot to commend it. To a public receptive to the lure of musical comedies its simple charm, pleasant romance, good comedy, plus an escapist angle, which proved to be the shape of things to come, it made quite an impression.

Now the play has been revived on the grand scale by Mr. Emile Littler. It had its premiere at the Coventry Hippodrome last night, prior to its London venture, and if the enthusiasm roused is any criterion, then "The Quaker Girl" is going to restore happy memories to the middle-aged and give delight to the new generation.

LILTING MELODIES

In some phases the show has been modernised. The comedy has been brought up to date and the third act scene reveals the 1944 imagination for costume and setting. Yet the essentials have wisely been left, the lilting melodies are with us still, and the main basis of the story structure is untouched. All in all Mr. Emile Littler has achieved much.

SWEET AND WINSOME

Patrons will no doubt speculate as to how Jessie Matthews would have played the rôle of Prudence, but such indulgences are futile. Celia Lipton is at any rate good enough for me. Lovely to look at, she is sweet and winsome in all that she does. Sincere as a Quaker girl in the first act, she merges into Paris life preserving her demureness. Her singing is delightful and never better than in the number, "Tony From America." The house rose to her.

There is more good singing from Joy Hayden (Princess Mathilda), who tempers vivacity with modesty—an admirable performance in every way. Ivy St. Helier is a joy as Madame Blum. Gesture, accent, and acting skill are all combined to provide laughter. April Ross makes a pleasing Phœbe, pert and competent, and Jasmine Dee adds beauty and deportment to the show as Toinette.

HAL BRYAN'S SUCCESS

Billy Milton is "Tony from America," but in voice and style his geographical traditions are much nearer home — say, the West End or Lancing College. He gives his part artistry and ease. Jeremiah, the wayward Quaker, is in the clever hands of Hal Bryan. He comes near pantomime comedy at times, even imitating a bit of "Itma," and gives new life to the old and familiar character. Geoffrey Dunn plays Prince Carlo with formality and sings "Come to the Ball" as we all desire it. There is a good study of the Paris police chief by Dimitri Vetter.

The chorus singing is splendid, and is not the least pleasure the play gives us.

A.W.

Quaker Girl "sweet as ever"

OPERA HOUSE

"The Quaker Girl" Again Delightful

AS "The Quaker Girl" came and conquered over 30 years ago, so will continue to do so as long as she is in such good hands as Emile Littler presented to a full audience at the Opera House last night.

Not a petal of the ageless flower of romance has been shed in this new version of the musical comedy which is smart, streamlined and thoroughly delightful.

To those who saw her in the Spring it is sufficient to ensure another visit to say that "The Quaker Girl" has practically the same cast this week.

Heroine Celia Lipton, stronger in voice and with just the right assurance, is the perfect Prudence, mixing the sorrowful with a rippling sense of fun: Billy Milton is an ideal Tony from America, and Hal Bryan's extremely amusing foolery finds plenty of outlet as Jeremiah.

Ivy St. Helier is a highly experienced performer who pleases greatly as Madame Blum, and ... McGrath would be an asset to any show.

Celia Lipton's Triumph

IN playing the part of Prudence, in which Gertie Millar appeared 30 years ago, Celia Lipton became a musical comedy star in a night in Emile Littler's delightful revival of "The Quaker Girl" at the Coliseum (writes A. E. Wilson)

Young singer's London hit

From Our Theatre Correspondent

Celia Lipton, 20-year-old singer, last night established herself as a star in a 30-year-old musical comedy, "The Quaker Girl," revived by Emile Littler at the Coliseum, London.

The lilting music of Lionel Monckton, plus a skilful energetic cast, clever staging and a brilliant direction, makes "The Quaker Girl" one of the brightest musical shows in London at present.

Bouquet Of Memories

MISS LIPTON rose at 6.30 this morning, and having read all the glowing notices of her success went back to bed again.

"I suppose I shan't realise how lucky I am for a day or two," she said when I rang her up to congratulate her.

"What cheered me immensely just before the show began was to receive a beautiful bouquet from Gertie Millar (the Countess of Dudley). It was accompanied by a kind message and a photograph of herself as the Quaker girl 30 years ago.".

FINAL SCENE from "The Quaker Girl," one of the most colourful presentations which has graced the Hippodrome stage for many years. It will open in London next week.

Always on my dressing table at the theatre, amongst the make-up odds and ends, the pictures, brushes, stood a jewel, a gift of unpretentious craftsmanship... six inches tall, a diptych. The outside of chrome, a replica of the Quaker Girl, inside at left in tiny boxes like mosaics the signatures of all the cast and facing this in gold and red and black, mediaeval style, these words

To our beloved Celia
on her Birthday
we offer our
thanks for your friendship
admiration for your talent
wishes for happiness... hope for the future
and our
Love to you

69

CELIA LIPTON and BILLY MILTON as they appear in *The Quaker Girl* at the London Coliseum. You can hear them this evening at 6.0 in a recording of last Tuesday's *Variety Band-Box.*

Gertie Millar, the original Quaker girl and later the Countess of Dudley, came to see me in the show one evening. This made me extremely nervous–wondering what she would think of my performance. I was relieved, delighted, and surprised–all at the same time–when I received her beautiful post (above).

Ivy St. Helier, Billy Milton, Celia Lipton and Hal Bryan in a scene from "The Quaker Girl."

Celia Met Her Good Fairy On The Ten-Fifteen

BLONDE Celia Lipton is 21, but she still believes in fairies — and especially that they travel about in railway trains. There was, for instance, the fairy who sat opposite her in the 10.15. That was the day she went from London to Coventry to open in " Skylark," a new George Doonan revue. The fairy was tall, dark and young, and when a general conversation opened up in the compartment he sat back and listened interestedly.

Occasionally he broke in with a quiet touch of reminiscence, particularly when the topic turned to travel abroad.

It was when a soldier learned from Celia that she was on the stage that the fairy took a closer interest. He monopolised her attention from then on, asked her a lot of questions, and found that Celia's ambition was to play the lead in a musical comedy.

He seemed sorry when Celia rose to leave at Coventry, but as he shook hands he said: " I hope you get your wish." Then he added, " I'm sure you will."

Heaven-Sent Chance

Some time later Celia planned a rest in the country; was only two days settled down when a telegram arrived. Jessie Matthews had left "The Quaker Girl," and some one was needed to take her place. Would Celia do it? Celia jumped at this heaven-sent chance.

Up to London she went to meet the sender of the telegram. It was her fairy of the 10.15— impresario Emile Littler!

When Celia confessed she had never played musical comedy before, let alone take over a title role, he said he knew that, but was convinced she could do it. Then he gave her ONE WEEK to learn the part; Celia was up half the night learning her lines. Shrewdness of Emile's judgment can be judged by the fact that "Quaker Girl" has played three times within a year in Glasgow alone—and to capacity houses!

News of Celia's father—ex-band leader Sidney Lipton, who joined the Army as a ranker nearly five years ago and is now a captain—is that he is in Brussels organising bands and shows for the troops.

Coloratura Found

Sidney has found what he calls " a number of brilliant Belgian artists," including one coloratura, whom he would like to bring to Britain for a new venture which he has in mind.

Having a personal preference for light orchestral music, he plans to form a dance band greatly augmented by a string section, on the same lines a America's Andre Kostelanetz.

He is due for leave in a few weeks and Celia tells me he may be demobbed within a few months.

When he gets an orchestra together again, Celia hopes to be able to sing for him at times.

The further progress of
CELIA LIPTON

By RUSSELL PALMER

I ENJOY meeting and knowing nice people, whether they are occupied in my own chosen branch of this journal's wide scope of activity or in some other.

I can feel a very definite admiration for an artist who rises to the top of his or her profession from one end of the scale to the other.

I detest mediocrity and half-heartedness.

Celia Lipton grew up with a father who had certainly risen to the top of his sphere of entertainment (before the war required his services abroad as an officer in the British Army) and done so with a degree of polished individuality and sound musicianship that brought credit to the whole business of making dance music.

The one thing he stipulated when she wheedled his consent to her taking up singing as a career several years ago, by the womanly device of sitting on his knee until his masculine objections had been removed (under which precise circumstances it would be difficult to refuse Celia very much) was that she should succeed unquestionably, or admit failure and settle down to any one of a dozen other occupations that he preferred her to follow. Sydney Lipton knew too much about the pitfalls obstructing the road to success to imagine his daughter would have an easy time; had too often seen in others the pain of disillusionment to wish her any such experience.

Of course Celia brought him certain evidence of her abilities or he might never have agreed at all. Without telling anyone she brought off a B.B.C. audition under her father's very nose, and took the results to him as proof that she meant to go on with singing if only he would permit it. When I first met the Lipton family in their London flat while Syd was on leave a long time ago, she had already justified his conditional agreement and "graduated" from singing with dance bands to appear on the Hippodrome stage in one of George Black's productions. She had piled up an impressive amount of stage experience on tour, from the now famous South of England to the principal towns and cities of Scotland. Working two theatres in the same week was quite a regular pastime for her.

Celia had, in turn, made her own decision. She wanted to sing in musical comedy and operetta; to "cast away the microphone and reach the back row of the gallery without artificial means" as I remarked in an article about her some two years ago. This meant study with a reputable singing master; hard practice at the piano—in fact most of the things that the majority of crooning young ladies hold in the lightest possible consequence. That a good many of our "popular singing" charmers should speak of reading music as something that only stupid people bother their heads about, has always left me profoundly amused.

Celia Lipton has worked—hard. Whether or not you admire her particular vocal ability, the fact remains that she has put a great deal into her training and studies. She still takes singing lessons. Five minutes after arriving home from a short holiday some weeks back she parked me in an exceedingly "sinkable into" armchair while she telephoned her tutor and fixed a lesson for the following morning. She wanted to discuss several points about her reading of the score of Show Boat, for the "starred" radio production of this famous musical play, in which she appeared with Pat Taylor on the 24th of last month. Heaven knows most of the girls currently rhyming "moon" with "tune" wouldn't know a G clef from a pig's trotter, bless their little hearts. As to Celia's Magnolia in Show Boat, who will not agree with me that she sang with considerable vocal facility to the requirements of the score? And something else. A keen musical intelligence that would not have been misplaced in higher realms of music.

She aimed at musical comedy as something that she could enjoy doing, and so it was that when Emile Littler presented his new version of The Quaker Girl at the Coliseum recently, she appeared in the part of demure Prudence Pym who became the toast of Paris, reviving a well-remembered musical comedy character originally created on the stage thirty-four years ago by Gertie Millar. Not an easy part by any means, yet her notices were uniformly good from London's "revival-hardened" critics. Now

Photo (and "Quaker Girl" cover) by Dorothy Wilding

that its run has been interrupted by present events, Celia and the whole company of sixty or seventy have toured the garrison theatres of the South under ENSA's guiding hand, taking Lionel Monckton's familiar melodies to the men of the Forces.

Earlier this year Celia played her first principal boy in pantomime, the production of Jack and Jill at the King's, Hammersmith, and had a lot of fun doing it; but of all her varied activities she told me she had the most pleasure in taking over for Glynis Johns in the name part of Peter Pan which had a nine weeks tour in the provinces—Manchester, Liverpool, Glasgow, Leeds and other large towns. It was quite a new departure for her to undertake an acting part, particularly one that has been portrayed by so many front rank actresses who have found it worthy of their serious attention, and I know she hopes to play it in London some time.

All things considered I should say she has every reason to be well pleased with her success; her five or six years of gradual development from the young lady who impersonated Judy Garland so realistically in radio adaptations of several films, to her position to-day at the age of twenty as one of London's latest leading ladies, is a story of real effort and ambition.

Ambition is a tricky human quality, so often a source of disappointment, but it has served Celia very well, largely because she has never been content to remain perched on the crooner's rickety pedestal of popularity. For crooning has the most fickle public in all entertainment.

In conclusion, perhaps you'd like to pay a short visit with me to the Lipton home in London, where Celia and her mother spend their time together, when engagements permit. You'll probably find Celia at the piano and perhaps she'll play something for you (as she did play two little folk song arrangements for me the other evening). A delightful atmosphere of informal hospitality in which only one thing is needed to complete the family picture—to have Sydney Lipton back from the Middle East, where he has been fighting in North Africa and Italy with his regiment. For Syd is no cardboard soldier. He joined the army to fight, and has been doing so abroad for the past eighteen months or two years.

As I said at the beginning I enjoy meeting nice people.

The Liptons certainly are, and in concluding this article essentially about Celia, I would like to say "Hello! Syd, wherever you are at the moment! Keep fit, and we'll be glad to see you home as soon as you've finished your job out there."

My father returned home from the war. To my mother, her hero had come home safe and sound. She had every reason to be proud of him, as was I. When I came back to England I was thrilled because my father was home to stay. I felt that we were a family once more. My mother, during my father's absence, had been not only a mother and a father to me, but also she had unselfishly endured those arduous days on the road as my chaperone. It is very hard to describe the joy my mother and I felt on my father's return.

One of the first things my father told me was the emotion he felt one day in North Africa, sitting in his tent on the edge of the desert. He said he felt an over-whelming wave of homesickness and tried to assuage it by turning the dials on his radio in an effort to tune into the BBC. There were tears in his eyes when he told me how suddenly his tent was filled with the sound of my voice saying, "Daddy, I hope and pray you will hear this song that I am about to sing just for you." The song was "Oh, My Beloved Father," an aria from "Gianni Schicchi" by Puccini.

This incident has remained etched in my memory as one of those inexplicable events that some may call coincidence. I have always felt it had a far-deeper signifi-cance, which to this day I am unable to fathom. Picture if you will–I in war-torn London at the BBC studio, missing my father very much and desperately wanting him to know it. Then, visualize my father, hundreds of miles away, in another battle-scarred arena, longing to see my mother and me again. At precisely the moment I went on the air that day, my father's radio picked up the BBC. And, for the rest of his tour of duty in North Africa, his radio was unable to pick up the BBC again as clearly as it did the day I sang to him over the airwaves.

After my stint with the USO, I rejoined the cast of "The Quaker Girl" and began touring the the United Kingdom. The show was an enormous success and we found that people were returning to see the performance several times. No matter which town we played, there was never an empty seat in the house. When the tour was over, I was asked to reappear in "Peter Pan." The London run of "Peter Pan" lasted about five months then we went on tour, appearing in theatres from Glasgow, in the north, to Northampton, in the south.

The tour seemed to be over in no time. I went from playing the part of Peter to a sultry singer, appearing with some of the great English bands. I also sang on the BBC with the Mantovani and the Melachrino Orchestras.

CASINO THEATRE
OLD COMPTON STREET, W.1

Under the direction of TOM ARNOLD and EMILE LITTLER
Licensed by the Lord Chamberlain to · · · EMILE LITTLER

EMILE LITTLER'S
ANNUAL LONDON PANTOMIME

MOTHER GOOSE

6D

DIRECTED BY CHARLES HICKM[...]

CASINO THEATRE

Chairman :
TOM ARNOLD

Matinees Daily at 2.30

Licensee :
EMILE LITTLER

Evenings at 6.30

EMILE LITTLER
presents
HIS SIXTH LONDON PANTOMIME

" MOTHER GOOSE "

Book and Lyrics by BYAM STREET
Music by JOSEPH TUNBRIDGE

Characters in order of appearance :

Troubles, the Village Policeman	... ... CON KENNA
Jill, Mother Goose's Daughter ...	... ROBERTA HUBY
Colin, Foreman on Mother Goose's Farm ...	... CELIA LIPTON
Mother Goose	... ... NAT MILLS
Tulip, a Dairymaid	... ... BOBBIE
Squire Skinflint	STANLEY HOLLOWAY
Witch Binding	MARJORIE FIELDHOUSE
Fairy Snowdrop	... JASMINE DEE
Priscilla, the Goose	... DOROTHY ELLISTON
Cup and Saucer, two snakes in the grass	
King Goose	DAVE & JOE O'GORMAN
Lord Chamberlain	ARTHUR TURTON
	JEREMY NICHOLLS

EUGENE'S FLYING BALLET
THE TERRY JUVENILES
THE TILLER GIRLS

Directed by CHARLES HICKMAN

Roberta Huby, Celia Lipton and Arthur Turton in "Mother Goose."

That Christmas, I appeared at the New Casino Theatre in the pantomime "Mother Goose," presented by Sir Emile Littler at the Casino on Old Compton Street. The well-known English comedian Nat Mills played Mother Goose. Stanley Holloway played the part of a villainous squire and I was cast to play Colin, the principal boy. My boyish figure and long legs were obvious physical attributes for the part. The principal girl was played by a lovely actress, who was to later become Lady Kathleen Grade, wife of the British television tycoon and movie producer Lew Grade (who later became a peer in the British House of Lords).

The cast was occupied at the Casino from opening night on December 20th until the end of February 1947. The BBC showed interest in the show, broadcasting a visit to a rehearsal on December 16th and then including a half-hour excerpt from "Mother Goose" in its pre-Christmas holiday schedule.

At the time, I was fascinated by the potential of television. So, I was more than pleased to accept a singing role on a television show "Kaleidoscope," produced at the Alexandra Palace by Dickie Afton. Debbie Reynolds and Eddie Fisher were also working there at the time.

WEST-END'S PRINCIPAL BOY

Celia Lipton stars in Emile Littler's all - star pantomime, "Mother Goose," at the Casino Theatre, London.

OUR ARTIST'S SKETCHES OF A FEW OF THE PRINCIPALS AT THE CASINO THEATRE, LONDON.

Rehearsal in mink

I WAS given a glimpse of the future when I called in at the Casino theatre to watch part of the first rehearsal of Emile Littler's pantomime, "Mother Goose." The principals were rehearsing in the bar —which, incidentally, was closed. There was no colour or glitter, no music.

Celia Lipton, principal boy, wore brown tailored trousers and a smartly cut jacket. Roberta Huby, principal girl, was in mink. Mother Goose was in a blue lounge suit. The book and lyrics are new, and what I heard I enjoyed.

On the stage, a host of young women were learning a dance routine.

"Mother Goose" is one of the few pantomimes in and around

Box-office now open for London Casino panto, "Mother Goose," which opens on December 20. Nat Mills, Bobbie, Celia Lipton, Stan Holloway, the O'Gorman Brothers, and Roberta Huby make this a "must" for the kids.

In my silver evening gown from "Skylarks"

Using a crane at Walton Studios, MacLean Rogers directs Celia Lipton and a bevy of beauties in a night club scene for the Nettlefold production "Paul Temple and the Canterbury Case."

While television was beckoning me, so was the cinema. I had taken my first screen test when I was 14 years old for Warner Brothers in London. I was tested by producer Marcel Hellman for the film "They Met in the Dark," opposite James Mason, who had starred in a number of films, and was later the leading man with Judy Garland in "A Star is Born." Before the cameras started rolling, my eyebrows were plucked off and then penciled in to create arches that seemed to reach my hairline. James was asked to stand on a soapbox, so that he and I would be the same height. Nothing came of the screen test, and at that time I was too busy appearing on stage to pursue a movie career.

Although, later I decided that after stage, radio, and television, it would be interesting to be in films as well. So I made my cinematic debut in the film "Tall Headlines," with Dame Flora Robson, who was a famous Lady Bracknell in Oscar Wilde's, "The Importance of Being Ernest." Then, I appeared in "Paul Temple and the Canterbury Case," produced by MacLean Rogers and filmed at Walton Studios. My role called for me to be murdered in the middle of singing a song. Fortunately, a stunt girl took over falling down the stairs on my behalf. Wherever that stunt girl is today, I want her to know I shall always be grateful to her.

I also appeared in "This Was A Woman," with Sonia Dresdel. In the credits, I was billed as, "Introducing Celia Lipton." My part was substantial—no singing—a dramatic role of a young woman who steals the heroine's husband. I enjoyed filming, but a stage career at the same time was impossible.

Through all this work and traveling, I tried my best to have some sort of social life, but it wasn't easy. Somehow, I never found much time to accept the many dinner invitations or to go dancing. The discipline of my childhood had certainly shaped my entrance into adulthood; work always came first. There was no time for fun and relaxation. I loved my work and the different roles I played.

That is not to say I did not attend parties—but, they were usually functions revolving around the theater, such as opening nights. Some of the great actors of that time including Sir Peter Ustinov, Sir John Mills, Sir John Gielgud, Trevor Howard, Lord Olivier, Vivien Leigh, Anna Neagle, were but a small sampling of the thespians who attended these functions.

It was at one of those opening-night parties that I met one of the nicest young men whom it was my privilege to know. He died at a very young age from leukemia, but I shall always remember him and his gracious family. His name was Bill Hanson, the brother of James Hanson, later a financial wizard who was made a life Peer, and was once engaged to Audrey Hepburn. I was on the road, appearing in a show near Huddersfield, where the Hanson's lived. Bill invited me to meet his family at a lovely house they were living in at the time.

I sang with bands, and appeared on television and in the movies. I did shows for the BBC radio, cut records, and was under contract to Columbia Records—recording at Abbey Road Studio. At this same time, with my recording and stage careers, I continued working in radio for the BBC including performing in the General Forces Programs "The Melody Lingers On" and "Variety Band Box." The shows were broadcast from the stage of the Queensberry All-Services Club.

From July until the end of October 1946, I appeared on the BBC "Light Program" in a weekly show for Forces in hospitals called, "Here's Wishing You Well Again." In August and September of 1946, I played Jane Lindon in a weekly series called "The Barnstormers" on the "Light Program." "The Radio Times" described

Starring as Lili in "Lilac Time"

the program as "The story of a theatrical venture" with book and lyrics by Gyles Adams, and music composed by Peter Akister. I also sang with Carroll Gibbons and his orchestra in his "Floor Show," broadcast on the "Light Program."

This continued for almost two years, and then I was asked to temporarily replace actress Phyllis Calvert at the Scala Theatre, where she was appearing as "Peter Pan." Phyllis had come down with the flu. I had two days in which to re-learn the whole of "Peter Pan." I did it, though, and I loved playing the role, flying across the stage to the delight of the audience and myself.

After I finished playing Peter, I concentrated on rehearsing for my next and most challenging role, that of Lili in the light operetta "Lilac Time" with music arranged from Franz Schubert.

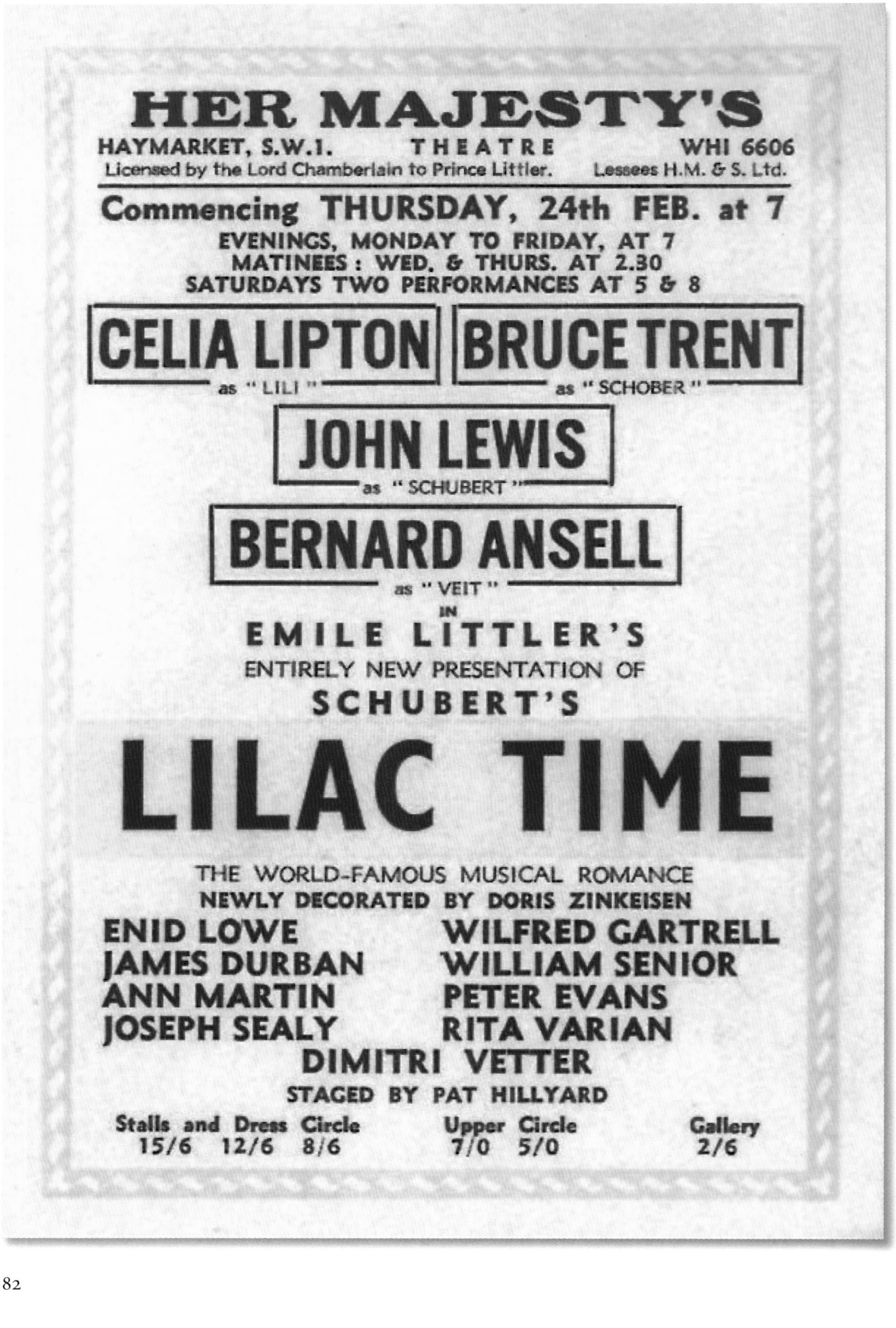

HER MAJESTY'S

HAYMARKET, S.W.1.   THEATRE   WHI 6606
Licensed by the Lord Chamberlain to Prince Littler.   Lessees H.M. & S. Ltd.

Commencing THURSDAY, 24th FEB. at 7

EVENINGS, MONDAY TO FRIDAY, AT 7
MATINEES : WED. & THURS. AT 2.30
SATURDAYS TWO PERFORMANCES AT 5 & 8

CELIA LIPTON   BRUCE TRENT

as " LILI "   as " SCHOBER "

JOHN LEWIS

as " SCHUBERT "

BERNARD ANSELL

as " VEIT "

IN

EMILE LITTLER'S
ENTIRELY NEW PRESENTATION OF
SCHUBERT'S

LILAC TIME

THE WORLD-FAMOUS MUSICAL ROMANCE
NEWLY DECORATED BY DORIS ZINKEISEN

ENID LOWE	WILFRED GARTRELL
JAMES DURBAN	WILLIAM SENIOR
ANN MARTIN	PETER EVANS
JOSEPH SEALY	RITA VARIAN

DIMITRI VETTER
STAGED BY PAT HILLYARD

| Stalls and Dress Circle | Upper Circle | Gallery |
| 15/6 12/6 8/6 | 7/0 5/0 | 2/6 |

Starring in "Lilac Time" at the Palace Theater, London

My producer, Sir Emile Littler, clung to the vision of me as "The Quaker Girl"– prim, proper, and submissive–and continued to cast me in that type of role. All the while, I longed to play a gutsy girl like Annie Oakley in "Annie Get Your Gun." That show was brought to London by Sir Emile, and my friend Dolores Gray played the lead role, taking London by storm. After seeing Dolores do such a great job, I felt that Annie had to be played by an American.

"Lilac Time's" Lili was the most difficult singing role I had ever attempted. After six months of rehearsals we opened at Her Majesty's Theatre in London, in 1949, to excellent reviews: "Her performance has been acclaimed as one of the best 'Lili's' in the history of the piece." We were only supposed to appear for a six-week run, but the show was so successful that we went on to the Palace Theatre in London.

Once again, the show and my performance were well-received. But, Sir Emile was a firm believer that, in order to have staying power, a show needed to conquer the United Kingdom. With that in mind, he booked "Lilac Time" on a long tour of the provinces, to play in most of the major cities. Doris Zinkeinsen, the renowned stage, set, costume designer, writer, and artist, designed the costumes and production set for "Lilac Time." She did an exquisite painting of me as Lili. Today, I am the proud owner of that painting. It was presented to me as a gift from Sir Emile.

Stardom
By JOHN BOLTON

PEOPLE in the entertainment business are always interested in what they now call "star quality." They will discuss it without necessarily being able to define it, except as something which one artist possesses while another, though perfectly competent by all outward standards, has not.

Sometimes, I think, you get the key to star quality if you talk with the artist under discussion. Its first essential, I would say, is the ability —knack, single-mindedness, or what you like to call it—to give the whole mind to whatever is in hand.

All the great music-hall artists I have known had it—Marie Lloyd, Nellie Wallace, George Clarke, Harry Lauder—but it isn't just something that accrues with age and long experience. I think it has to be there from the start.

You get it in a stage artist as young as Celia Lipton, now happily back in "Lilac Time," and at Leeds Grand Theatre this week, asserting more and more of her hold on audiences at every performance, though she says she still felt shaky from her illness when the week began. With her, too, the star quality comes out even in casual private talk. Point is that she is keenly and vitally interested in every topic.

And she works hard at her job. Those around her believe she will go much farther, and say she is only at the beginning of a brilliant career

Billy as Cha the E...

OUR ARTIST'S SKETCHES OF SOME OF THE PRINCIPALS APPEARING AT HIS MAJESTY'S THEATRE, LONDON

"Lilac Time"

TIME CANNOT KILL THE LOVELY MELODIES OF "FRANZ SCHUBERT" —THAT'S WHY THEY'RE SUCH HAUNTING REFRAINS (JOHN LEWIS)

"VEIT LOVES BABIES —ESPECIALLY THOSE BORN 20 YEARS AGO (BERNARD ANSELL)

WE FOLLOW THE COURT-SHIP OF "TILLI" AND "WILLI" FROM "YOO-HOO" TO "I DO" (ANN MARTIN AND PAMELA WHITE)

"LILI" THE GIRL WITH THE HIGH EYE CUE —THAT LIVELY LOVELY CELIA LIPTON

"MARINI" GETS TANTRUMENTAL

ENID LOWE

THAT "NOVOTNY" ONE-MAN ESCORT SERVICE (DIMITRI VETTER)

THE FOOLANDERING "BARON" IS PLAYED AND SUNG BY BRUCE TRENT —AND TIP-TOPERATIC HE IS

"IF SCHUBERT WERE AS SMALL IN STATURE AS HE PROTESTS HE IS, HE'D BE HIDDEN IN THE NAP OF THE RUG!"

Doris Zinkeinsen, who designed the costumes and production set for "Lilac Time," did an exquisite painting of me as Lili. The painting was presented to me as a gift from Sir Emile Littler.

A picture of me taken from the book "Spectacle" by A. Crooks Ripley.

After reading the proposed tour schedule, I knew I had to get away and take a holiday before embarking on the backbreaking, two performances a day, over a six-month period tour. I left London armed with letters of introduction and flew to New York. Upon landing in New York and traveling from the airport into the city, I was struck by the peacetime noise of sirens, horns, and the bustle of all the people. America, I decided, was far more lively than England.

After arriving in Manhattan, I reserved a table in the Plaza Hotel's dining room. I intended to sample all my favorite foods that had been almost non-existent during wartime in England. The delicious salad and vegetables tasted like rare delicacies. But, after a few bites of what looked like a gigantic slab of sirloin—the first steak I'd seen in years—I began to feel quite ill.

Unwilling to give up completely, and confront the reality that my stomach was not prepared for the onslaught of all that food, I ordered a banana split. I realized then how limited food had been in Britain, and I felt sick and guilty about all the food served to me at The Plaza, food that I was about to leave to waste. Indeed, this was a stark reminder of my homeland where food was still hard to buy even after the war.

During my three-week stay in New York, I never ceased to be amazed at the amount of food Americans seemed to be prepared to waste without a moment's guilt or hesitation. When my mother finally visited the States, a few years later, her reaction was identical to mine. She found, as I had, that the portions Americans are accustomed to being served were simply too large. So my mother, with typical Scottish frugality, lived up to the tenet of "waste not, want not."

I never have believed in wasting anything. Not food and definitely not opportunity. I spent my first few days in America following up on my letters of introduction. Most of the people I contacted encouraged me to leave England and find my niche in the US. I was not sure I really wanted to leave England. But, instinct told me it was the ideal time to test the transatlantic waters…to go on a fishing expedition, of sorts, and see what career opportunities awaited Celia Lipton. I vowed to come back to America once I had finished the "Lilac Time" tour in Britain.

My first American introduction led me to Warner Brothers, and to Harry Meyer, a very powerful man in the entertainment business. His cheery office did not foretell what was soon to become a chamber of horrors. I showed him all my press clippings and after a minute, or two, he shut the book. Then, re-enacting the old cliché of what happens to young actresses in Hollywood, he proceeded to chase me around his desk. I stopped long enough to retrieve my portfolio of clippings and, summoning as much British manners as I could muster, icily said, "Thank you very much and good day."

I strode out of his office, and was half-way to the elevator when I heard footsteps behind me. I quickened my pace. Then I heard Harry Meyer somewhat sheepishly say, "Wait just a minute." There was no one else in the vicinity. Thinking this was just another ploy on his part, I gripped the heavy, press-clipping book with both hands, ready to hit him over the head with it if he tried any more amorous advances. But, when I turned and looked at him, I realized he was indeed contrite as he offered, "As a matter of fact, an act at the Strand Theater is sick. They show movies there. But, it has a stage show as well. If I send you over there, would you fill-in for him just for tonight?"

Figuring I had nothing to lose, I agreed to fill-in for the ailing performer. But, just as I was ready to enter the elevator, Meyer said, "I'll send some agents in tonight to watch your act…but, for God's sake, try to lose that damn British accent." How wrong he was.

After "My Fair Lady" burst onto the Broadway scene, a British accent in the American theatrical world proved to be an asset. Meyer's off-handed, disparaging reference to my accent did not dampen my excitement. All I could think of was, "I am in America, I am going to appear on Broadway tonight, and I have had no rehearsal with the orchestra!"

During the hours prior to my appearance at the Strand Theater, I alternated between being scared and euphoric. But, when it came time for me to go on stage, somehow, I lost my case of nerves and confidently sang, "How Are Things in Glochamora?" The audience responded so well that I went on to do some impersonations that really pleased the crowd. As Harry Meyer had promised, there were some agents who caught my act that night. An agent from the William Morris Booking Agency had seen me on stage at the Strand, and within less that a few days, William Morris, Jr. sent me a letter of request to represent me.

All this was pretty heady stuff for an actress who had just a week before stepped off the plane from England. Even more so, when the trade newspaper, "Variety," reviewed my performance, and called me another "Gracie Fields."

And so it was, my visit to New York, which I had intended to be mainly a holiday, turned out to be a working holiday. A television writer, I had met only briefly, recommended me for a part on the Milton Berle Show. Before I could catch my breath, I was rehearsing for the show in which I would walk out on a red carpet as Marie Antoinette with "The Three Musketeers," played by Milton Berle, Morey Amsterdam, and Henny Youngman. My part required that I sing "Queen of France" that contained the lyrics, "strong as Atlas." The song was dramatic, and I decided the finale should contain a gesture, which in Britain was completely innocuous. In America, however, the gesture had a far more different connotation.

Before I knew what was happening, Berle, Amsterdam, and Youngman became so convulsed with laughter they could barely stand up. While they were falling over their fake swords, the feathers festooning their three-cornered hats began poking their eyes. This led the three to start groping each other, and I, not realizing what was going on, thought it was part of the act. Finally, the producer got hold of me and took me off the set. He explained, as delicately as he could, just exactly what the gesture I had made at the finale meant in America. Needless to say, the "vulgar" gesture was eliminated from my song.

Career aspirations aside, I had a wonderful time in New York, attending many parties where luminaries were always in attendance. On one occasion, I was invited to a charity benefit on a boat that sailed up the Hudson River. Someone told the chairman of the event that I could sing, and shortly thereafter, I was prevailed upon to entertain the guests.

Among those on-board were Mary Pickford and her husband Buddy Rogers. Mary, at the time, was Chairman of the Board of Universal Studios, and when she asked me to join her table after my performance I felt I had been given a very special honor. I was immediately put at ease when Mary said that I could easily have been her daughter, and that our coloring was identical. I was tempted to say, in that case, you could help me become as famous an actress as you are. Instead, British diffidence took charge, and I made some simpering remarks of gratitude. After all, at that time Mary Pickford was one of the greatest living movie actresses.

It also turned out that she was something of an amateur fortune-teller, and wanted to read my palm. She told me that she saw a life that would be filled with lots of happiness and tragedy, and a life devoted to helping others. I remember her asking me if I had ever wanted to be a doctor. When I told her that all I ever wanted to be was an actress, she scolded me. She then told me I was a giver and not a taker, and that I would become wealthy. But, then she cautioned me to beware of the vultures who would circle round me. (There certainly have been vultures aplenty since that time.)

Just before I left New York, I was invited to a party given by one of the Annenberg sisters, Mrs. Paul Ames. It was a lovely, eclectic event. Leonard Bernstein played the piano, and Mary Ford and Les Paul sang. (I never dreamed then, that years later, Mrs. Ames' sisters—Evie Hall, Janet Hooker, and Enid Haupt—would become my good friends and neighbors in Palm Beach.) Reluctantly, I bade America farewell—like it or not. I was under contract, and duty compelled me to return to England to fulfill that contract with Sir Emile Littler for "Lilac Time."

England was starting to rebuild its cities, towns, and industries after the devastating consequences of the war. Coming back to my wounded country was a sharp contrast to what I had seen in America—a country physically unscathed by the horrors of World War II. There was very little time to wish I was back in New York, because I had to prepare for "Lilac Time" and its tour through the United Kingdom. Compared with the exciting time I'd had in America, the tour was as dull and taxing as I had expected. I contracted a variety of low-grade fevers and my throat began to suffer. Traditionally in opera, a singer should only appear in a part three times a week. More performances can be too much of a strain on the voice. I began to fear that singing Lili for eight performances a week, over such a long period of time, was damaging my voice.

I was so absorbed in my work that I was unaware of the changes taking place in the British theatre, which would later become a radical transformation. London, long the home of innocently sweet musicals, was deluged by glitzy American Broadway musicals, bursting with brashness and big budgets. One after the other they arrived in London—"Oklahoma," "Finian's Rainbow," "Annie Get Your Gun," and "Brigadoon." When my tour with "Lilac Time" ended I returned to London, only to find that the theatre scene was dominated by American musicals, and British artists were not even invited to audition. Those of us in the theatre were utterly dismayed at this turn of events and unsure of how to react in the face of these American musicals.

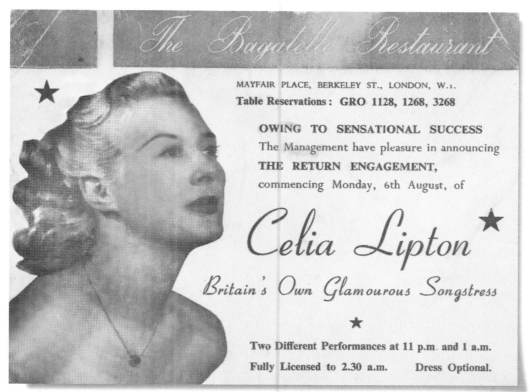

Singing in a cabaret was not my favorite kind of performance, but it was work. I headlined at The Bagatelle in London, and later at The Ritz-Carlton in Montreal, and the St. Regis in New York.

I was advised to retreat into the relative security of performing cabaret and, although I didn't relish the prospect of singing to audiences clanking knives and forks and drinking, I nevertheless invested the considerable sum of £500 in a new wardrobe–despite clothes rationing. Then, I promptly accepted an engagement to appear in cabaret at the Empress Club's Dove Room. I followed that with three performances at the famous Bagatelle. "Variety," the show business weekly, singled me out as "A talented impressionist."

The Bagatelle was chic, as well as elegant, and the patrons seemed to enjoy my singing. Although my voice was getting husky, everyone said it was seductive. When I sang the lyrics to "The End of a Love Affair"–"I smoke a little too much and I drink a little too much"–it sounded as if the song had been written just for my new torchy-sounding voice. But deep down, I knew my voice was in trouble.

While I was appearing at the Bagatelle, two prominent men came to hear me sing. One of them was director Richard Brooks, and the other was Pandro S. Berman –one of MGM's top producers. They asked me to sit with them after the show and seemed genuinely interested in my future career plans. Instead of saying, "I would love to make a film in America," all I volunteered was, "How nice of you to come and see my show." Talk about British reticence! That interview was classic!

After appearing at the Bagatelle, I went back to the Empress Club's Dove Room. One night, the entire room was reserved for a party by a contingent of stars from America. I was extremely nervous. Some of the stars who were expected to see my act included Jack Benny and Eddie Anderson (who played Rochester on the Benny radio and television shows), Alice Faye, Phil Harris, Julie Wilson, and Bea Lillie. The show began with a talented conjurer who met with great applause from the celebrities. But, when it came time for my act, all the lights fused and the room went completely black. The stars never saw my performance that night. Instead, I just sat in my dressing room and cried.

A few days later, columnist Noel Whitcomb wrote: "Only girl I felt sorry for at the party was young Celia Lipton, who was doing the cabaret. Celia was terrified. Sitting around the tables were some of the world's shrewdest judges of a cabaret act. And this was only Celia's third week in cabaret. But she had one little secret, which buoyed her up. She had figured—quite rightly—that the reason why most English cabaret acts don't go down so smoothly as American acts is because they don't get such expert production. So she had telephoned lighting-expert Bob Nesbitt and asked him to rig some special lighting for her, because he is a big shot in the lighting world. Very decently Bob had agreed. He fixed some lighting for Celia that added 100 percent to her act. So Celia came on to the floor ready to show these international impresarios what a British girl can do when she has a really slick production. And then the lights fused all together and only candlelight was left."

Undaunted by the embarrassing experience at the Dove Room, I was booked into the Embassy Club. Jack Hylton, my manager, suggested he throw a party for me prior to the opening—I readily agreed. Among those invited were Caesar Romero, a chatty man, and Clark Gable, who was as handsome in person as he was on screen. He truly was a very charming, friendly, and dignified gentleman.

My opening at the Embassy was well-received. The reviews were so good that one night Noel Coward called the club ahead of time to find out what time I was on. Unfortunately that night, of all nights, my pianist never showed up. What was worse, he had all my music with him. After waiting for a long time to catch my act, Noel Coward came to my dressing room and demanded to know when I was going on. I explained my pianist was missing with my music. That was not the answer he wanted to hear after waiting for hours in the audience. He promptly turned on his heels and left. It made me sad that he never saw me perform. Later, I heard that my pianist, on his way to work, had been mugged by a bunch of thugs and pummeled into unconsciousness.

I started to realize that my voice was changing and becoming progressively worse. Maestro Cunelli had also noticed and wondered whether I was developing nodules on my vocal chords. I had, after all, suffered several bouts of flu and had been working almost non-stop. It is easy to be wise after an event. My voice was still developing and I was pushing it too hard. But, I was young, I was becoming well-known, and wanted to make the most of this wonderful world—even though all British towns and cities were blacked out for the six-year duration of World War II. Unless you saw Piccadilly Circus without its brilliant neon lights, it is hard to imagine just how dark the nights were. Clubs and theatres became little oasis of brightness and laughter, in an otherwise, unremitting country at war. I didn't want to be out of this milieu even for a week or two.

But, the Maestro convinced me that I should see a top London throat specialist. The doctor confirmed our fears, and I underwent an operation whose after-effects were devastatingly painful. One of my first visitors was the actor Trevor Howard, who rose to international prominence just after the war in the movie, "Brief Encounter." He told me lots of funny stories to cheer me up, but I was not allowed to laugh or speak.

For months afterwards, I didn't speak or laugh at all, and I began to fret that I might never sing again. I couldn't even tell the Maestro my fears, but he seemed to instinctively understand. As my voice began to mend, the Maestro said that singing again would be like learning to walk, and that we would have to work very hard together.

And, we certainly did work…practicing, trying to get my voice back into shape. Much of the time I felt demoralized and disheartened, alarmed by the future, and increasingly doubtful about the prospects of regaining my singing voice. After months of work the Maestro thought I was ready, and I agreed to do a broadcast for the BBC of "Shipmate's Ashore," with Deborah Kerr and Leslie Howard. Yet, it seemed that my career in England was not progressing as quickly as I had hoped.

The British theatre scene was filled with new musicals coming from America. I was tired of appearing in revivals and wanted to work in a new show.

I had been very independent for some years. My father had been away in the war and my mother had been a wonderful chaperone, for much of my formative time in the theater. But, singing in musicals, performing eight shows a week, was very hard on my vocal chords. It was then, after the long hours, throat surgery, and in a state of pure exhaustion, I thought I'd rather act and give my singing voice a rest. So, off to New York I went.

New York City

MY SECOND LIFE

My cabaret stage photo by Bruno of Hollywood, N.Y.

Chalfonte-Haddon Hall, Atlantic City, New Jersey

I found work immediately upon my arrival in New York—appearing in one-night engagements at Grossinger's in the Catskills, and at Chalfonte Haddon Hall in Atlantic City. After working the resort areas for a while, I was asked by Nat Abramson, head of the New York's WOR Radio, to appear at Constitution Hall in Washington, D.C. as part of a two-and-a-half-hour production called, "1952 Broadway Review." The program was sponsored by the Women's Army and Navy League, to raise money for the men and women of the armed forces. The show was a great success. Nat Abramson told me later that President Harry S. Truman was in the audience and was apparently so impressed with my act, that he wondered if he would be good enough to accompany that "little English girl" at the piano.

Tactful to the core, Nat assured the President that he was more than capable of accompanying me at the piano, but talked him out of inviting me to the White House. Nat figured if a photo appeared in newspapers around the country, showing the President accompanying me at the piano, this might not sit well with Americans. I was not yet a citizen. It would not have been appropriate for a Brit—particularly a Brit who only had a temporary, work permit—to be invited to perform at the White House when there were so many top-notch American artists, who hadn't been invited. Obtaining a permanent work permit was difficult. Finally, an immigration lawyer advised me to go to the Bahamas, and from there emigrate to the U.S.

So, I headed to the Bahamas aboard a cruise ship, where I was part of the entertainment complement, and received free passage. It should have been a fun-filled experience, but it wasn't. I had realized earlier, on my voyage to New York, that I wasn't a natural-born sailor. My journey to the Bahamas was no different; I was sea-sick most of the time. But, as queasy as I felt, I was still able to do my act. I landed in Nassau, and had a singing engagement at the British Colonial Hotel, where I was billed as "England's Charming Singing Star."

During the six-week stay, one of my most memorable experiences was meeting Nancy Oakes. Her father, Sir Harry, was murdered in mysterious circumstances in 1943. His body was found on the beach, and no one was ever caught.

After Nassau, I returned to the United States with my papers in order and the determination for a career on Broadway. When my New York agent told me that there was a part coming up in Rodgers and Hammerstein's "South Pacific," and I would be required to audition, I was nonplussed. I hadn't banked on being auditioned because, after being styled as England's Judy Garland in the BBC performances, I never had to audition again. I was a "known" in England. I soon swallowed my pride and auditioned. (In those days most everyone in the U.S. auditioned regardless of their star status.)

I knew I would be up against very stiff competition; just ahead of me was a young, beautiful blonde, with a fantastic voice. She turned out to be Florence Henderson, who became a popular star, on stage and small screen. I didn't get the part, because the producer thought my accent too British, but I gave the audition my best shot singing, "I'm In Love With A Wonderful Guy." And, even though I did not get the role, I did not lose my resolve. I went on to audition for the role of Lady Sybil in John Fearnley's production of "Maggie," based on Sir James Barrie's play, "What Every Woman Knows." I felt some comfort in the audition, knowing that a British accent would be advantageous, or perhaps it was a feeling of well-being that, once again, I would be acting a part conjured up by the writer whose legendary "Peter Pan" enthralled audiences around the world.

It was a difficult and demanding audition, and the competition was keen, but I got the part. However, there was a stumbling block—I was not a member of American Equity. After 50 American actresses had been tested for the role, and had been found unsuitable, American Equity (in an unprecedented move, subsequently reported in "The New York Times") got special permission to allow me to play the part of Lady Sybil, even though I was not a member. "Maggie" opened in 1953 at the National Theater on Broadway.

Starring as Lady Sybil in the Broadway production of "Maggie."

A scene from "Maggie" at the National Theater.

FRANKLIN GILBERT and JOHN FEARNLEY
present

BETTY PAUL   KEITH ANDES

CELIA LIPTON

in

Maggie

A New Musical
(Based on J. M. Barrie's Play "What Every Woman Knows")

with

BRAMWELL FLETCHER   **JOHN HOYT**

FRANK MAXWELL   **JAMES BRODERICK**   **ALICIA KRUG**

and

KATHRYN LEE   **MARC PLATT**

Book by **Hugh Thomas**   Music and Lyrics by **William Roy**

Directed by **MICHAEL GORDON**

Sets and Costumes by **RAOUL PENE duBOIS**

Choreography by
JUNE GRAHAM

Musical Direction by
MAURICE LEVINE

Orchestrations by
DON WALKER

Lighting by
LOUIS POPIEL

Production Associate
HARRY ZEVIN

THE CAST
(In Order of Their Appearance)

ALICK WYLIE	BRAMWELL FLETCHER
JAMES WYLIE	JAMES BRODERICK
DAVID WYLIE	FRANK MAXWELL
MAGGIE WYLIE	BETTY PAUL
JOHN SHAND	KEITH ANDES
MRS. MacPHERSON	ANITA ELLIS
PROFESSOR DUBOIS	HENRY HAMILTON
MRS. MacLAUGHLIN	JENNY LOU LAW
MADAME MARSTONNE	IRENE BORDONI
SYBIL TENTERDON	CELIA LIPTON
WILLIAMS	GENE HOLLMANN
VENABLES	JOHN HOYT
JOHN SHAND (IN BALLET)	MARC PLATT
MAGGIE WYLIE (IN BALLET)	ALICIA KRUG
SYBIL TENTERDON (IN BALLET)	KATHRYN LEE
PORTERS	GENE HOLLMANN, HENRY HAMILTON, ORAN OSBURN
CONDUCTOR	PAUL UKENA

Playbill from "Maggie" – music and lyrics by William Roy

"Maggie" then went on the road, and I loved my role. My character was like that of Alexis Colby of "Dynasty," a period piece in which I was adorned in chinchilla, jewelry, and beautiful hats. We played Boston and Philadelphia, and I was receiving thunderous applause at every entrance and exit. I was delighted that there were huge pictures of me outside the theater. I sometimes had to pinch myself to believe that I was actually awake and not dreaming, and that I was really starring in a Broadway show.

But, there was a problem at the National Theatre in New York. The scenery didn't fit. On opening night, the people in the first five rows could hear the stagehands swearing. It was very sad and, although Rodgers and Hammerstein were very much behind the show, it closed after a week. Despite the brief run, for me the show was a triumph. Reviewing the musical, Walter Kerr wrote in "The New York Times," "I did like the handsome Celia Lipton, who played Lady Sybil with great aplomb."

The role in "Maggie" would have established me in the American theater, but while I was very disappointed at the show's closing, I knew I had to keep trying. I also missed my parents and talked to them a great deal on the telephone. They were very supportive and encouraging. I knew I must not give in to my disappointment and homesickness, and run back to England because of this one failure. My philosophy was, as it still is, "onward and upward." To add to all my problems, American Equity had a rule that anyone who was not an American citizen had to wait six months after a show closed before being allowed to resume work.

Unable to survive financially without work, I went to Montreal, Canada and, as I knew some French from holiday's years before, sang in French at the Ritz Café at the Ritz Carlton. One critic labeled me a "Top favorite and welcome newcomer" and another, "A lively blonde girl from England, Celia Lipton holds down the show assignment at the Ritz Carlton Hotel and shows herself to be a very accomplished performer…It's some time now since we've seen a cabaret artist with such a good sense of what people want in the way of songs and comedy and knows how to put it across. Showmanship and fine-timing are two of her attributes and they made an unbeatable combination when it came to putting lines across the footlights."

Once the six months were up, I left Canada and came back to New York, where my agent had arranged an audition for me at the St. Regis Hotel's nightclub—the

The Maisonette
After the theatre
LONDON'S CHARMING
Celia Lipton
AND HER SONGS
appearing at
DINNER and SUPPER

MILT SHAW AND
HORACE DIAZ ORCHESTRAS
Special theatre dinner
$4.00 from 6 to 8 P.M.
(no entertainment tax)

HOTEL
St. Regis
FIFTH AVE. at 55th ST.

RITZ CAFE
Celia Lipton; John Gallant; Joseph Settano Trio.

Only a handful of British vocalists have scored any sort of success on this side of Big Ditch. Lovely Celia Lipton is one of them. The daughter of famed London orchestra leader Sidney Lipton, the songstress seems to have rehearsed for years just to play this gathering place of Montreal's social register.

Miss Lipton, a shapely blonde with a charming personality, starts her show by singing a neatly-written introduction as she circles the ringside handing flowers to the guests. This is a neat trick that has been used here before but never so neatly as Miss Lipton's version.

Most of her songs have specially written lyrics and are beamed at an Anglo-Saxon audience. For instance she includes a slightly ribald Scottish song, The Tilt In Your Kilt, as well as semi-serious Cockney dialect number, in her repertoire. And, like most visiting vocalists, sings a French language number. In Miss Lipton's case, however, she sings in flawless French.

Weekend customers apparently enjoyed her Mad Dogs and Englishmen number best of all her offerings. Her medley of other Noel Coward selections also received a heavy round of applause and her pleasant informality — in the best Mayfair supper club tradition — set her up as a top favorite, and a welcome newcomer, to the city's cafe circuit.

CELIA LIPTON

Maisonette. I was to follow Julie Wilson, the club's regular performer who was a talented cabaret singer. Singing in a cabaret was not my favorite kind of performance, but it was work. Actors have to keep their name up as best as they can or they may be forgotten. I longed for a theatre, and playing to thousands of people, no matter what the circumstances.

Fortunately, the director of the St. Regis, Pierre Bultnick, renewed my contract at the Maisonette for another three weeks. I endured the run singing my Noel Coward medley and "Everything stops for tea of course if it's Lipton's," which had been written especially for my cabaret act there. Although the reviews were good, I still found it annoying to cope with the noise of clinking glasses, knives, forks, and clumsy waiters—nevertheless, I thought it was a good experience.

Lee Mortimer in his "Nightlife" column wrote, "Celia Lipton is a welcome windfall from Britain. The British have sent us Celia Lipton, who may be heard in the St. Regis Maisonette these nights…ironically, when she goes into the American torch numbers, show tunes, and impressions of our film stars, she scores strongly."

Tips on Tables

Miss Lipton Suits Role to a Tea

By ROBERT W. DANA.

Two of our singing stars, Dolores Gray and Julie Wilson, went to London after their American triumphs on stage and in night clubs. As sort of a reverse lend-lease, England has sent us Celia Lipton, British musical comedy star, who opened last night in the St. Regis Maisonette.

Miss Wilson, who has been doing her customary topflight job as the opening attraction in the room, apparently was elsewhere at last night's dinner show. But Miss Gray was on hand with a gay party to see her protege, daughter of England's popular bandleader, Sidney Lipton, make good in a big way.

A Fetching Blonde.

I like Miss Lipton very much. The audience was wholeheartedly in favor of her. While she is English, she seems to have the American temperament and style of showmanship best adapted for a room like the Maisonette, which requires a performer to be beautiful, gowned and coiffured for the ultimate satisfaction of a social crowd, then downright entertaining.

With, perhaps, one exception, she filled the bill admirably. In a black tulle gown with appliqued velvet bows, black tulle halter top and bouffant skirt, the blond singer was vivacious and fetching.

The only number that struck an adverse chord was Irving Berlin's "Only for Americans," which she prefaced with the remark that she meant no offense. However, its special lyrics still packed topical food for thought that was distasteful to some.

Breezy Manner.

Frankly, I was amazed at the ease with which Miss Lipton swung into her program, winning her audience immediately with breezy friendliness in song that was much more American than British. For a few moments I could scarcely believe she wasn't one of our own.

"Isn't It Great That Everybody Loves Everybody and Nobody's Mad at Anyone?" she sang. It was a perfect setup for Phil Moore's "Everything Stops for Tea." And here we had the English girl, pulling out all the stops with a beverage that is a mark of life for Britishers, adapted to the American sense of humor through use of allusions to situations both there and here.

She sang a ballad, "A Nightingale Sang in Berkeley Square" and followed with the most delicious number of all, called "Nobody Thinks I'm a Mermaid, But I Am, Honest and Truly I Am."

And Versatile.

Further showing her versatility, Miss Lipton sang "That's What Makes Paris Paris." Full of rhythm and clever lyrics, she reminded me much of Hildegarde on this one.

I think Miss Lipton will be a real success in the Maisonette and thank Miss Gray and Miss Wilson for sharing their scouting bounty with us.

THE Hollywood REPORTER

Thursday, October 23, 1952

Broadway Ballyhoo
by RADIE HARRIS

MAD-HATTAN MEDLEY: The Sardi set is abuzz over the reason behind the divorce of publicists Dorothy and George Ross. Quel histoire! . . . Celia Lipton in the Maisonette Russe of the St. Regis, and Sophie Tucker, back at the Latin Quarter, are welcome additions to the nitery scene. Celia, a British import, isn't hot potato British——is pretty, poised and can sing English and American songs with equal charm. Sophie is still the "Reddest Hottest" Mama of them all. Her naughty songs are naughtier——her schmaltzie songs are schmaltzier——and after 40 years in show biz she still has more zing than any ingenue. And when it comes to sequins and orchids, who's counting!

Appearing now in the Maisonette of the Hotel St. Regis is Celia Lipton from London and she is a definite hit with the patrons of this elegant room. This blonde English beauty is making her American debut. She has charm and poise and a pleasing voice suited to the little satires of her repertoire. Wearing a black tulle halter gown, she sings straight numbers with scarcely a trace of accent. Opening cheerily with "Isn't it Fun When Everybody's Friends With Everybody?" Miss Lipton varies her program with Cockney songs and others of the romance type. Her imitations of Katharine Hepburn, now on Broadway, and Bette Davis, soon to be there, are clever as is her salute to Noel Coward, admired on both sides of the Atlantic.

In his "New York Here and There" column, critic Russell Rhodes wrote, "Celia Lipton, blond English beauty, makes her major American debut in the St. Regis Maisonette in the style cut to the patrons of this elegant room. She has charm, poise, and a voice suited to the little satires of her repertoire." As soon as my contract at the St. Regis ended, I went straight into John Murray Anderson's "Almanac"—a review in two parts with 25 scenes, set to open at the Imperial Theater in New York. The cast included Hermione Gingold, Nanci Crompton, Polly Bergen, Billy de Wolfe, Harry Belafonte, Orson Bean, Jonathan Winters, Monique Van Vooren, Kay Medford, and Tina Louise. Tina was a beautiful redhead who went on to star in the television show "Gilligan's Island," as well as appearing in many movies.

Part of my role included reading Oscar Wilde's "The Nightingale and the Rose," while ballet dancer Nanci Crompton did hundreds of pas de deux all over the stage. We started out in Boston, and did five weeks there. John F. Kennedy, then a young and popular Senator, came to see the show with Michael Grace, one of the show's producers. The Senator and Michael came backstage to visit with the cast. (Michael was a member of the well-known Grace shipping family and was a wonderful friend.)

Hermione Gingold, who remembered me from my childhood days, was very kind and insisted on everyone calling me, "Baby Cel." When we finally opened in New York, Harry Belafonte's dressing room was right next to mine and, for a while, I couldn't understand why so many beautiful showgirls seemed to suddenly want to spend time with me in my dressing room. Then it dawned on me that they were all interested in Harry.

He was already a household name, and did "Hold 'Em Joe" in the show. Offstage he'd put on a British accent for my benefit and ask me whether I had any eyebrow pluckers to pluck out the gray hairs on his head. Kay Medford was also adorable, and would bring food in for the cast every day. In earlier rehearsals, Polly Bergen joined the show, and she and I shared a dressing room. Then, Jonathan Winters took over for Orson Bean (who went back to nightclubs). Jonathan was a darling and brilliantly funny.

"Almanac" ran for a year on Broadway. "The New York Times" said, "Celia Lipton combines beauty with an infectious comedy sense."

Rehearsing for the Broadway review "Almanac" with Director Cyril Ritchard, Hermione Gingold, and Billy de Wolfe.

Billy de Wolfe and I in a comedy skit from "Almanac."

John Murray Anderson's Almanac

De Wolfe is a convulsing antic-mate, whether portraying a dimwit Daphne du Maurier hero (in "My Cousin Who?"), a frowsy old dame in a British railway coach, the muscle-flexing he-man in a "Pic-nic" takeoff or the stupefied butler drinking toasts for five in a laugh-able bit titled "Dinner for One."

Among the gifted, engaging fea-tured performers there are such notables as Polly Bergen, a comely singer with a sultry style that grows more interesting through the evening; Orson Bean, an inno-cent-faced but droll monologist; the fresh and likable young dance team of Carleton Carpenter and Elaine Dunn; pert little ballerina Nanci Crompton; impressive char-acter-vocalist Harry Belafonte, and Celia Lipton, who combines beauty with an infectious comedy sense.

Celia Lipton

A comparative newcomer to our shores, Celia Lipton scored a fine success on Broadway in the short-lived "Maggie," the musical adaptation of Barrie's "What Every Woman Knows" produced last season. Prior to this she made her American debut at New York's smart St. Regis Maisonette. Daughter of Sidney Lipton, musical director of London's Grosvenor Hotel and a native of Edinburgh, Scotland, she began her career as a girl of fifteen when she played Judy Garland's part in "The Wizard of Oz," and later had roles in "Babes in Arms" and "Strike Up the Band." She played the Palladium in "Applesauce," a lead at the London Hippodrome in "Get a Load of This," and starred in "The Quaker Girl." She enacted the title role in "Peter Pan," the lead in "Lilac Time" and was seen in English films, in addition to being a London supper club favorite at the clubs Bagatelle, Embassy and Empress. Recently she scored in Canadian supper spots.

Following "Almanac," I played the female lead in a "Goodyear Playhouse" television production, opposite Kevin McCarthy and with Robert Coote. The show was produced at CBS television. After the broadcast, Delbert Mann, the American movie producer, wrote me a letter saying he hoped that we would work together again. I hoped so too.

The "Goodyear Playhouse" television production, "The Personal Touch"

David Wayne, of "Teahouse of the August Moon," and Miss Audrey Hepburn, of "Ondine," receive Tony Awards for the best acting in stage plays of the past season from Miss Fay Emerson at the annual dinner of the American Theater Wing.

Miss Celia Lipton and Billy de Wolfe, stars of John Murray Anderson's "Almanac," attend the Tony Awards dinner, which benefited the American Theater Wing.

(D'Arlene Studio)

Critics Aren't Such Show-Offs Now

Max Beerbohm Was in a Lively Era Of Geniuses Fresh in the Bud

By JOHN CHAPMAN

Nobody likes a drama critic until he has died or retired, and when one of these happy things happens people begin to rejoice and remember what a wonderful fellow he was. Today on Broadway there never have been, since their time, such critics as J. Ranken Towse (a most verbose old fool), Alexander Woollcott (an egophile of totally erratic judgment), Percy Hammond (who would hunt through a dictionary clear back to its glue binding to find a word nobody ever heard of, including Percy), H. T. Parker (the Bostonian who wrote in agate type), Heywood Broun (who never quite knew whether he was reviewing Broun, baseball or Broadway), or Bide Dudley, or William Winter (who could be dull longer than anybody).

Today's writers about the theatre are a sorry lot and will remain a sorry lot until they drop dead or are forced by Social Security to quit. Then they might gain a little in fame. It does happen that three or four—at the outside—of today's paid playgoers write well, have wit and possess a sound understanding of the theatre. But these three or four will go unsung until they are out of business. A future generation will have the joy of remembering them too late and publishing ponderous collections of their works.

This week's critic is Sir Max Beerbohm, the cocky fellow who followed—and never quite caught up with—the cocky G. B. Shaw as the play reviewer for the Saturday Review of London (not to be confused with the Saturday Review of New York, where John Mason Brown has spent so many years in admiration of Charles Lamb). Simon and Schuster have published a 579-page volume titled "Around Theatres," which is a collection of Beerbohm's (call him Max for short) pieces in the Saturday Review between the dates of May 28, 1898, and April 16, 1910. This is quite a long time and quite a long book.

Struck a Pose.

Beerbohm was a sprint of 25 when he took over Shaw's job writing theatre pieces for a hebdomadal publication devoted to the arts. On the day of his debut in 1898, being a young and fancy artist, he announced, with majestic readery, that it was something awful to be following G. B. S. Then, with boyish candor, he declared, "Frankly, I have none of that instinctive love for the theatre which is the first step toward good criticism of drama. I am not fond of the theatre. Dramatic art interests and moves me less than any of the other arts. . . . In drama I take, unfortunately, neither emotional nor intellectual pleasure."

A fine man for a job, Max. Something like hiring Robin Hood to be a bank guard. But this introductory piece must have been a boyish prank to gain attention, like a juvenile delinquent setting fire to the school or Lucius Beebe wearing an ermine-lined boater. Max grew up between May 28, 1898, and July 9, same year. On that date he wrote the most moving, most knowing and most profound appreciation of Rostand's "Cyrano de Bergerac" and of Coquelin's appearance in it that can be found in print. No man who was not fond of the theatre could have done it.

A Young Fake, Anyhow.

Max was a young fake, and now, as Sir Max Beerbohm, age 82, he may be an old fake—but I shall have to wait for S. N. Behrman's biography of him to find out. He did have the theatre and understand it and write gracefully and wittily about it. He was more concerned than we are now with actors. Modern criticism in New York is almost totally devoted to playwrights; actors are mentioned if they can be praised and are not mentioned at all if they are lousy. We are kind to actors, but Beerbohm wasn't. He didn't even call them actors, let alone people; he called them, with grand detachment, "mimes." The only modern critic who ever tried this stunt was Percy Hammond, who once wrote, "The more you praise an actor the more it despises you."

Beerbohm's greatest admiration, and it was rightly held, was for the man whose job he got—Shaw. He was touting G. B. S. in London when only us Americans knew and appreciated him. In 1901 Beerbohm wrote of Shaw, "I care not that he is in his forty-fifth year; he is, I assure you, a young writer; he is still in an early state of development." Second judgment. A few weeks later he wrote, "Assuming that Mr. Shaw will live to the age of 90 (and such is the world's delight in him that even then his death will seem premature) I find that he has already fulfilled one half of his life span." Wrong guess here, by four years.

Wrote for His Own Amazement.

Beerbohm's pieces were about mimes and plays and dramatists, ostensibly, but mostly they were about himself, which is why his old reviews remain lively in the new book. To Gordon Craig he wrote, "Whether the play I criticized was by Shakespeare or Mr. Tompkins"—a fictitious hack—"must not matter to me, so long as I (underlined) was what I must bear in mind." In a piece about soliloquies in the drama, such as Hamlet's, he wrote, "Talking to oneself has this obvious advantage over any other form of oratory or gossip: one is assured of a sympathetic audience."

A few of today's critics are wise, literate and witty, but none is the show-off Beerbohm was. They all are fierce egotists, but they mask themselves in the impersonality which has become—except for columnists, who are hired freaks—the tradition of today's journalism. This personal coldness—or personal insecurity—on the part of playreviewers may be one of the things which are wrong with the theatre. If the theatre isn't fun to read about, as it was when Beerbohm was writing, how could it be fun to see?

Perhaps "Max" had the answer to this question on June 7, 1902, when he wrote, "To a certain extent, an art is affected in its welfare by the quality of its critics. Good critics are good for it, bad critics are bad for it. But only an art that is by way of doing well can hope to have good critics."

WELL, IT'S SPRING, AIN'T IT?—Here's a bouquet of lovely ladies in Broadway shows. At left, Celia Lipton, singer in "John Murray Anderson's Almanac." Above, left, is Doretta Morrow, a singing star of "Kismet." Next to her is Deborah Kerr, warm heroine of "Tea & Sympathy." Over to the right and all the way from her top to her tootsies, is Deedee Wood, a "Can-Can" dancer who can. And below is the tall and luscious model of "The Solid Gold Cadillac," Charlotte Van Lein.

English 'Falstaff' Thursday Night at The City Center

Going into its fourth season at the City Center, the New York City Opera Company presents a new English translation of Verdi's last opera, "Falstaff," on Thursday night. Chester Kallman has made the translation, which was a matter of turning Boito's Italian adaptation of Shakespeare's "The Merry Wives of Windsor" back into the original tongue. Richard Wentworth will sing the title role, Fenton will be played by Jon Crain, Ford by Walter Cassel, Mrs. Ford by Phyllis Curtin, Mrs. Page by Rosemary Kuhlmann and Anne by Madelaine Chambers. Otto Erhardt is staging the work and the sets and costumes are by John Boyt. John Butler has designed the choreography and Joseph Rosenstock will conduct.

"Carmen" is a Friday night's City Opera bill with Gloria Lane in the title role and Walter Fredericks opposite her as Don Jose. "Show Boat" will be repeated Saturday afternoon and "La Traviata" will be sung that night with Eva Likova and John Druary as the lovers.

THE GOLDEN DOZEN

Contest how long has with number of performances as at last night.

DRAMATIC

"The Seven Year Itch"	573
"The Fifth Season"	582
"Tea and Sympathy"	396
"Teahouse of August Moon"	260
"Solid Gold Cadillac"	172
"Sabrina Fair"	161

MUSICAL

"Wonderful Town"	466
"Can-Can"	382
"Comedy in Music"	270
"Kismet"	140
"Anderson's Almanac"	122
"Girl in Pink Tights"	53

Final Met Week

The Met winds up its 22-week season this week with the following bills: "Aida" tomorrow, "Barber of Seville" Tuesday, "Marriage of Figaro" Wednesday, "Norma" Thursday, "Parsifal" Friday and Saturday afternoons and "Il Trovatore" Saturday night.

A Little 'Rope'

Patrick Hamilton's thriller, "Rope," will be revived by William Gass at the Gallendor Studios, 39 W. 67th St., for a limited run beginning Tuesday night.

Discuss Change In Tix for Crix

There is a move afoot to consolidate the first-night and second-night press lists to Broadway openings, with everybody who rates as a critic or theatrical writer coming on the first night. The long-standing present system is to have the daily newspaper critics and columnists on the first night, and the weekly and monthly magazine writers on the second. The Theatrical Press Agents and Managers union will have a preliminary discussion of the problem Tuesday afternoon.

Orchestra Returns

Back from a two-week tour of the South, the Philharmonic-Symphony returns to Carnegie Hall this week with Dimitri Mitropoulos conducting and with violinist Tossy Spivakovsky as soloist, Thursday night and Friday afternoon.

Chamber Opera

"Dido and Aeneas," with Jennie Tourel, and "The Witch of Endor" will make up a double bill of chamber opera to be presented at Town Hall tomorrow evening as the last program in a series by the American Chamber Opera Society.

*I was cast as Esmeralda in "The Hunchback of Notre Dame"
for NBC television.*

In the midst of building a career in America, opportunity beckoned once more. My agent arranged a reading for me at NBC television for the role of Esmeralda, the heroine in "The Hunchback of Notre Dame"–a Robert Montgomery production, to be broadcast live. The great writer and television host, Dominick Dunne was the producer. I got the part, and the show aired two hours each, in two segments. It was also significant in that it was the first television production broadcast live to have the largest mob scene ever filmed.

I was back on Broadway in 1954. (I was reminded of this by a clipping from the April 11th edition of the "Sunday News," where I was described as "one of a bouquet of lovely ladies in Broadway shows." I also appeared on television around this time. Much to my surprise, many years later in 1989, I was persuaded to do a guest appearance in "B. L. Stryker," starring Burt Reynolds, in the "The Dancer's Touch" episode. The reviews were good, and I added another tip-top credit to my resumé.)

It was wonderful working with Hurd Hatfield in "The Hunchback of Notre Dame," he was such a great actor.

"The Hunchback of Notre Dame," based on Victor Hugo's novel, was produced by Robert Montgomery with the assistance of Dominick Dunne. I worked with a stellar cast, including Bramwell Fletcher and Hurd Hatfield. The show aired live across America and Canada.

In New York, I found a good friend, Iris de Flores, one of the most unusual women I have ever known. Costa Rican by birth, Iris was blessed with flashing white teeth, lustrous black hair, and a vivacious personality. I met her when we were both guests, one weekend, at the Manhasset estate of Michael Grace, who always attracted interesting and talented people, such as John Murray Anderson (who discovered actress Bette Davis).

Iris could have gone onto stardom. She was an extremely talented singer and guitarist, but concentrated on inventions, banking, and real estate instead. She seemed to know half the movers and shakers in New York. It was a great comfort to have Iris around, ready to chat away for hours on the phone and cheer me up. Some nights when I was feeling melancholy, I'd throw on my warm coat over my granny nightshirt, pull on a pair of boots, then hail a taxi, and zip around to Iris' for a cup of tea and girl talk. We would spend hours talking about music and the theatre. Iris was so flamboyant that it was difficult to keep up with her latest admirer. I, on the other hand, had early on forgone an active social life – much less, love – to pursue my stage career.

I had always liked reading–novels, poetry, and plays had been a refuge during lonely hours as a child–and books, once more, provided a balm. (Men and women have often credited books with changing their lives, and I feel the same way. Indirectly, books altered my destiny, and transformed my life into what Mary Pickford said she saw in the palm of my hand.)

It all began because I had borrowed some books from Iris. Today, I can't remember what they were, only that on one New York night Iris called and asked me to bring them back, adding, "By the way, I won't be alone because I've got this important scientist coming over." Before I could ask why, Iris breathlessly went on, "I can't remember if I've told you, but I've invented a blueprint brassiere shaper. You put your brassiere onto it after you wash it, then it won't lose its shape when you put it on again."

Torn between disbelief and hysterical laughter, I assured Iris that she was a genius, that I'd bring the books back that evening and that I'd like to have dinner with her and, as she'd hurt her knee exercising and wasn't able to get around, I would help prepare the dinner. Iris lived on the top floor of an apartment building and, invariably, the elevator was broken. That evening was no exception. Although I can't remember the number of stairs, I do know that by the time I got to the top floor I was breathing heavily, and almost banged straight into a ladder standing right outside Iris' front door.

Looking up, I saw a man with black curly hair and the most expressive, brooding, brown eyes that seemed to momentarily flash a sign of recognition, while he stood on top of the ladder. He was in the midst of repairing the skylight and, noting his rolled up shirtsleeves and open shirt, I thought to myself what a good-looking plumber.

The door to Iris' apartment was ajar, but I rang the bell before I walked in and, to my surprise, the good-looking plumber-man followed me in. I didn't have time to wonder what was going on because Iris was right there saying that she wanted me to meet her friend, Victor Farris, the scientist. She introduced me to the man on the ladder that night.

Apparently, Iris' apartment had been burgled the previous night, and her friend was making it secure. I think I commented that it was very nice of him to help her. Victor and I then raided the refrigerator, and managed to concoct a fairly decent meal out of the leftovers we found. All the while, I sensed that Victor, the scientist, was analyzing me. He told me he made valves. Valve-making was a million miles away from the Broadway theater scene, and was the ultimate conversation stopper.

Iris broke the ice by producing her brassiere-shaper blueprint. Courteously, Victor examined it, treating Iris and her invention with the utmost respect. But, as soon as she left the room he flashed me a conspiratorial grin. I had thought Victor was one of Iris' latest beaus. I can't remember much of what Victor and I talked about that first evening. I just remember his eyes–probing, searching, and investigating my very soul, or so it seemed. His questions, too, were piercing. Later, when I knew him better, I learned that Victor was so accustomed to interviewing job applicants, that he employed similar techniques in relationships–weighing every answer in an attempt to assess whether he could trust someone.

When it was time to leave, Victor offered to drive me home. I didn't accept immediately, so Iris stationed herself behind me and began prodding me in the back, indicating that I should take him up on his offer–so, I accepted. As we left Iris' apartment, I guessed that Victor had offered to drive me home because I must have passed some kind of test. Then, I saw Victor's car. It was the most awful-looking, pale-blue Cadillac I'd ever seen in my life. It bore the scars, dents, and scrapes of endless battles for limited parking space on Manhattan's streets and avenues. It was certainly not the type of automobile I would have expected a scientist, inventor, and industrialist to own. Once in the car, Victor turned to me and asked if I would like to have coffee with him at the Westbury Hotel.

Over coffee, he asked me about my career, and I told him that I was an actress—reeling off my credits in the self-promoting style I had observed in Americans, and was beginning to master. Victor silenced me. He said emphatically that anyone can act. I was so overwhelmed by Victor's forcefulness that I didn't think to contradict him. But, I made a mental note to bring up the subject later, and to convince him he was wrong.

It was still early and, as we sat having coffee at the Westbury bar, we were facing the men's room. Every time a man came out, Victor pretended he was knocking them off with a machine gun. He had me in convulsions. Our one-cup of coffee seemed to last for hours, with much laughter. We both found a new camaraderie. At one point, Victor dropped his voice and told me he didn't spend all his time in New York. He said he also worked in Chicago. Sensing the implication, my eyes widened and I asked if he knew any gangsters. He implied some of his best friends were gangsters. I imagined scenes from the "Godfather" at that moment. I was uneasy and very uncomfortable with his answer, and he sensed it.

By the time Victor dropped me off at home that night—shaking my hand like a perfect gentleman—I was convinced that he was a Mafia Don. After all, he had told me that in America it was nothing to belong to the Mafia, and he had darkly hinted at his own involvement. He mentioned unspeakable crimes for which his conscience was not entirely clear. All night long my heart pounded, and I thought, "I'm falling for a gangster, I'm falling for a gangster, I'm falling for a gangster! What would my father say?" I spent most of the night tossing and turning.

Finally, I had found a man who swept me off my feet, but fate seemed to decree that I must never see him again. After all, I was "The Quaker Girl," how could I possibly date a gangster? All these thoughts were running through my mind when the phone rang at 3 a.m. It was Victor "Mafia Don" Farris, solicitously enquiring how I was. He called me "puppy." I tried to be nonchalant and said, "I'm fine." There was a long pause while I wrestled with my head, which told me to slam the receiver

Victor and I on the town.

down, and never talk to this gangster again. But, my heart melted at the very sound of his voice. Relenting at last, a chastened-sounding Victor told me softly that he was pulling my leg. He wasn't a gangster at all. Victor wanted to prove to me that "anybody can act." He certainly convinced me that "HE could act."

A formal date came next. Victor took me to the Pierre Hotel, telling me it was one of his favorite restaurants. I still didn't know much about him. All Iris had told me, before flying off to see a new beau in California, was that Victor Farris was taking care of her blueprint for the brassiere shaper, and "he's a brilliant man." (Incidentally, Iris eventually married Rudolph Schirmer of Schirmer Music). I assured myself that Iris must be right. Later, Victor told me that he was helping Iris patent her brassiere shaper. Ultimately, she sold her invention to a very interested company.

Victor was a macho man whose toughness co-existed with humor and sweetness. It was only when we crossed the Hudson, and went to New Jersey, that I got some insight into the real Victor Farris. He lived in Tenafly, New Jersey, but his factory was in Palisades Park and, with an endearing, little-boy impatience, he told me he couldn't wait to take me around there. The idea didn't exactly enthrall me because I had sung in many factories in England, called "Worker's Playtime" on the BBC radio. But it was clear that Victor lived and breathed his work, so off we went to tour his factory.

First, we had dinner at one of his favorite restaurants in Englewood Cliffs, which also happened to be Cary Grant's favorite as well—who happened to be at the restaurant that night, and we met him. It was late by the time we had finished, and when we arrived at the factory it was completely deserted. Exhilarated, Victor climbed into a jeep, motioned me to sit beside him, revved up the engine and, like a kid at a fun fair, began roaring around the factory—picking up huge valves and, then, gently putting them back on the ground.

The valves were as big as I was, and Victor handled them lovingly. Victor was very proud of the fact that he had paid for every piece of machinery he owned and didn't owe anybody anything. The boyish enthusiasm in his voice, and the fun we had together, captivated me. That first night, in the empty Farris factory, I fell in love with that man. Victor Farris of Tenafly, New Jersey, a man who made valves for a living, it was a very long way from "The Quaker Girl," and an entirely new experience for me.

Eventually, I learned all about the Farris empire: how Victor had built it, and exactly who he was, and what he had achieved. Victor was born in Buffalo, New York, in 1911. His grandfather, on his mother's side, was a high official in the French government. His father was a successful businessman, and had as his partners George Rand (who started the original Marine Trust Bank) and E. M. Statler (of the Statler hotel chain).

Victor's factory, Farris Engineering Corp., Palisades Park, N.J.

But, Victor was entirely self-made. He once said that he wasn't born with the proverbial silver spoon in his mouth. His mother and father both felt that their sons should be productive, and "make their own way." Victor's brothers did, indeed, make it. Dr. Louis G. Farris, one of them, became an American Board obstetrician and gynecologist. He was elected to the top societies in his profession, and honored several times in his fields by the American Medical Society in his state and nationally. He was a Fellow of the American College of Obstetricians and Gynecologists. The journalist, Quentin Reynolds referred to him as, "One of the best known specialists in gynecology and obstetrics in New York State, with a reputation that goes beyond its borders."

Victor's older brother, Dr. Edmond J. Farris, became internationally known for his work in genetics, anatomy, and human fertility. He was one of the first doctors to successfully perform artificial insemination. He was nominated for the Nobel Prize, and founded the Farris Institute for Parenthood in Philadelphia, in 1956. Victor was wonderful to Ed and helped him publish his book on fertility, which became a standard textbook in every medical school.

His third brother, Emile M. Farris, became President of American Viscose Corp. He was also a member of the flying troupe, the Lafayette Escadrilles. Emile was honored by the Civil Aeronautics Board for his outstanding work in civil aviation. He staged and managed The World Air Show in Philadelphia, in 1948, and is remembered for news-making flair and headlines, the world over, for the "Farris Touch." He was the quintessential showman.

Victor himself had attended Massachusetts Institute of Technology and was only 17 when he sold his first invention to the Ford Motor Co.—a dashboard for the Model A Ford. But, his most famous invention (out of more than two-hundred patents he would ultimately hold) was the milk carton. Watching his mother wearily lugging milk bottles home from the store, he made up his mind to lift her burden by inventing a lighter container. After testing a series of containers, he did just that.

Victor founded the Farris Engineering Corp in 1943. The company produced safety and relief valves, testing devices, plastic-manufacturing machinery, and was the largest company of its kind in the world. One of Victor's other illustrious inventions was a machine which wrapped cigarette packages in cellophane. Most of his other inventions were hydraulic and pneumatic devices.

Farris Engineering Corporation

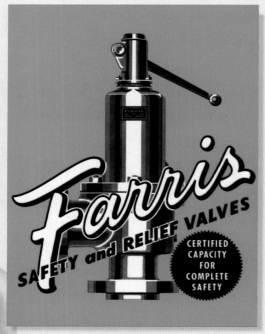

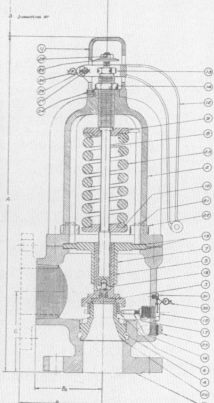

Since 1943, Farris Engineering Corporation has designed and produced a wide range of safety and relief valves. Used as safety devices, valves prevent over pressurization of vessels, pipelines, and equipment. Victor Farris, inventor of "Farris Valves," worked from his factory in Palisades Park, N.J., once considered "the most modern factory exclusively devoted to the manufacturing of safety and relief valves in America." Today, "Farris Valves" are used worldwide by every major sector of business and industry, and various branches of government.

Victor and his invention, the "Farris Valve"

At 31, Victor was a millionaire, eventually owning seventeen companies and was the recipient of the National Free Enterprise Award, given annually to the ten most outstanding businessmen in America. When America was drawn into World War II, in December 1941, there was a severe shortage of safety-valve instrument manufacturers. Victor became a consultant to the United States Navy, and was instrumental in designing the heat-balance system for Liberty Ships.

Victor implemented a series of inventions that were the basis of the intricate safety and relief valves used to control the flow of chemicals, steam, gases, and hydrocarbon vapors. He also helped to design the DD 445 Class Destroyer. The Farris welded steel valves are still used on British and American battleships (as recently as the Gulf War).

During the early 1950s, Victor acquired the well-known Pickering Governor Corporation, which he later merged with the Pierce Governor Company (which was listed on the American Stock Exchange). The United States Navy and industries throughout the world used millions of these governors as speed controls on diesel engines in power stations. Manufacturing plants founded by Victor, are still located across the United States and, through stock holdings and licensing agreements, in England, France, and Australia.

Victor Farris

Victor was the recipient of the National Free Enterprise Award in 1959, given annually to the 10 most outstanding businessmen in America.

Thursday, July 23, 1959

Farris is Honored as One of Outstanding Successful U.S. Men

Victor Farris, president, founder and sole owned of the Farris Engineering Corp. and affiliates, of Palisades Park, was one of 11 men throughout the United States to be honored Tuesday in the Waldorf-Astoria Hotel, New York City.

The 11 received "American Success Story Awards" offered by the Free Enterprise Awards Association, Inc., for men whose up-from-the-ranks careers symbolize the rewards of success possible under the American free enterprise democracy. The presentations to the 11 men picked from all walks of life across the nation, were made by Talbot T. Speer, a Maryland newspaper publisher.

Following the presentation ceremonies, the recipients, who started as mechanics, sign painters and in other humble jobs to rise to owners and heads of multi-million dollar industries, took a fleet of cars to the Russian Trade Fair in the Coliseum to show the Russians staffing the Fair how American free enterprise made their success possible.

With rolled-up sleeves they handed out statements written in Russian and wrote a few strong opinions in every guest book to invite comment.

The citation honoring Mr. Farris as one of the 11, read as follows:

"Victor W. Farris, 49, president, founder and sole owner of the Farris Engineering Corp. and Affiliates, with plants in Palisades Park, Houston, Tex., and London, England. Residence, Tenafly. Started in 1943 with three valve patents, now has 100 patents. His genius built 19 Farris corporations, a multi-million dollar business in safety and relief valves to prevent over-pressure and explosions. Produces flexible rubber pinch valves to carry and control flow of chemicals, fluid and dry materials, Farris Pickering governors, diesel speed controls and others used by the U.S. Navy, oil producers, refiners and most fields.

NEWS BULLETIN

FarriScope

MAIN OFFICE & FACTORY: PALISADES PARK, N.J.
Factories in England • Canada • France • Australia

Founder is Man of Many Abilities

A few years ago, the New York Herald Tribune published an article about Victor Farris which gives an insight into the dynamic founder of Farris Engineering.

Ken McKenna, The Business Editorial writer for the Tribune, described Victor Farris as "an inventor who considers himself a business man but has enough credentials to qualify in either field." Acknowledging Victor Farris as the world's foremost manufacturer of safety and relief valves, Mr. Mc Kenna listed some of Farris's other qualifications. He wrote, "These include 14 personally owned corporations, encompassing three real estate companies, a publishing house and factories... On the creative side there are his more than 200 patents. His inventions range from automotive and aircraft industries to the packaging and hydraulic fields. Some years ago he patented a paper milk bottle whose design is still in use."

Other newspaper articles have noted his achievements in the field of real estate development. For years the downtown waterfront area of Nyack, New York had lain idle and abandoned, a veritable eyesore. Victor Farris seized the opportunity to inaugurate his own urban renewal plan. He created a complex of private marina, marine hardware, swim club, restaurant, shopping center and service station. Adjoining property, formerly used by the Tidewater Oil Company, was also acquired and underwent extensive restoration.

VICTOR W. FARRIS

INDUSTRIALIST

Farris's development of Hudson River waterfront has been hailed by the Nyack Planning Board and civic leaders as a significant contribution to the revitalization and future growth of Nyack.

The Newspapers' Community News sections have also frequently mentioned Victor Farris. He's hyper active in his home community and serves as a trustee of Englewood Hospital, a director of the Peoples Trust Company, a director of the YMCA, a fellow of Fairleigh Dickinson University and a member of the National Council of the Boy Scouts of America. He also serves as president of the Victor W. Farris Foundation and is active in many charitable fund-raising campaigns.

Perhaps his dedication to his principal of "Progress Through Honest Purpose," and his contributions to his fellow man were best noted by the Free Enterprise Awards Association of New York when they presented him with their American Success Story Award a few years ago. The award is presented to the man whose career symbolizes the success possible under the free enterprise democracy.

Victor relaxing in his office just before the Christmas holiday.

Victor's personal philosophy—the backbone of his business success—was based on integrity. He once summed it up by saying, "If you departed from the truth, you must eventually come back to it, and in doing that, you could waste years of accomplishment. If you were a person of truth you would make progress. Integrity was something that could not be compromised." You were either a person of integrity or you were not. Some people, he said, thought that integrity could be bartered. It could not. Integrity reached into all facets of life—including business.

There was never a time in the operation of any of his companies that a bill was not cash-discounted, or his failure to see that one of his products was properly serviced. He would send a man across the country to service a $50 item because his name was at stake, and his personal integrity. He also knew that integrity and truth were not always promptly rewarded.

When I met Victor, he had been divorced for eight years. He had always worked very hard and, after the divorce, he immersed himself in his inventions and his companies—allowing himself no time for the dating game. I was the first girl Victor started to date seriously after his divorce. He would often say he fell in love with me because I had no guile, and that he found me thoroughly decent. And, I fell in love with him because he was a very special person—strong and assertive, sweet and kind. He was a man of integrity who created an aura about him that was, in its way, spiritual.

I don't want to give the impression, though, that Victor was the strong, silent type. He was strong, yes, but not silent. In many ways he was: a renaissance man; a gifted inventor; a talented musician (although he never studied music); a painter with a distinct flair for detail; and, as I discovered on our first meeting, a very good actor. He had an incredibly mischievous sense of humor and would have made a great comedian, actor, or politician.

I hadn't contradicted Victor's assertion that anyone could act, but he must have read my mind and known that I wanted to challenge him. So, although I had stopped myself from contradicting him, Victor had still made it his business to prove me wrong, and to prove himself right. And, in a strange way, I liked that.

Until now my career had been a blessing, teaching me discipline among other things. But, dedication to my career also had a negative side. I'd been working since I was 14 years old, and although I loved my parents, they had been far too much in love with one another to really spend much time nurturing me, and directing my life in any way. As a result, since my early teens, I had taken charge of my own future and had allowed no one else to control it for me.

Now this man had burst into my life, this Victor Farris, a Humphrey Bogart-like figure. Victor was tall, dark, and handsome; a man who had swept me off my feet, and who took no contradiction from me—not even an unspoken one. I knew I could lean on him. I sensed that Victor Farris was exactly the man I needed to make my life complete. During our first few months together, Victor and I were just like any other young couple in love. He was romantic and, although he didn't shower me with gifts or gigantic bunches of flowers, he would spend as much time with me as possible.

I was still living in Manhattan, and it used to infuriate Victor that he couldn't find anywhere to park his horrid, old, pale-blue Cadillac. Later, I used to joke that he married me because he couldn't find a place to park. Right up until our wedding day, I would lean out of the window and watch the curb and car fenders, and go crazy while Victor drove round and round in circles. It did cause me to wonder why Victor didn't just stick the car in a parking lot and save himself all the bother of driving around to find a parking space. But then, that was Victor.

One day, when we were sitting in the garden in Tenafly, where he lived on, ironically, "Bliss Avenue," Victor suddenly pulled me into his arms, kissed me, then put me on his lap, and almost shyly asked whether I would like to "get hitched." Did he mean get married? Without a doubt that is exactly what he meant! I joked that he had evaluated me like one of his pieces of patented machinery. He laughed at that. His proposal and my acceptance was starting to sound like a Vaudeville act. He admired the way I'd soldiered on in the war, entertaining troops and civilians, building my career, and even coming to America and playing the Broadway stage. Well, who could refuse such a man, especially a man I was in love with?

Victor asked for my father's phone number in London, and called him to ask his permission to marry me. He spoke to both of my parents. They told me later, when I got on the phone, that they felt his warmth, his quick mind, and sense of humor. My father's early question in the conversation to Victor was, "Can you support her?" "I'm a millionaire," he snapped back at my father. My mother and father were very happy that I was getting married. My father, who lived for his work, asked me, "What about your career?" I replied, "I'm not thinking about that right now."

Victor's attitude was not so different. Although he knew that I had been actress in England, and that I had appeared on Broadway, he wasn't the least bit interested. He didn't even bother to read my voluminous reviews. He just laughed, ruffled my hair, and called me his "Puppy." I'd always prided myself on my career, success, and early stardom. Performing was part of my life—it was my vocation. Up until this time, love had come from an audience. Yet, here was this fascinating man, who has me ignoring my career and acting as if it had never happened. Victor seemed to be unaware that Celia Lipton, who had been on stage, and made radio and television broadcasts—on both sides of the Atlantic—was the same woman he loved.

I found the strangest thing was that we were like ships that had passed in the night. Ironically, we had both been in Nassau at the same time years earlier, but never met. I was performing in the ballroom of the Hotel that week, and he had seen me from the garden, but could not hear me perform.

In a perverse way, Victor's attitude tickled me. He wasn't remotely impressed by my success, or my tunnel-vision determination to become a great actress. He had come along at the right time for me. Even though Victor never once suggested that I give up my career, I knew our marriage wouldn't work if I continued. How could it if I was on the road all the time?

What Victor was looking for was a wife, somewhat old-fashion, yet at the same time, romantic. He was not interested at all in a career girl who spent half her time traveling and the other half at the theatre—not an actress who would require him to pick her up after the theatre at midnight. Although we never broached the subject, I knew instinctively that Victor wouldn't have taken kindly to any of that. He wanted a traditional wife, actually the kind my mother was. I wanted to be that for him.

From the moment I agreed to marry Victor, I gave up my career. I was proud of my achievements, and happy to become Mrs. Victor W. Farris.

Victor and I were married on January 14, 1956, at his home on Bliss Avenue, in Tenafly, New Jersey. My parents were as emotional as was I at the ceremony. Iris was my maid of honor. Among the guests were Michael Grace of Grace Shipping Lines, Billy de Wolfe (the comedian), and Lord (James) Hanson. All during the ceremony, I remember praying that the marriage would be successful.

Our wedding portrait

My parents enjoy a good laugh as I give Victor a giant slice of cake.

I knew that for me divorce would always be out of the question. Victor had been divorced. My best example, that marriage was to last until death, was my parents' commitment to their marriage.

When the British press learned of our wedding they called Victor and asked if he was a millionaire. Laughingly, he confirmed that he was and, "many times over." The British papers carried the headline, "Celia Lipton Marries a Millionaire." I cut out the stories and filed them away. Celia Lipton was past history. Now, there was only Mrs. Victor W. Farris.

Our honeymoon was spent first on Victor's boat, sailing down the Intracoastal Waterway to Miami, where we stayed at the Fontainebleau Hotel. That boat, quite simply, was the love of Victor's life. He even used to carry a picture of it around in his wallet. He joked that he carried a picture of his boat, and not his wife, because he had the boat longer.

Victor and I attending a formal event.

Victor Farris, Celia Lipton, Wed

Many notables of both this country and England last Saturday afternoon attended the marriage of Victor W. Farris, head of the Farris industries in Palisades Park, and Miss Celia Lipton, noted British actress.

The wedding ceremony took place in "Windward," Mr. Farris' estate in Tenafly. It was a model of simplicity, in the warm atmosphere of the living room, while about 75 guests, among them some leading stage stars and famous industrial leaders, looked on. The Rev. George Hassey, minister of the First Presbyterian Church of Palisades Park, a schoolmate of the bridegroom in Buffalo, officiated.

The bride, who has attained widespread fame on the stage in both England and this country, was charming in an heirloom bridal gown of Southern Belle fashioning in candlelight coloring, made by a famous couterie. She was attended by Iris de Flores, grand-daughter of the president of Costa Rica, who wore a gown of ice blue silk taffeta.

Mrs. Farris is the daughter of Capt. and Mrs. Sydney Lipton, of London, who flew from England to attend the ceremony. Capt. Lipton is well known throughout England as head of the Sydney Lipton Orchestra, which has performed for the Royal House of England for many years.

She will be best remembered on the English stage for her performance as Peter in "Peter Pan," and many television appearances, both in England and the United States. She recently appeared on Broadway in John Murray Anderson's "Almanac" and was also seen with leading dramatic appearances on the Robert Montgomery Show, the Ed Sullivan Show, the Goodyear program and many others. She plans to retire from the stage but may continue some TV work.

Mr. Farris is one of America's outstanding young industrialists and has developed an industrial empire which started in Palisades Park, where his plant has expanded to an amazingly successful point in the past decade, spreading to Houston, Texas. He is an inventor of note, as well as the head of 15 successful corporations and has attained a leading rank both as an inventor and as a consultant in American and English shipbuilding. His affiliated industries contribute heavily to the atomic energy, aircraft, petroleum and chemical industries throughout the world. He is a director of an Englewood bank, and a member of the New York Athletic Club, American Society of Mechanical Engineers, American Chemical Society, Association for the Advancement of Science, and other similar or-

Mr. and Mrs. Victor W. Farris
—Photo by Eastwest Studio

American Chemical Society, Association for the Advancement of Science, and other similar organizations.

Mr. Farris' best man was his brother, Dr. E. J. Farris, famous medical scientist and a former candidate for the Nobel prize, who is also famous for his books and lectures. Another brother, Dr. Louis G. Farris, head of the staff in obstetrics and gynecology at Millard Fillmore Hospital, Buffalo, also attended with his wife.

Among other guests were Delores Gray, movie star, and her mother, former U. S. Senator John Milton, a personal friend of Mr. Farris; Mr. and Mrs. Michael Grace, of the Grace shipping family; the Countess de Beaumont and the Countess de la Grand Prey, Mr. and Mrs. Poole, the former being director of the Gotham Hotel, New York; Dr. and Mrs. Lee Solworth, of Englewood; James Hanson, industrialist of London, New York and Toronto; Billy de Wolfe, noted comedian, who recently made a picture with Bing Crosby; Bramwell Fletcher, famous on the stage and now doing a series on TV; Rudolf Schirmer, head of the Schirmer Music Publishing Co.; Mr. and Mrs. Rolf Moroni, who own factories in the United States, France, Germany and Italy; Dr. N. F. Fogler, vice president of Allied Chemical and Dye Corp. and Mrs. Fogler, and Mr. and Mrs. James MacFarlane, of Muncie, Indiana, the former being vice president of the famous Ball Brothers, representing one of America's largest fortunes.

GOURLAY

E PICTURE IN THE MAN
LLET WAS OF
YACHT…NOT HIS WIF

nay

nber

often I
r a man
made a
ne from
l milk
fact I
ell admit
Farris
ca is the
e encoun-
s made
at all
ard milk

he things.
simple one,
d lucrative
aim back in

antages," said
re lightness,
possibility. I
nt and the
e production.
ght on. I
of infringe-
atent which

Celia Lipton
.. from ditties to duties

expired five years ago. By that
time I'd made quite a bit. They
sell about 5,000,000 of the things
every day in the States."

HER DUTIES

MR. FARRIS has other,
weightier claims to dis-
tinction.
Starting his career as a
mechanical engineer and inventor, he now has about 200
inventions and patents to his
credit, including disc brakes.
He is the multi-millionaire
owner of 23 companies which
range from engineering to publishing. One of his companies

is the largest manufacturer of
safety valves in America. He is
also married to Celia Lipton,
daughter of bandleader Sydney,
who gave up a promising career
as singer for him.
I met them in a West End
hotel suite of contemporary
style which must have been
created by a colour-blind
designer.

HIS GIFTS

MRS. FARRIS said: " I've
never had a 'moment's
regret since I gave up my
career four years ago when I got
married. I'm devoted to my old
man and fascinated by his
career.
" He's always dreaming up
something new. Gets up in the
middle of the night to sketch it.
I'm proud of him. I think he's
a genius. Mind you we have our
rows. Then I scream that I'm
walking out and going back to
show business.
" But I never get further than
the door with my suitcases."
Neither of them said so, but
it may be that he has invented
a gadget which trips her up
when she gets to the door.
Mrs. Farris went on: " Of
course he spoils me.
" Look at these. That's a
Cadillac in value. And that's a
Rolls-Royce."
She was displaying a diamond-
and-ruby brooch (Cadillac) and
a diamond-and-ruby bracelet
(Rolls-Royce).
" Put them away. Hide them."
said Mr. Farris. " Valuable
possessions just worry you."
He then produced a photo-
graph of his own most-prized
possession—an impressive diesel-
engined sea-going yacht.
" I'm the kind of guy who
carries a picture of his yacht in
his wallet, not his wife. But,

then, I had
She's a bea
gadget you ca
are my own M

While he h
Farris has be
British invent
to promote in
incinerator
anything, in
without smoke

" Could be
disposing of
tives. Or wive
" Or husba
Farris.
They laughe
looks of aff
affection.
I don't pre
expert on m
obviously they
recipe for
matrimony. A
respect and
with a hea
bantering hun
the sentiment
Plus, of cou
encrusted bre
husband—not

Wolf Mank
satile and
business
including
Linder, scri
Norden, an
Dahlberg,
into the ni
restaurant b

They are
London's
where busi
far from g

Captain Victor Farris and his 65-foot yacht, The Kerida.

Victor had bought his first boat in 1922, a captured rumrunner, for $800 at a sheriff's auction in Buffalo. In March 1969, he was interviewed in "The New York Times" about boating and said, "Boating is 90 percent maintenance and 10 percent cruising." He loved each and every boat he owned.

At the time I married Victor, he owned a 65-foot yacht called the "Kerida" which, in Spanish, means "Dear One." The "Kerida" was an old-fashioned vessel, which Victor berthed in the Englewood Cliff's boat basin. It was also a very old boat with an oil burner. (I believe these are no longer manufactured.) The "Kerida" made an awful mess, showering black soot and ashes everywhere. When we were coming into a marina, or going out to sea, almost everyone around us complained about the soot that was emitted by the boat. But, Victor just didn't care. He was having too much fun, and his boat could do no wrong.

On the other hand, I couldn't believe the way Victor had decorated the boat, with its sticky, blue, kitchen-papered, stateroom walls. Later, when he purchased his second boat, "The Victorious," an 85-foot Burger, I did my best to have some input on the decor. Other than that, I fully accepted that Victor's boats were male bastions, ruled by Victor and George, his German captain who, ironically, was as rotten a sailor as I was.

An inner-ear problem heightened my difficulties at sea. However, I never could figure out how a man prone to seasickness ever became a captain—although Lord Nelson, who was always seasick, became the most successful admiral in British history. Trafalgar Square in London, is named in honor of his greatest victory in 1805.

Hoping for calm seas

Victor's only other interests, apart from boats, were race cars, gears, and, of course, machines and inventions. He was never dull and his sense of humor seemed boundless. At the Fontainebleau, Victor made a great joke of the fact that the hotel emblem, the letter 'F' (as in Farris), was inscribed on everything: the napkins, the soap, the sheets, and all the silver.

"Let's make a good haul," he joked. We didn't, but it was like Victor to make a joke about something. During our honeymoon I began to see how unique this man truly was. Rather than send his handkerchiefs off to be laundered, he would engage in a most unusual ritual. He would vigorously wash them in the bathroom sink, then carefully place them on the dressing-table mirror, smooth out all the wrinkles, and then wait for them to fall off the mirror–that was the sign they were dry.

We had great fun at the Fontainebleau; swimming, playing tennis and golf. I was blissfully content and in love with the man I had married. I wanted to make him happy and give him a son.

On the surface, Victor appeared to be a man who had everything. But that wasn't true. The one thing Victor lacked, the one thing I most wanted to give him, was a child. His first marriage had been childless, but I swore to myself that his second marriage would be full of happiness and children.

"Happy! I see land."

"Where is my wife?"

Victor and I with Captain George and our dog Pokey, posing with Victor's 85-foot Burger yacht, "The Victorious."

Enjoying Victor's great sense of humor

Deciding that our chances may be good to conceive a child, we consulted with Victor's brother, Dr. Edmond Farris, an expert on fertility. Much to our surprise and joy, he told us that if I was fertile, we might well be able to conceive. Although I was hell-bent on getting pregnant on the honeymoon, Ed's advice came as an unwelcome shock when he suggested that we abstain from making love on our honeymoon. Well, as newlyweds that did not sit well. Yet, his brother said if we waited until the right time, during peak fertility, I had a very good chance of becoming pregnant.

The ensuing drama was farcical. Time and time again, amid giggles and embarrassment, we would call Ed and lament that it had been three days, then ask, "Hasn't it been long enough?" Dr. Ed remained adamant. We had to wait two more days. Our waiting paid off, I conceived on our honeymoon.

Back from the Fountainebleu, our married life began in earnest on "Bliss Avenue" in Tenafly. First, I had to cope with having to live in the same house where Victor had lived with his ex-wife. Apart from the memories of Victor's past, the entire place screamed of a lack of good taste. The master bedroom was decorated with black-and-white wallpaper with harlequins on it, and the draperies matched the wallpaper. The entire room made me dizzy. I used to wonder, who in the world would have this wallpaper? Yet, the answer was clear, Victor.

I had come from a reserved, sophisticated, British background, and had grown up in elegant homes that were finely furnished. Now, I was living in a house with a psychedelic bedroom.

The living room was a site to behold with its floor-to-ceiling picture of Carmel, California, and eclectic furnishings. Every night before I went to bed, I would pray that someday we would move to a new home, one that I could decorate and furnish more appropriately.

By now I was very pregnant and enjoying every minute of puttering around the house, cooking up a storm, and doing my utmost to become the kind of wife to Victor that my mother was to my father. We lived a fairly mundane lifestyle, going to New York once in a while to have dinner. I also joined the Englewood Women's Club where I was welcomed and quickly made many new friends.

I had very little in common with Victor's business colleagues. Most of them were far older than I, and not much interested in someone from the theatre. I couldn't talk show business with them. Discussions seemed to focus on business, families and children.

I didn't miss my career for a very long time. It was as if I had suddenly left a kind of ordered, military regime of time-keeping, entrances and exits on cue. I was enjoying a different kind of life. I was thoroughly relaxed. Celia Farris was a completely new person and Celia Lipton had disappeared. I stopped singing completely. I started smoking. I could never do that as a singer. In those days I had observed the Maestro's cardinal rule, "Never smoke, never drink, and never stay up late." Suddenly, I could relax and break all the rules, and I did just that!

The experience was new and exciting! At the time I relished my life; relaxing, having fun, not working, laughing, enjoying Victor, being in love and being his wife. Later, I did give up smoking, but Victor would not. He had to have his cigars; eventually, he did quit.

I tried to establish a relationship with Victor's family, which was a challenge. Victor's parents were not living, and most of his family at that time resided in Philadelphia. We went to visit Emile, Victor's brother, who was a member of the exclusive Union League Club. Having grown up in England, I didn't understand the significance of American clubs and wasn't impressed.

After a few months of marriage, I was able to form a clearer picture of the complex man I'd married. Victor was a man of dynamic ideas. He had a warm heart and truly cared about others, even though he considered himself a tough businessman. One of his employees had a daughter who was a gifted pianist. Victor found out that the employee couldn't afford to buy a piano for her. So, he quietly purchased a piano and had it delivered her house. That was the kind of man Victor was.

A myriad of contradictions co-existed within him, as they do many of us. He loved to bargain, yet, he could be a big spender. He could be stern or he could be jovial. Victor could be very impulsive or calculating and analytical. He could be cool, with a frightening look, or genial. At times Victor was very understanding and agreeable, yet, when he dug his heels in, he was the most stubborn and unrelenting individual one could know.

The moodiness of men, in general, was new to me even as a married, pregnant wife. Vic was consistently flamboyant, living life on a roller coaster, in a hurry to accomplish as much as possible before his family history of circulatory disorder caught up with him. He had great presence. When he walked into a room everyone knew he was there. Above all, Victor was scrupulously decent and honorable.

Despite his keen intellect and self-confidence, he often used me as a sounding-board. Not knowing a nut from a bolt, I took to repeating his last sentence. Whereupon he would reply, "Puppy you just hit the nail on the head." I spent a great deal of time listening. Victor was a genius and to listen to this genius explain an idea was thrilling. Becoming his sounding-board, as well as being someone he loved and trusted, helped Victor make that ultimate decision, which was always his.

My parents had come over from England to visit, and I was enjoying every minute of being Mrs. Victor Farris, soon-to-be mother. I was six months into my pregnancy and everything was going normally—eating like a horse, cooking up a storm, and everyone telling me "you look great." Although, I was not particularly enthusiastic about my doctor and thought he was a trifle off-hand, the nurses swore by him.

My favorite Standard Poodles–Tony and Pokey

My parents on holiday with us.

One particular Sunday, Victor was insistent that he wanted to take my parents out on the boat. Tentatively, I tried to explain to them that I didn't feel well–remembering that even during the best of times I was not a good sailor. Now, in the last stages of my first pregnancy I just couldn't face going out to sea. But, my mother, mindful that my refusal to go out on the boat would plunge Victor into a bad mood, didn't want to upset him. She insisted that I join them on the boat, so I did.

We boarded, and I was careful not to mention my nausea to Victor as he was notably unsympathetic to my ailments when it came to the boat. He constantly made it clear that he thought women were a pain in the neck when they were seasick. It wasn't that Victor was uncaring. I couldn't have loved a brute like that. But, he was a strong-minded and hearty man–quite a bit older than I–and part of his appeal to me was his strength, stamina, and fortitude to always plunge forward. Once aboard, and cruising up the Hudson, everyone kept running around the boat like mad, and no one paid any attention to me. Suddenly, my mother strained her back and cried out in pain. Victor immediately became concerned and volunteered to fix her back. However, no matter what he did for her, it only seemed to make the pain worse.

Meanwhile, I was doing my best to cope with a new puppy we had brought on board. The puppy was running everywhere and I was worried that he might jump overboard. This, as well as my mother's condition, seemed to make the time on board, to that point in the day, very stressful. As the captain began to prepare lunch, I was suddenly in unbearable pain, my water had broken, as the Kerida was roaring up the Hudson past West Point. At that moment, I thought I was in the throes of labor. This was my first baby, yet, I thought to myself I could not be having the baby, I am only six months into my pregnancy. It has to be something else. I was terrified, in pain, and had no idea of what to do. There was no telephone on the boat. So Victor, immediately realizing the severity of the situation, got on the radio and arranged to have an ambulance waiting for my mother and me. He took control, turned the boat around, and throttled her as high as she would go toward Englewood Cliffs.

When we arrived, there was only one ambulance waiting. The pain I was experiencing had eased dramatically. Yet, my mother was still in agony. My father and Victor were on both sides of her, supporting her off the boat. They put her on the stretcher and she was taken away by ambulance.

I sent Victor and my father to the hospital after my mother, and told them I would drive myself to the doctor. He examined me and then sent me immediately to hospital, where my mother had been admitted for her strained back. My mother was treated and discharged some time later.

However, I was not. I was in labor for 30 hours before I giving birth to our daughter. She lived only 24 hours. Had I stood my ground and refused to go on the boat that day, perhaps I could have saved her life. I should have insisted that I stayed in bed that morning, but I didn't.

I saw the tiny, baby girl for a brief moment in the mirror above me, before she died. She was still attached to the umbilical cord. Then, it was severed and there was nothing, nothing but emptiness. It was the emptiest feeling in the world.

Victor seemed unmoved by the death of our first child. Victor and his brothers looked at many things in a scientific way. I thought to myself that maybe this was how these type of men manage a loss. I later learned that he believed, "The next time we will get it right."

To get over my loss, I channeled all my ambition and drive—that had once served me so well in the theatre—into Victor and giving him a child. His brother Dr. Ed, advised me not to get pregnant after the loss of this baby. I did not listen to him, or anyone for that matter. I was impatient to give Victor a child, and within months I was pregnant again.

In retrospect, I should have taken the advice that I had received from many individuals during my pregnancy. "Take it easy and stay in bed until giving birth," but I didn't. When I was six-months pregnant, I spent time aboard the "Kerida," once again—cooking for Victor and doing my best to have fun. Again, I suffered excruciating pain, blood was pouring out of me, and I felt as if I was bleeding to death. I was rushed to the hospital in severe pain. There, I gave birth to a son.

The moment he was born, Victor began celebrating. He rushed all over the hospital, handing out cigars. A few hours later our son died; he was premature. Perhaps, with the medical breakthroughs of today the baby would have survived. The emotional devastation was so great that I attempted to block the entire event out of my life. I didn't want to remember. I still don't. It's the way I was able to cope and carry on with life. After two failed pregnancies, Marian came to us and I was overjoyed to be a mother.

I kept trying to give birth—ten more times in all—each attempt ending in failure. Had it not been for the joy of having Marian, I don't think I would have been able to overcome the severe bouts of depression at the loss of each baby. I wanted so desperately to give Victor a child. Bearing him a child would have been the ultimate gift I could have given him. My heart was broken. This was a time in my life where I felt useless and inadequate, feelings that had never come over me before.

Rose Kennedy, who was a friend, used to say that "God never gives you more suffering than you can handle." She was correct in this statement, as Rose was indeed a woman of great strength, character, determination, and kindness. It is often said, "As one door closes, another opens." That statement has been most applicable throughout my life, and particularly significant during these times of such great loss.

I loved and cherished every minute of being with Marian. Victor, on the other hand, was not that enamored with the new addition to our small family. I soon learned that it's the attention that a child requires that can make a husband irritable.

Victor liked to be the center of attention at all times. If I divided my love between him and Marian, Victor seemed to resent it. At times, his resentment tore me apart. So did his lack of interest in the child when she was a baby. I didn't expect him to change her diaper. I never would have asked him to. But, after what I had gone through to give him a child, I wished Victor could have been more enthusiastic about having a child. He loved Marian dearly, but had no idea how to react to to a

An evening with Victor was never dull.

baby girl. Victor had grown up in a family with three brothers.

It was only when Marian was about two-and-a-half-years old and began talking in coherent sentences that Victor really started to show his love for her and took an interest. By then we had, yet another, new member of the family—Cecile Victoria, "Ce Ce" for short. Now I had two young babies, just a year apart in age, and my life as a housewife, mother, and chauffeur to the children began in earnest. I delighted in taking them to the dentist, the pediatrician, and later, when they were older, to school, ballet classes, sporting activities, and to visit their friends.

I had met Dr. Kilton Stuart through my friend Iris. Kilton was a brilliant man and a friend of Margaret Mead, the famed author and anthropologist. He was an anthropologist, a psychologist, and a Mormon who looked like Ernest Hemingway. Kilton wore sandals all the time, without consideration of the climate. His expertise was human dreams. People thought he was bit crazy to study them. Later, Kilton taught me how to analyze my children's dreams. He also helped me with Marian, who was a sleepwalker. Sometimes, I would be woken by an ear-splitting, dog-like snore coming from outside my door. Tiptoeing across the room, I would open the door to find Marian curled up in a heap, asleep.

"Helicon Hall"

Victor finally agreed to move out of the house that he had shared for years with his former wife. "Helicon Hall," our new home, was the former residence of writer Upton Sinclair. I loved it and we made many new friends. I discovered that Victor felt at ease with people from show business, and he became the life and soul of many parties by playing his Wurlitzer organ.

I found it funny that he could only play the black keys, yet he delighted in playing at the drop of a hat for anyone willing to be his audience. With no formal training, Victor had learned to play by ear. It was amazing to watch him play; his feet went back and forth along the pedals, creating wild rhythmical sounds of drums crashing, and clarinets moaning. He was in the moment, entertaining and making people laugh as he played.

Personalities who came to our home included Gordon and Liz McCrae, the great Estée Lauder, Johanna Revson, Millie (Mrs. Robert) Considine, Elizabeth Schraft, Beatrice Lillie, Anna Marie Alberghetti, Melanie Kahane, the Duke and Duchess Pini di San Miniato, and the great Ethel Merman.

Victor and I at "Helicon Hall"

Playing the organ

Victor was the life of the party, quick at the keys and on his feet.

Victor loved nothing better than a good practical joke.

Victor, Marian, Ce Ce, and I

By CeCe
Farris

(+)

My Life So Far

Farris

2 N 4- G-7   MORT KAYE STUDIO

At the age of
9 months

Marian

Ce Ce

Victor knighted as Commander of the Sovereign Order of Cyprus...our family

Lighthouse Yacht Center,
Nyack, N. Y.

AUG · 66

Welcome To
Lighthouse Yacht Center

Telephones		Telephones
Yard Office		Restaurant
(914) 358-5200		(914) 358-8995
Art Gallery		Boutique
(914) 358-5360		(914) 358-7620

This center is for your enjoyment; we hope you will visit often. Your suggestions are graciously received.

Compass Course, coming north:

From Tappan Zee Bridge, steer 320° magnetic, to Lighthouse.

FACILITIES ON THE PREMISES:

Coffee Shop — Breakfast, Luncheon, Dinner
Restaurant — Luncheon, Dinner, Banquets, Private Parties
Boutique — Fashions from the fashion centers, Gifts
Art Gallery — Objects d' art
Pool — Fresh Filtered, Heated Water
Paved Parking — for a clean basin
Fuel — Diesel — Accessories
Repairs — Engines, Electrical, Carpenter Shop

Before leaving, please check at the Yard Office to settle your account.

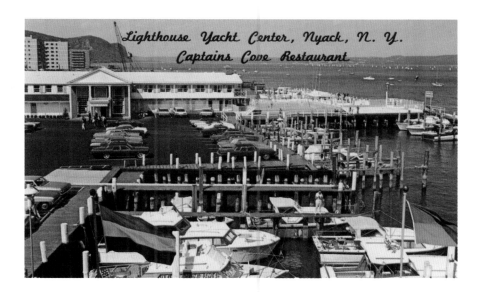

Victor's boat continued to be one of the focal points of our lives. It was anchored at the yard in Nyack, alongside another vessel that was owned by Laurance Rockefeller. (I once boarded the Rockefeller boat and was amazed by its sparse interior. The boat was unlike anything one would have thought a Rockefeller would have owned.) Victor was always a businessman adept at acquiring land. He purchased an anchorage in Nyack. He had a yacht basin dug to berth his latest 85-foot boat, "The Victorious," and then enlarged the yard to accommodate 150 yachts, a restaurant, and a marine supply store.

Things developed very quickly and soon I was spending most of my time in Nyack. I was happy that Victor was so involved in his boat and boating. For me, discussions among his boating cronies about ropes, anchors, paint, and marine supplies, were of limited interest. Reasoning that other "boat wives" may also be "in the same boat," so to speak, I hit on a brilliant solution for myself and for other women like me. Our property included a lighthouse, the perfect setting for a boutique, which I aptly named The Lighthouse Boutique.

I tested the market by displaying a few garments in the window. They sold immediately. I knew this was the start of a successful venture. For the opening-day launch, Victor and I invited friends and members of the New York press to a champagne brunch on the "Victorious." Then, we cruised up the Hudson to Nyack, while models showed clothes from the boutique. A fashion writer from "The New York Times" and numerous other publications covered the opening of The Lighthouse Boutique, and the business just took off.

Opening-day launch of The Lighthouse Boutique

My Lighthouse Boutique

We broke even fairly quickly. I made a few mistakes along the way, but forgave myself because this was my first venture into the retail world. Yet, I was ecstatic at the prospect of shopping on Seventh Avenue and looked forward to delving into a "Guys and Dolls" world. The fashion business was new to me, and I secretly expected the boutique to lead to a few extra perks, such as buying my entire wardrobe wholesale from manufacturers.

I was a size 10, and on learning from my Seventh Avenue suppliers that I couldn't buy individual pieces wholesale, and had to buy 10 outfits in each particular size, I ordered complete wardrobes. I made sure there was at least one of every outfit in a size 10, so I could keep one and sell the other nine in the boutique. Victor thought this was very funny, and advised me that I should carry larger sizes. Some American women he said, "have big asses!" So, I improved my inventory to carry up to size 16.

I ordered outfits in a run of sizes that sold out almost immediately. I tried different angles in newspaper advertisements, as I had no experience in marketing—I was an amateur. But when I placed an ad that read, "Why go to New York? Come to us!" they did. I also staged fashion shows in the Yacht Center's restaurant, and they were very well-received. Business at The Lighthouse Boutique was booming and I was happy—we were a success!

The boutique added variety to my life. Victor would spend many a day checking the boatyard while I happily worked away at the boutique. In between, we would often sit on the roof of one of the buildings and catch the sun. One day when I was sunbathing on the roof, I watched a yacht pull into a slip. (I loved watching boats berthing, through binoculars.) Imagine my surprise when I saw Frank Sinatra and his wife at the time, Mia Farrow, leaning over the railing, watching the vessel being tied up at the dock.

When the gangway was lowered, Sinatra sauntered off the yacht and headed for our gift shop. Victor happened to be in there holding down the fort. He was a great fan of Sinatra. The usually loquacious Victor admitted later that he became tongue-tied. However, Sinatra was charming and put Victor completely at ease. They had a lengthy conversation that covered just about everything from music to boats. Sinatra gave Victor a gold money-clip that had the name Sinatra inscribed on it. And there I was, sitting on the roof soaking up the sun, instead of basking in the gaze of "Ol' Blue Eyes!" (I would later meet Frank Sinatra in Monaco and Hollywood.)

Victor and I in front of my boutique at the Lighthouse Yacht Center, Nyack, N.Y.

Lighthouse Boutique

Main St., Burd St., at the Hudson River • NYACK, N.Y.

AT THE Lighthouse Yacht Center

The Genius of *Gino Paoli* **ITALIAN COUTURE KNITTER**

At Easter Time . . . Step out in style with this beautiful Gino Paoli 3 piece knit suit $134.95

DUE TO INCLEMENT WEATHER . . .
Our CLEARANCE SALE Will
CONTINUE TO SATURDAY, MARCH 25TH

WELCOME ABOARD
AMPLE FREE PARKING

CCP   CHARGE ACCOUNTS INVITED!   •   DAILY 9:30 to 6 OPEN FRIDAY 'TIL 9 p. m.

Victor was approached about a business venture in England. The British were interested in producing his valves there. He had arranged to meet with Sir Leon Bagrit who was world-renowned in the field of automation. He had built his company, Elliot Automation, into one of the largest of its kind in the world, and had written several highly regarded books on automation. He was also renowned for establishing the first company of its type in Europe.

Prior to our departure for England, I cautioned Victor that he was not going to enjoy doing business with the Brits. I knew little about this particular type of business, but I knew the British have a far more leisurely attitude about conducting business. "They stop for tea every day," I explained to Victor.

So, off we went to London, the first time we would visit there together. We arrived late in the afternoon, but decided not to go out. Instead, we retired early so that Victor would be well rested for his meeting with Sir Leon in the morning. By the time I awoke, Victor had already left for his meeting.

Anxious to hear the result of the meeting, I decided to stay in the suite until Victor returned. Upon his arrival later that day, Victor looked drained, as if he had not slept all night. When he began speaking, his voice was strained, his face almost ashen. "What do you mean, the British stop for tea and lunch? They are brilliant merchants and know exactly what they are doing and talking about," Victor proclaimed. He looked as if he had been zonked sideways. I couldn't help but chuckle inwardly, thinking that the British had probably shown even the brilliant Victor Farris a thing or two about doing business. He was stunned to find that British businessmen were more rough and tough than he was. Victor took his revenge by delighting in shocking some of the more stuffy members of the British establishment that we encountered at social gatherings.

One such event was a party that an English aristocrat, who had once asked me on several dates when I was single, was also attending. That evening when he learned that I was married, he looked Victor up and down and patronizingly asked him, "And, what do you do?" Victor replied, "I run a string of whore houses!" The aristocrat's jaw dropped. Nothing more needed to be said. Victor was in his element being terribly funny.

We attended many events while in Great Britain, including the Royal Ascot where Prince Charles was playing polo that day. Victor enjoyed the parks and

At Royal Ascot

"people watching." However, he did not like the smaller portions served in British restaurants. Invariably Victor's solution to this dilemma would be to gleefully ask the waiter, "Why is there not enough meat on the plate?" I would sink down in my chair with embarrassment as this happened in nearly every restaurant.

Victor admired British tailoring and went to my father's tailor on London's Saville Row, who was also the tailor for Cary Grant and the Duke of Windsor. He bought a suit from the tailor and then complained that it didn't fit properly. The truth of the matter was that Victor lacked patience. He couldn't be bothered to keep going back for fittings. Every time he wore that suit, he would mutter, "British suits! Ha!" Victor told me one day that he was going to buy a Rolls Royce, proclaiming that he was going to "beat them down on the price." I explained, "We don't do that in England." "Well, we do in America," he retorted, and proceeded to negotiate the price. That day we drove home in a wine-red Rolls Royce.

Anything French was another matter. Victor's family originally emigrated to the United States from France. In France, he felt a sense of home. When Marian and

Victor dressed as Napoleon at a costume ball.

Ce Ce were older, we all flew to Paris and spent an afternoon on the Bateaux Mouches (riverboats that cruise up and down the Seine). Onboard, the waiters served everyone, including the children, wine and brandy. Victor proceeded to drink all the bottles of wine and brandy, including mine. When the boat finally docked, the three of us carried a thoroughly inebriated Victor off the vessel. Smashed, Victor kept chanting, "Vive La France! Vive La France!" and he meant it!

I would recall my stage career, as a singer and actress, when friends from England came to visit. But, my life as a wife and mother was wonderful, overshadowing those difficult years of my first life on the stage. Caring for Victor and my two daughters added a joy to my life that was exhilarating. There was never a dull moment being married to such a genius.

When our daughters had their school holidays, Victor would always think of something special for all of us to do. One special trip was sailing the Intracoastal Waterway to Charleston, South Carolina, and then on to New Orleans. It was my first visit to that historic city.

Victor only belonged to clubs where he could tie up his boat.

Marian, Ce Ce and I loved the quaint buildings, jazz music and Creole cuisine. We eventually moved to Palm Beach after enjoying our winter visits to the area for many years. Victor decided it would be nice to have a home on the beach. After looking at a number of properties, we settled into beautiful house located on the north end of the Island. This would be our second home away from home.

We had talked about Victor retiring from his business for quite some time. He worked tremendously hard and looked tired, white and drawn from the long hours and stress. I had hoped when we decided to take a second home that he would begin to take it easy, at least while we were in Palm Beach.

Although Victor loved his boat, beyond that he wasn't really much of a man for traveling. He was too involved with his businesses and inventions to want to leave home for long, or without a purpose related to his companies. For me this was a blessing. I'd had my share of being on the road, and to this day I really do not care to travel. Yet, Victor really loved life in Palm Beach and his biggest pleasure was his boat. He would only belong to clubs where he could tie up his boat, so he belonged to the Sailfish Club in Palm Beach and, of course, the New York Yacht Club.

We entertained on the yacht and soon made new friends in Palm Beach. From

One of my new friends in Palm Beach was Mary Sanford.

the first time I met her, she was referred to as "The Queen of Palm Beach." Mary Sanford, was charming to me and a very strong woman. She announced, shortly after meeting me, "A pretty girl like you should be doing something!" And, the next thing I knew, I was serving on a plethora of committees. One of my first appointments was chairman of an advertising book for the Good Samaritan Hospital Ball. I began selling advertisements for the program book. It was an assignment that I quickly grew to greatly dislike because it involved asking for money. (To this day, I still don't like asking for money.)

I hated the job and found that the beleaguered merchants were so fed up with appeals from charities, that they would firmly say "No" before I could complete my request. Victor, however, being an Aquarius and a humanitarian, encouraged me, saying, "It will do you good Goofa." After all, raising money for charity had been a long-standing tradition in Palm Beach. In fact, during the season, the Town raises millions of dollars for charity.

Victor eventually merged Farris Engineering with Teledyne and we moved to Palm Beach and, for the most part, lived there year-round. One weekend, as we were relocating everything to Palm Beach, Victor drove our 17-year-old standard poodle,

Pokey (who had about three or four teeth left in his mouth), from Englewood, New Jersey, to Palm Beach in his Rolls.

We had moved into an enormous Spanish-style home in the estate section of the Island. Our new home overlooked the ocean, was just a few minutes from all the shops on Worth Avenue, and, most importantly, was designed by the renowned architect Maurice Fatio. The house was enormous, beautiful, and had breathtaking views of the ocean. However, it had one very peculiar feature. The staircase to the second floor bedrooms was on the outside of the house.

Casa Del Mar, our new spanish-style home in Palm Beach, was designed by renowned architect Maurice Fatio and built to the order of Mr. Allen Kirby of Allegheny Corp. fame.

The ocean-view estate had a formal, marble entrance and a staircase which led to an atrium thru a wrought iron gate to the vaulted loggia with a beamed balcony. The estate featured 19 rooms – 9 rooms on the first floor and 10 rooms on the second. It had 6 master bedrooms with 6 baths and 3 maids quarters. There were 4 magnificent coquina fireplaces. The ground floor was complete with a wine cellar that had a vaulted steel door, and storage/laundry facilities.

The property had a beautiful pool and cabana pavilion on the ocean that was served by a tunnel from the main house. The pavilion was complete with a kitchen, shower, and dressing rooms; a lovely place to entertain. Above the garage was a beautifully decorated apartment.

Gate to entrance foyer

Loggia

Casa Del Mar, facing East

East view

Drawing room

Library

Dining room

Master suite

Atrium

Pool and cabana pavilion

Ambassador and Mrs. Arthur Gardner were our neighbors across the street and often entertained the Duke and Duchess of Windsor as their houseguests. Victor liked to take care of his own car right in front of our house. Of course, as an engineer and inventor, he knew everything about the engine of a car. He could have taken it apart and put it back together, had he wanted to. Victor washed the car himself, as well. He would take the hose out and wash the Rolls in our front driveway nearly every morning. The Ambassador's chauffeur would look on with disdain as he did this. One particular morning, I reminded him that The Duke and Duchess were houseguests of Ambassador and Mrs. Gardner, so maybe he should not wash the car in the driveway. Victor responded with "I will wash my own car, in my own driveway, and I don't give a damn who is visiting across the street or watching." That was Victor, no pretense.

Around this time Victor decided to purchase a larger yacht, which was to be named the "Victorious." We came up with the name after, of all things, the "HMS Victorious," a British aircraft carrier that was launched during World War II in 1939.

Much like the "HMS Victorious," Palm Beach also had a rich history—from the beauty of its Spanish-style architecture, to the waters of the Atlantic Ocean that surround the Island and were once navigated by the likes of Ponce de Leon, who discovered Florida, and Columbus.

The Island's enchanting history progressed at the hands of Henry Morrison Flagler at the turn of the 20th century. Flagler and John D. Rockefeller, who co-founded Standard Oil, began developing the coast of northern Florida, in particular St. Augustine in the late 1800s. Flagler built a number of hotels for people of affluence to enjoy during the winter months.

To bring them to Florida, Flagler built the Florida East Coast Railroad, linking the northeast United States to northern Florida. Eventually, Henry Flagler extended the railroad all the way to Key West. Along the way it came to Palm Beach, where he eventually built the luxury resort The Palm Beach Inn, later renamed The Breakers. In addition, he built a magnificent estate for his third wife, Mary Lily and himself, which he named Whitehall.

Upon its completion in 1902, "The New York Herald" proclaimed it as "more wonderful than any palace in Europe, grander and more magnificent than any other private dwelling in the world." Today, Whitehall is The Henry M. Flagler Museum.

Rose Kennedy was gracious and down to earth.

The Kenan Family still owns The Breakers, which is one of the greatest resort hotels in North America.

I learned a great deal from Mary Sanford. She was a great lady, a former movie actress, a friend, and a powerhouse at organization. Mary never lost sight of the goal at hand. Mary shared her wisdom, that anyone who wants to raise money for their favorite worthy cause should treat the project as a business. She was the "Queen of Palm Beach" for many wonderful reasons, including all the tremendous work she did for the Town and for charity.

Rose Kennedy was one of Mary's best friends. Rose had suffered through so many heartbreaking tragedies, yet was a lady of great faith, strong will and courage. She was a sweet, wise and wonderful woman. Rose was gracious, down to earth and we became very good friends.

One particular day, Rose invited me to her home for tea. We had a marvelous afternoon together. It was always that way with Rose. When it came time to leave Rose walked out with me. During the course of the afternoon the gardener had left a huge pile of lawn debris in front of my car. I got stuck as I was trying to pull out of the driveway. Rose, noticing my predicament, and always resourceful, walked into

Anne Douglas White and I became friends in London, years earlier.

the street and began directing traffic. She began waving cars on so that I could get out. However, her help had somewhat of a reverse effect. All the drivers passing by sat bolt upright in their cars, not believing what they were seeing, mouths open in amazement at the sight of the venerable Rose Kennedy directing traffic. As a result, every single driver stopped and stared, refusing to move north or south, they were hypnotized by the sight of Rose, looking typically chic in her pink suit and hat.

Perhaps the greatest lady I've ever been privileged to know was Marjorie Merriweather Post. I met her through Anne Douglas White in Palm Beach. Anne and I had become friends in London many years prior to this. Anne was then a Red Cross nurse and had asked me to sing for the troops at every Red Cross Club in London. She had seen me in the "Quaker Girl." Our friendship had remained strong throughout the years and now we were both living in Palm Beach, where her husband, Bob White, was the President of the Everglades Club.

I can't find the words to express how charming and kind Marjorie was. She was a totally captivating lady. Victor and I were invited quite often as her guests at Mar-a-Lago, her home in Palm Beach. On the surface, her existence at Mar-a-Lago may have seemed rarefied; she had priceless antiques and lived in a splendor-filled

Marjorie Post was totally captivating.

setting. But in reality, Marjorie, as she liked to be called, with her strong Midwestern accent and values, was completely down to earth and cherished simplicity. She was beautiful, gracious, looked like a queen, and was the epitome of a stately lead in an epic film.

I found Marjorie to be a very interesting woman, whose life experiences were most unique. The more I knew about my new friend, the more fascinated I became. She was the daughter of C.W. Post, the cereal tycoon, who owned such brands as Grape Nuts, Postum, and Post Toasties. Her marriage to E.F. Hutton began a new chapter in her life. Marjorie took the reins of the company at the age of 27. She built it into an empire that included General Foods and Birdseye Frozen Foods.

Upon her passing, interestingly enough, Marjorie's largest holdings were in IBM, which was the result of her great business acumen in sensing the technology shift and emerging growth in America and other nations.

Marjorie Merriweather Post's beauty, wealth and great warmth provided her with worldwide recognition and respect, but she never took that for granted. She had traveled extensively and owned a home in Washington. Marjorie was a most grand and gracious hostess. As the wife of Joseph Davies, ambassador to the Soviet Union,

she became one of the first women to help represent America in that part of the world. She possessed the diplomatic skills of an ambassador herself.

When I met Marjorie, my parents were living in Palm Beach. I introduced them to her; she enchanted them by saying, "You did a good job on her."

Marjorie had it all: wit, style, sophistication, sincerity, simplicity and warmth. I can vividly remember her at the Red Cross Ball held at The Breakers in Palm Beach. Marjorie looked magnificent in a grey taffeta gown, accessorized with a diamond-and-sapphire necklace and matching earrings. Her grey hair was coiffed in an elegant French twist on top of her head. She looked every inch like a queen.

There was also another wonderful side to Marjorie, one that her closest friends were privileged to know. Every Thursday night, Marjorie invited Victor and me to her square-dance party. She greeted guests wearing an off-the-shoulder, lace blouse and a pretty cotton skirt. Of course, we all wore petticoats. Marjorie, who had a hearing disability, must have felt the music through the vibrations on the floorboards. She delighted all with dancing exhibitions. I was a natural born, trained dancer, so I had no trouble mastering square-dancing.

However, Victor could not square-dance if his life depended on it. I tried everything! First, trying to teach Victor myself but that effort proved to be unsuccessful.

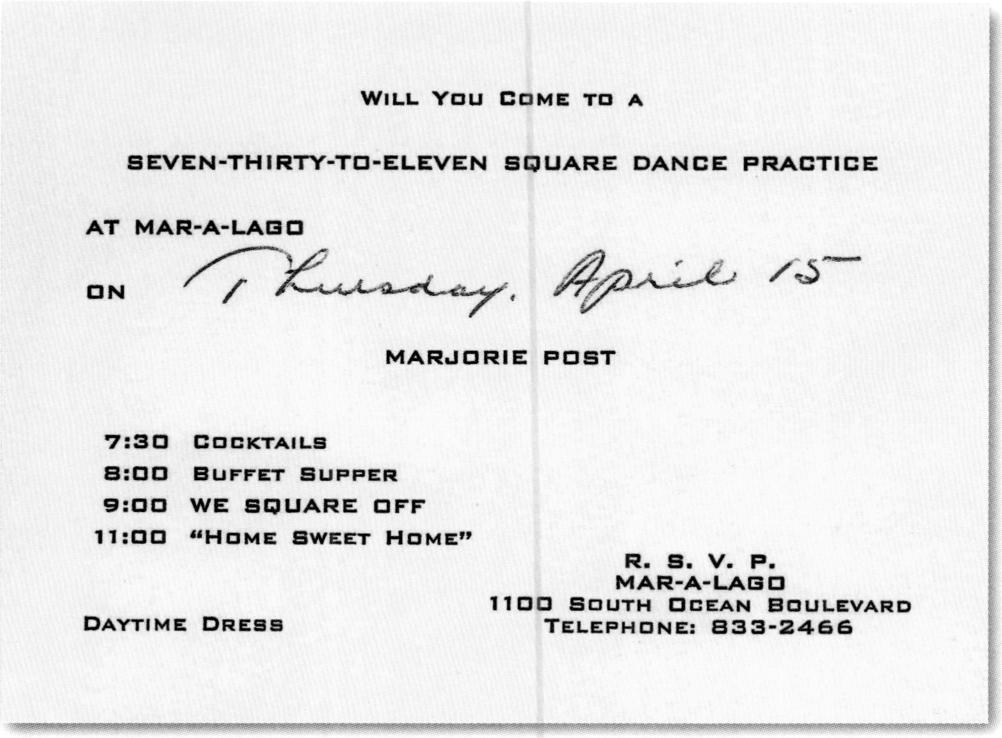

WILL YOU COME TO A

SEVEN-THIRTY-TO-ELEVEN SQUARE DANCE PRACTICE

AT MAR-A-LAGO

ON *Thursday, April 15*

MARJORIE POST

7:30 COCKTAILS
8:00 BUFFET SUPPER
9:00 WE SQUARE OFF
11:00 "HOME SWEET HOME"

R. S. V. P.
MAR-A-LAGO
1100 SOUTH OCEAN BOULEVARD
TELEPHONE: 833-2466

DAYTIME DRESS

So, I left him in the hands of the professional dancers that Marjorie hired each Thursday night. This was all for naught, Victor just could not square-dance, period. As a result, I spent those nights at Marjorie's hanging onto Victor for dear life. I was terrified that he would swing straight through the French doors and land in the bushes. I can remember being very relieved when Marjorie did dos-à-dos, which signaled that the evening was over.

Every Thursday evening, a couple was invited to dine with Marjorie alone in her library. This was considered a great compliment. Towards the end of her life, Victor and I spent many hours alone with Marjorie. Although she had great difficulty with her hearing, Victor could still make her laugh by putting a napkin over his hand, drawing a mouth and eyebrows on it with lipstick, then puppeteering. He made the most extraordinary expressions and the elegant Mrs. Post would explode in laughter. After dinner, the four of us–Victor, Marjorie, her secretary and I–would watch movies about birds.

On a very special occasion, I hosted a birthday for Marjorie. She preferred to do most of her own entertaining, and rarely accepted invitations. I was honored to celebrate her birthday at Casa del Mar, our home in Palm Beach. Marjorie must have enjoyed herself, so much so that she left her fur wrap behind.

Topridge, Upper Saint Regis, Franklin County, N.Y.

Marjorie invited Victor and me for a weekend at her house, Topridge, in the Adirondacks. We traveled in her private plane, and when we arrived at The main house it was in the shape of a tepee. It was decorated with Native American treasures, with bear rugs on the oak floors, lit by large fireplaces. At Topridge, Marjorie had separate guesthouses for visitors, with her favorite fittingly named, "Dina's House" after her beloved daughter Dina Merrill. We were served caviar, sour cream, and blintzes for breakfast, followed by a cable-car excursion to explore a nearby mountain. During breakfast one morning, Victor and I kept rushing from the table into the kitchen to look at the only (tiny) television set in the entire house. We wanted to witness John Glenn being the first man walking on the moon. The entire weekend was unforgettable, just like the wonderful Marjorie.

Estée Lauder, another memorable woman and friend, was a tremendous businesswoman and fascinating personality whom Victor and I came to know when we moved to Palm Beach. I vividly remember the afternoon in which we had been invited to a luncheon at her home. Suddenly, during the middle of the meal, when my mouth was full of cucumber, Estée pointed at me and said, "Sing!" (Apparently she must have found out that I was a singer.) I couldn't refuse, so while seated at the

Estée Lauder and I

table, I began to sing "Where or When." Victor, on the other side of the table, joined me, singing in harmony. Victor had a great ear for harmony. Estée's guests, enthusiastic about our little performance, all applauded and dubbed us as "cute."

At a charity ball some time later, Estée and I were seated next to each other in front of a mirror in the ladies lounge. I took out my lipstick (Estée Lauder, of course) and was preparing to apply it. With great authority, Estée took the lipstick out of my hand, reached for a tissue, and thoroughly wiped the lipstick container clean. Then, she politely handed it back to me. Not a word was spoken, but the point taken: An Estée Lauder lipstick container must be clean!

Palm Beach has always been a great place for fashion. At one particular gala I entered the ballroom to find that I was wearing the identical Scaasi gown as my friend Mary Lou Whitney. Mary Lou and I burst out laughing. I lived close by, so I dashed home and changed into a different Scaasi gown. I was back at the gala in 15 minutes! (Arnold Scaasi is a great American fashion designer today. He has dressed First Ladies as well as the First Lady of cinema, Elizabeth Taylor. Scaasi's partner, Parker Ladd, was a television host, commentator, and has written numerous books and columns. And, Scaasi's book, "Women I have Dressed (and Undressed!)," has been well received.)

Seeing double... Mary Lou Whitney and I both wore Scaasi.

Raising funds for the Salvation Army Ball

It wasn't always easy to convince Victor that I needed a new dress or gown for this event or that party, or a new suit for a ladies luncheon. Victor did not appreciate the whole fashion scene. He often said of shops on Worth Avenue, "You're only paying for their expensive rents. Just go over to Macy's." To him they had the same thing in all the stores.

The noise of the great genius would roar through the house as he was cutting his own hair. He liked to be his own barber. "Come and see if this is all right," he would say. To my chagrin it was not, "all right." Victor had curly hair, which stood up like a poodle's in the wind. After he had cut it unevenly, it was an utter mess. He wasn't saving money; he simply did not want to waste time in a barber's chair.

On another occasion, we were on the boat and he encouraged me to "cut his hair." I thought to myself, "OK, I can probably do better than he." So, I found a large bowl and put it over his head and began to cut around it. The boat was moving, the bowl was slipping, and the back of his head was a mess. A barber I was not!

Victor was a great humanitarian who accomplished an enormous amount in his life. His genius had been praised throughout the world and, on March 16, 1972, he was honored in a unique way. He became the 35th American ever to be knighted with the rank of Commander of the Sovereign of Cyprus. The history of the Order, and what it represented was defined by the Honorable Frank J. Brasco in the House of Representatives:

> "The Sovereign Order of Cyprus, one of the oldest orders of chivalry, was founded in the year 1192 by Guy de Lusignan, King of Cyprus and Jerusalem, and confirmed by Pope Innocent 111 in the year 1200, who imposed upon it the dual mission of spreading the Christian faith and acting as a bulwark of the

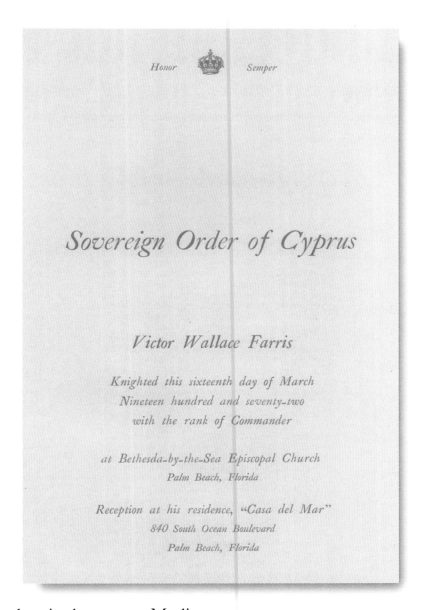

Honor 👑 *Semper*

Sovereign Order of Cyprus

Victor Wallace Farris

Knighted this sixteenth day of March
Nineteen hundred and seventy-two
with the rank of Commander

at Bethesda-by-the-Sea Episcopal Church
Palm Beach, Florida

Reception at his residence, "Casa del Mar"
840 South Ocean Boulevard
Palm Beach, Florida

Christendom in the eastern Mediterranean.

"Three hundred men of noble birth were inducted as Knights in the New Order and allowed to wear the red, eight pointed cross of the order at the throat. The Sovereign Order of Cyprus, today a modern organization, which is based on ancient principles and traditions, is dedicated to the building of schools, hospitals, churches and other charitable, spiritual and educational institutions. It honors writers, artists, and men of science, culture, education and medicine, leaders of the free world from every walk of life regardless of race, color, creed or national origin. However, in its nearly 800-year history, only 900 men have received this coveted knighthood and cross."

Sovereign Order of Cyprus

EXTENSION OF REMARKS

OF

HON. FRANK J. BRASCO

OF NEW YORK

IN THE HOUSE OF REPRESENTATIVES

Wednesday, June 14, 1967

Mr. BRASCO. Mr. Speaker, under leave to extend my remarks.

The Sovereign Order of Cyprus, one of the four oldest orders of chivalry, was founded in the year 1192, by Guy de Lusignan, King of Cyprus and Jerusalem, and confirmed by Pope Innocent III in the year 1200, who imposed upon it the dual mission of spreading the Christian faith and acting as a bulwark of Christendom in the eastern Mediterranean. The order was created on the model of the Hospitaller and military orders such as those of the Temple, and of St. John, installed in the Holy Land. Three hundred men of noble birth were inducted as knights in the new order and allowed to wear the red, eight-pointed cross of the order at the throat. They were obliged to defend the island route to the Holy Land and to prevent attack and infiltration by the infidels. The order also consisted of men-at-arms, chaplains, and serving brothers who, with the knights, were organized in commanderies. The distinguishing mark of the knights was a blue mantle with the red cross of the order upon it. The order attracted to its ranks some of the most vigorous nobles of Christendom, and these knights were to take an active interest in the affairs of the Holy Roman Empire and of the Byzantine Empire in addition to their defense of the pilgrims and their charitable works.

Under a succession of able grand masters, for more than three centuries, the deeds and influence of the Sovereign Order of Cyprus were enormous and its members played an important role as a stabilizing force in the political life of the Levant. After the annexation of Cyprus by Venice, the order entered a period of decline and its members dispersed throughout the Balkan States and Western Europe. More recently the order was reactivated by the descendants of some of its most illustrious knights with the blessings of the Holy See and dedicated to the unique values of Christian civilization and the spirit of ecumenism. Its reorganizers, like their famous ancestors, felt obliged, in the face of the many dangers which beset our culture and our institutions, to reestablish this venerable and tradition-laden order of chivalry, springing from one of the most respected shrines of Western thought, affirming in this way, the continuity of Christian effort against terror and injustice.

The Sovereign Order of Cyprus, today a modern organization, based on ancient principles and traditions, is dedicated to the building of schools, hospitals, churches and other charitable, spiritual, and educational institutions. It honors writers, artists, men of science, culture, education, and medicine; leaders of the free world from every walk of life, regardless of race, color, creed, or national origin. However, in its nearly 800-year history only 900 men have received this coveted knighthood and cross. For the propagation and spread of its principles, the order has created an Institute for the Study of Moral Philosophy and Social Sciences—Academie des Etudes Superieures—which it subsidizes.

Mr. Speaker, it gives me particular pleasure to inform this House that it was in recognition of the dynamic spirit of American patriotism, and the modern day crusade in which we Americans seek to bring freedom from oppression to the peoples of the world, that Michel Paul Pierre Count de Valitch, grand chancellor of the Sovereign Order of Cyprus, heir to the rich traditions of this ancient order, authorized the establishment of an American commandery of the order more than 3 years ago. Count de Valitch personally attended to its inauguration and has, since then, personally overseen its affairs.

At this point, I would like to enter in the RECORD the names of some of the outstanding members of this order both in the United States and abroad:

His Royal Highness Prince Louis de Bourbon.

His Imperial and Royal Highness Prince de Ligny Luxembourg.

His Excellency Paul P. Barrenechea, Minister for Foreign Affairs, Republic of Peru.

His Execellency Stephan Brunet, Secretary General, Union of War Veterans, France.

Mr. Francis Bellon, distinguished industrialist, Paris, France.

Archbishop Charles Brearley, Sheffield, England.

His Excellency Baron Francesco Caponera, Diplomat, Rome, Italy.

Dr. Charles P. Covino, Space Research Pioneer, New Jersey.

Archbishop Louis Canivet, Paris, France.

General James H. Doolittle, United States Army, Retired.

Right Reverend Monsignor Aloysius C. Dineen, New York City.

Honorable Joseph Eden, Diplomat, London and Paris.

Mr. Henry Evans, Author and Professor of International Relations, New Jersey.

Monsignor Patrick B. Fay, New York City.

Honorable Ludovic Huybrechts, Conseilleur de Commerce, Antwerp, Belgium.

Honorable Jean-Louis Jammet, LL.D. Professor of Law, Paris, France.

Dr. Serge Korff, Professor of Nuclear Physics at New York University and President of the Explorers Club of New York.

Dr. Hugh R. Kailan, Professor of Education, London, England.

Honorable Edward Thompson, Justice of the Supreme Court of the State of New York.

Dr. Pasquale Zaccara of New York City.

Mr. Monty Winslow, President of Transojet Tours of New York.

Mr. Lowell Thomas, Author, New York.

Honorable Enrique De Los Heros, former ambassador of the Republic of Peru in Spain.

Rear Admiral Gordon McLintock, Commandant, United States Merchant Marine Academy, Kings Point, New York.

Mr. Georges Levai, distinguished authority on Art, Paris. France.

Mr. Nicolas Alexandre Manic, industrialist and patron of the arts, Paris, France.

Colonel Le Baron R. Matyn de Lionel, Grand Chancellor of the renowned Royal Order of St. Georges de Burgogne of Belgium, Brussels, Belgium.

Rear Admiral Alfonso Navarro Romero, Republic of Peru.

Count Stephen Potocki, diplomat, Paris, France.

His Highness Prince L. Radziwill, Rome and London.

Reverend Frederick P. Erkhardt, D.D., New York City.

These distinguished contemporaries typify the caliber of men holding this high honor. I wish to congratulate Count de Valitch and the members of the Sovereign Order of Cyprus and to wish them continued success in their efforts toward bringing about a better and more peaceful world.

Victor and I on the evening he was knighted as Commander of the Sovereign Order of Cyprus.

The award ceremony took place at the Church of Bethesda-by-the-Sea, in Palm Beach. After the ceremony, we hosted a reception in our home, inviting many friends to share in the joy of this very special occasion.

Victor and the Sheriff

Victor, my chivalrous Knight

His Excellency
The Most Rev. Lorenzo Michel de Valitch
Titular Bishop of Ephesus
Grand Chancellor

requests the honor of your presence
at the investiture of

Victor Wallace Farris

as Chevalier Commander

in the

Sovereign Order of Cyprus

at the

Episcopal Church

of

Bethesda - by - the - Sea
Palm Beach, Florida

Thursday, March 16th, 1972 at 7 o'clock

RSVP

Black Tie
Decorations

Mr. and Mrs. Victor Farris

Victor and Ce Ce

A Little Camelot In Palm Beach

Continued from Page B1

There were 200 at the church and 170 gathered later at the Farris home. All the beautiful people breezed about with high officials of the order.

The heavens had dared to open up on the rich. At 7:30, just before the guests left the church, the rains came. And back in the Farris courtyard, soaked damask table covers were being whisked off by the dozens.

But all ended well. The rain stopped and by the time guests arrived, no one would have known it all had happened. Everyone congratulated Farris, and Raymond F. Kelley and Donald Armstrong who had added to the grandeur of the ceremony.

Sir Alister Ewing and Lady Ewing swept into the courtyard where twinkling lights played on the tall fountain after greeting the hostess, Celia Farris, and the Farris daughters, Marian and Cee Cee. Celia was lovely in a black organza with ruching around collar and wrists by Sarmi. And the little girls were wearing tea roses in their hair — to go with the bouquets they carried at the church.

Guests paused as they descended into the courtyard where Sid Ziering and the orchestra strolled about playing romantic music on those violins.

They commented about the beautiful appointments — red carnations and ruby red crystal candelabra, the framed apostolic benediction from the Pope, the scroll and the sword and those grand robes of the order.

Each table, a miniature of the main one, was festooned with red and royal blue carnations and the red crystal candelabra. In the center the fountain was draped with red and royal blue ribbons and flags of the order.

Guests, carried away with the mood, sang in French and Italian. Everyone was having a grand evening.

Fashions reflected both the solemnity of the ceremony and

Mary Sanford breezed about in a Scaasi's black mirrored creation; Mrs. Philip Luken and Mrs. Allen Manning in lustrous greens.

Much like a Renoir painting was Mrs. John Perry Jr. whose hair was piled high above a swishing black organza gown. Actress Pamela Curran was there in a black halterneck dress, saying she likes writing better than acting. Seated across from her was Ted Peckham and Sir Ewing and Lady Ewing.

Judy Schrafft wore her gold Moroccan jewelry and a black jersey dress. In contrast was Mrs. Raymond Kelley, all in white and draped in maribou with lots of gold jewelry and gold leaves in her hair.

Those white gowns stood out — Mrs. William Battin in a white jeweled creation, Alice Godfrey blazing in gold trimming on her white. Malcolm Starr and Mrs. Arthur Pierson in white with elegant pearls.

Huldah Jesse was in black satin. In fact, there was a lot of that old black magic — Victoria Schrafft, her mother, Brownie McLean in a slinky black jersey; Mary Howes in black organza; Maggie Hayes, Mrs. Joseph Neff and Pamela Rank in black prints.

Ann Hamilton wore that smashing Cardinali pajama with white fox trim. And there were those pretty garden prints, Barbara Stranahan Holmyard, Mrs. Harold Payne Whitmore and Mrs. Richard Cowell.

Mrs. Arthur Burck designed the white satin dress she wore

Dancing at one of the Palm Beach balls

The Rosarian Academy Golden Anniversary Ball was the first gala I chaired. Many people still ask me how a Charity Ball is organized. To adequately outline this would take another book. But, in short, the chairman forms a committee of friends who wish to help a particular charity. Planning takes from six months to a year prior to the Ball. The chairman should arrange cocktail parties, dinners, luncheons, or teas, to build up the charity supporters and guest list. Many of the finer stores may enjoy hosting an event to honor the chairman and the committee, to build loyalty, and community support. "Save the Date" cards and invitations should be attractive, in good taste, and in the mail very early. The "Save the Date" cards should be mailed out six months prior to the event, and the invitations in the mail no later than three months prior. In Palm Beach, there are many other benefits competing for charity donations and attendance during the season.

Events that I have taken the responsibility of chairing, I have diligently worked to publicize by sending notices to newspapers and magazines, and working closely with a public-relations committee to benefit the charity.

To make a Ball successful, a chairman has to spend much time on the telephone, and call people and invite them to come. A budget must be prepared as well, and expenses watched very carefully. The goal is to raise as much money as possible for the charity. Conceptualize a great theme for the event, including magnificent floral arrangements, unique decorations, and appropriate music for dancing that enhance the event's theme. Not to be forgotten is the menu, a most important make-or-break of any event. A pre-tasting of the chef's menu is highly recommended. If you know any celebrities, invite them to attend the ball. I've found their presence draws people to the event. My nightmare has always been that no one is going to show up! Here's hoping you have a successful benefit. Oh, and make sure you thank everyone profusely along the way and on the night of the event.

I encountered a major challenge when I chaired the Rosarian Academy Ball in that, with the exception of Rose Kennedy, many Palm Beachers were not especially interested in supporting a small Catholic school in West Palm Beach. I knew I would have to do something very special to attract Palm Beach residents to the Ball, and to make it a success. I drew on my show business friends. I called Milton Berle first, and he agreed to be there. My next call was to my friend Perry Como, everyone's favorite singer. He was more than happy to help the moment I asked him. My final coup was Gordon McCrae of "Oklahoma" movie fame. The Ball was a great success.

The children from Rosarian participated in the evening performing a medley from "Oklahoma." They were dressed so beautifully in white outfits, the girls with white ribbons in their hair.

When Milton came on, he brought the house down. However, I worried beforehand, begging him not to tell one single dirty joke. "There are nuns around here Milton," I said. He was charming, beginning his act with the words, "What's a nice Jewish boy like me doing here at this benefit tonight?" It was Gordon's birthday, so the children of the Academy presented him with a surprise birthday cake. Then Perry came out, and I sang to him "Dear Mr. Como You Made Us Love You."

The evening raised a quarter-of-a-million dollars for Rosarian Academy (which was a great deal of money for a Ball at that time). I was given my first Palm Beach Chamber of Commerce Award for that Ball.

Mr. and Mrs. Perry Como at the Rosarian Academy Ball

Chairing my first ball

Victor and Gordon McCrae

Victor and I at the "April in Paris Ball" in New York.

Lord Hugh Cudlipp and Lady Cudlipp at my party, and Winston Churchill (center)

Victor enjoyed attending charity events in Palm Beach; especially the more down-to-earth type of affairs, such as the Fraternal Order of Police's Barbeque with pork ribs, apple pie, and plenty of talk about business. This was especially appealing to him. Victor was a diehard Republican, and once suggested that he run for Mayor of Palm Beach. I quickly dissuaded him, "Vic, you will have to give up your boat, and become a public servant. You will have to forfeit all privacy and entertain every night." Amazingly enough, he listened to me.

Our social life was full of contrasts it seemed, from hosting the English National Opera Company and its patron, the Queen, to Lord Hugh Cudlipp the proprietor of the "London Daily Mirror." Lord and Lady Cudlipp visited from England and stayed as our houseguests while working with Generoso Pope, owner and publisher of the "National Enquirer." Lord Cudlipp was consulting with Pope on upgrading the tabloid, which was at that time based in Lantana, Florida. Today the "National Enquirer" is owned by American Media. Chairman and CEO, David Pecker has done a brilliant job with the publication. Richard Valvo, Mr. Pecker's public relations counsel, keeps positive news constantly in the press about the Chairman and the publication.

Rose Kennedy and I

Sir Emile and Lady Littler

Sarah Churchill, her friend, and I

Ce Ce and I at the Royal Poinciana Playhouse

My mother and father at Mar-a-Lago

Victor and I celebrate the holidays

Ce Ce the debutant

There were so many unique and contrasting personalities in Palm Beach, including John Lennon and Yoko Ono who had been visiting the Island for years before eventually buying an ocean-view estate here. The Lennons, dressed in jeans and tanks tops, and wore long hair. They did not seem to want to mix with Palm Beachers and socialized with very few people. They were rarely seen except when frequenting a local health-food store from time-to-time.

Just when my life seemed so perfect, I was overcome with fear when I found a lump in my breast. After seeing my doctor, he immediately sent me to a specialist in New York. Then, I was referred to the Memorial Sloan-Kettering Hospital. The surgeon there informed Victor and me that he would operate. After the surgery, it took 36 hours to wait to find out if I would need a mastectomy. Those hours were the longest I have ever known. But, I was resigned, what would be would be.

Victor looked worried, as did so many other couples in the waiting room that day. For some reason, I wanted a bath. I will never forget my husband Victor, my American tough guy, washing my feet, and telling me "it will all be fine." He was kind and tender. For as long as I live, I'll never forget how loving he was to me during those hours.

They operated and I kept my breast. Victor and I went home and resumed our lives. However, I never forgot how fortunate I was. I have also coped with skin cancer and would caution all women to have regular examinations and protect themselves from the sun. My personal battle with cancer motivated me to donate to and raise funds for cancer treatments, research and therapies. I never forget to thank God each day for my health.

Indeed, my life had its many twists and turns, good and bad. Even marriage, as wonderful as mine was, had its moments of great testing. One of the worst arguments Victor and I had was during a visit to a theatre in New York. Looking back, it was one of those silly arguments that couples get themselves into. I said "I am leaving you and going back to the theatre." Of course, Victor, as tough as nails replied "go ahead." On the way home, I was silent.

When we arrived at home I would pack all of my cases with feather boas, chiffon dresses, sequined gowns, high heels, my music, press clippings, theatrical makeup, preparing for my departure. Obviously, I had enjoyed a few drinks at dinner, which did not help the situation. The next morning—when I had cooled off—I would

My mother and I at my first student show held at the Norton.

unpack the suitcases only to find that everything I had packed was strictly theatrical costumes or evening wear; nothing for the daytime. I was bluffing, and Victor knew that I would never leave him and the children. Whenever we had a big battle, I'd go through the same ritual, packing, but never leaving.

Our temperaments were creative in their different ways, and sometimes tempestuous. Victor's creativity was nurtured every day with his work. Whereas, despite my sense of fulfillment as a wife and mother, every so often I hankered after work of my own. Living in Palm Beach changed some of that for me, however I needed a creative outlet.

It was also during this time that I began to paint. I had discovered a medium where I could release my artistic creativity and energy. I studied with Wallace Bassford and Robert Moore at the Norton Museum of Art in West Palm Beach. I was part of a group exhibition at the Norton and James Hunt Barker Gallery.

The art critic Lawrence Dane of the "Post Times," which today is the "Palm Beach Post," wrote about my work, saying "Celia Farris, a charming lady, who has been known to arrange society events and who came to us through the London theater had a sell-out at Jimmy Barker's gallery...Celia was happy to part with oil landscapes she had on display and plenty of people would have bought more had they been available. She studies hard with Wallace Bassford and Robert Moore. I don't know any society dame with a greater esthetic urge, she will go far."

"Contemplating Paris"

"Picking flowers in the field"

"The day Judy Garland died 1969"

"Boats in San Remo"

"Mrs. Celia Farris, a social figure who studies hard with painters Robert Moore and Wallace Bassford, progressed from disbelief to ecstacy upon learning that three of her canvases had been sold at Palm Beach Galleries. A leafy landscape, which he friends said looked like a Cezanne, a charming study of two females sitting on grass, and a portrait of a florid girl you might think was a Renoir at first, composed the Farris range."

CELIA LIPTON FARRIS
One Person and Group Exhibitions

Phillips Gallery
James Hunt Baker Gallery
Ambassador Galleries
Norton School of Art
Art for America, NY
Palm Beach Galleries

"Twenty minutes"

"Time for thought"

"Two girls at the beach"

"English village"

"Two girls having a picnic"

"Crocheting in the garden"

"The Italian Lady"

"Flowers in a blue vase"

"Little Girl Picking Flowers"

"Remembering September 11, 2001"
I cried on 9/11. I knew America was now vulnerable.

"Remembering our heroes"

I tried to paint on the boat, on canvas that is. It was just Victor and me that day, there was no captain onboard. I remember I was down below, as they say in boating, trying to paint the light in the eyes of my subject. As I looked out the window, Victor had stopped the boat and was on the deck, tying up his 85-foot yacht all by himself. It was a very windy day. I am now all alone on the boat, still painting, and cannot believe what I am seeing outside the window.

The scene looked like a Charlie Chaplin movie. Victor dashing to tie up the ropes on the dock, then running back onboard, then rushing back onto the dock again, tying up the other end of the boat, then jumping back on board and finally silence. I kept envisioning myself drifting out to sea, alone, with Victor still on the dock. Immediately, I staggered up to the wheelhouse, hearing only the rush of wind outside. There stood a disheveled Victor. "It's amazing, how did you do it?" I asked. "Oh," he replied, "It's nothing at all. I can run this damn boat myself."

Lesly Smith (who later became the Mayor of Palm Beach), myself, and Tina Fanjul preparing for a benefit.

For fun during this same period of time, I went back into the recording studio in West Palm Beach. Victor wanted to come by and listen to me record. I warned the sound engineers that Victor wouldn't listen to me at all. Instead, he would be fascinated with the board and all its colorful knobs, because he was an engineer. True to form, Victor arrived and was instantly enamored with all the sound equipment. He wasn't listening to me, or so I thought. Then suddenly he looked up during the session and said, "Is that you? You sound like Lena Horne. I am going to take you to the William Morris office."

The recording sold very well and Victor enjoyed taking the CDs around and sharing them with friends and acquaintances. In hindsight, the thought always occurred to me that we could have had great fun making records together, Victor the great engineer and I the singer.

By this time, we had moved to another home, a Regency-style home that was the former residence of Consuelo Vanderbilt, the Duchess of Marlborough. She married the French General while living in the home and became Madame Balsan. Although we were not directly on the ocean, it was just a short block away. I spent many months decorating the house and beautifully furnishing it for entertaining. Victor saw no need for the expense of the new furnishings, draperies, carpets, artwork or decorator. He was much more interested in an office and garages for his cars.

Harry Benson, the world renowned photographer and my great friend,
took this photo of Victor and I at our new home in Palm Beach.

Victor and I moved into our third home, an elegant Regency-style residence in Palm Beach which was formerly owned by Consuelo Vanderbilt after she became Madame Jacques Balsan.

The home was built in 1941 for Mrs. Audrey Emery, formerly Princess Ilyinsky, wife of Russia's Grand Duke Dmitri and the mother of the former town Mayor, Paul Ilyinsky. It is a notable example of the work of Clarence Mack, AIA, who designed several Palm Beach homes.

The English Sitting Room

The three-story residence has 24 rooms, in addition to several staff rooms. Each room reflects the home's rich history. The second floor hallway has three 18th century oils of French noblemen, and through the doorway is an 18th century oil painting of the Duke of Marlborough. The Oriental Room has the original wallpaper, chosen by Madame Balsan and has been carefully preserved over the years. In the Loggia is the organ on which Victor often gave impromptu concerts. The home also features an elevator.

The Loggia

The Oriental Room

The Grand Salon

Many beautiful memories were made at our new home... Marian's wedding.

A portrait of me in the loggia for the cover of "Manhattan" magazine.

Victor at the organ.

The children were no longer children by this time. Marian and Ce Ce were young women, one with a family of her own. Things seemed to be changing all around me, and soon, would forever change the life I had known with Victor.

One evening, after Victor returned home from a day in Miami, he came to me saying he was feeling awful. His face was pale and pinched. He thought he had eaten too much dinner. I remember putting my arm around him, suggesting that he do some breathing exercises. His brother had recently died of heart disease, and had been required to carry oxygen with him constantly. I broached the subject with Victor, telling him we should get some oxygen in the house. Victor agreed, saying, "Tomorrow we will definitely go and get the oxygen."

Despite some temporary relief, Victor's pain that night increased. Our beloved granddaughter had just been to visit, and her child's chair was next to the bed. I gently held Victor and helped him put his feet up on the small chair, and then I covered him with a blanket.

I couldn't sleep that night because Victor's condition worried me. I phoned the doctor, and urged Victor to pick up the phone and explain how he was feeling to the doctor.

Our personal doctor was away that evening, and another doctor was taking his calls. Listening carefully, I heard Victor explain to the doctor that he had already taken four nitro-glycerin tablets. "I am still in pain," he explained. Unable to contain myself, I was yelling on the phone, asking the doctor, "What to do?" His instructions were clear, call the paramedics. I did so immediately. Hanging up the phone, I quickly got dressed and waited for them. Every minute that passed, seemed like an hour. Suddenly the telephone rang. I answered it, and heard the voice of a paramedic urgently explaining that they had been driving around West Palm Beach and couldn't find us.

Half out of my mind, in a rage, I screamed, "How couldn't you know where we are? You are in WEST Palm Beach. We are in Palm Beach!" He replied, "There is a street with the same name in West Palm Beach." I did not know this, and told him, "Please hurry." Then I slammed the phone down, and once again, began frantically waiting for the paramedics to arrive. Suddenly, Victor let out a loud gasp. He was sitting up on his bed with a look on his face that, for as long as I live, I will never forget. His face was yellow, lips blue, his tongue hanging out of his mouth. He was desperately trying to breathe. The pupils of his eyes were dilated. I felt helpless, afraid to touch him, fearing I would make things worse.

A thousand thoughts raced through my mind. What should I do? I was paralyzed and had no answers. All I could do was put my arms around Victor, and try to comfort him. As I gazed into his eyes, his pupils were fading in and out. Then I said, "I love you." My entire body was shaking when I ran downstairs to open the front door for the paramedics.

I don't know if Victor ever heard my last words to him. I was in a daze of confusion that seemed to get worse. The paramedics could not get into our driveway. The truck was too large. My heart was racing as I kept thinking, "we are losing critical time." When the paramedics finally got into the house, they could not fit their equipment into the small elevator. So, they climbed the stairs to the second floor, carrying their equipment and stretcher.

At the time my parents were living with us. The commotion that night woke my mother who, by that time, had lost her sight. She stood in the hall, asking repeatedly if we were being burgled. I remember quickly guiding her back to her room, so that the paramedics could pass through the hallway.

The paramedics slid Victor off the bed and onto the floor, and began pounding on his chest. They worked on him for what seemed like hours as I watched from the bedroom door. I can remember shouting, "Hang on and fight."

Victor was then lifted onto the stretcher, and carried down the stairway, and into the waiting ambulance. I noticed that someone had parked a car, blocking the driveway. I urgently pleaded with them to move the car, as neighbors, alarmed by the flashing lights of the ambulance, began to gather on the street.

The paramedics stopped me from joining Victor in the ambulance. I was told I would have to drive myself to the hospital. This was a nightmare. "Wake up Celia," I kept saying to myself.

When I arrived at the hospital it was deserted at that late hour, with only a guard at the door. I flew down the corridor, yelling, "Where is Emergency?" "That way," he indicated, pointing. "That way" turned out to be the longest journey I had ever taken.

I finally found the emergency room, and by that time everything seemed to go into fast-forward. It was awful. The doctors told me they were working on Victor, doing all they could to save him. I was in a blind panic. I was crying and beseeching the medical staff, one by one. I must have been a nightmare to confront in the corridor that evening, but the staff seemed to understand. Then, came the words I had heard in a hundred movies. I can't remember whether it was a nurse or a doctor, who spoke the fatal words, "I am sorry your husband...," then, "Would you like a cup of coffee?" Any other spoken words, more words, washed over me and meant nothing.

I kept thinking this is not possible. "Please, can I see him?" I asked. A young man took me into a cubicle where Victor lay, and to my annoyance, hovered there before leaving. I kissed Victor on his brow and found it was still warm. Grasping at hope, I screamed, "My God, he is still alive!" In relief, I yelled to the young man, "Please come back. He is still warm!" A nurse came into the room and gently explained, "Mrs. Farris, he is still warm because of all the work we have been doing on him."

Pushing away a lock of his lustrous hair, I kissed him for the very last time in my life; just once, a kiss to end a lifetime. Our entire existence flashed through my mind and ripped open my heart. All the images of him, we, and our family together, flashed before me as tears streamed down my face.

I walked out of the hospital, got into my car, put my head on the steering wheel and sobbed. Finally, after what seemed like hours, I started the car and drove into the bleak, dark night across the Intracoastal bridge, back to Palm Beach. That five-minute drive home seemed like 500 miles.

When I arrived home, all I could say to my parents was a broken, "He's gone."

The next morning, I woke with the realization that Victor was truly gone. I couldn't bear to think of it, so, I fixed my mind on the tasks ahead of me. I called my daughters and ask them to meet me at Quattlebaum Funeral Home in West Palm Beach.

This was the first time I had confronted death, and I had never been faced with the bleak prospect of choosing a casket. We were led into a room that was filled with coffins. The three of us clung to each other as we looked at the selection. There were coffins lined in red velvet, lined in blue velvet, ornately decorated with gold and silver–none of them suitable to what Victor would have wanted.

I said to the girls, "Your father was a plain man. He would have liked to have a simple, well-varnished wood, like the wood on the boat." In my mind, I privately wished we could have buried him on the boat where he was so happy. Instead, we chose a plain mahogany casket that day, then left that horrible room.

Victor's funeral service was attended by more than a thousand people—some from as far away as New Jersey. It was a beautiful service. The room was filled with so many flowers. Our bouquet of red and white carnations and orchids was placed on the casket, along with a small, sweetheart bouquet from his granddaughter.

The highly-respected Judge James R. Knott read a truly memorable speech, commemorating Victor's life. Afterward, the Judge told me he could barely get through his speech without weeping.

I didn't invite anyone home after the service. I knew I couldn't be polite and listen to condolences. I wanted to be alone and knew that from then on, I would be.

For three years, following Victor's passing, I couldn't bring myself to part with his clothes. Later, I learned that nearly all widows have similar feelings after they lose their husbands. In my grief, I also realized how truly blessed I was to have enjoyed 29 years of a wonderful marriage to Victor.

My husband was a special man who gave a great deal to his family, community, and country. In his memory, in 1985, I endowed the Victor W. Farris Medical Center at Good Samaritan Hospital in West Palm Beach. The building houses the most up-to-date equipment, patient-care facilities, and laboratory for the treatment of catastrophic illnesses. I stated that the Center would be, "A living testimony to Victor's profound belief in man's ability to overcome the problems of our times."

Victor W. Farris

In Victor's memory I endowed the Victor W. Farris Medical Center at Good Samaritan Hospital.

In 1994 my mother passed away and within one year my father joined her. The only answer I had to my great loss, was to concentrate on the future.

A painting I did of my mother.

My beautiful mother visiting Scotland.

A painting I did of my father.

My father

MY THIRD LIFE

"All the world's a stage
And all the men and women merely players,
They have their exits and their entrances;
And one woman (man) in her (his) time
plays many parts…"
"As You Like It"– William Shakespeare

I decided to go home to London. I leased a lovely apartment in Arlington House overlooking London's Green Park. Every morning, I strolled through the Park–the weather was warm and the sky was a beautiful blue. Young office workers from nearby Piccadilly would have lunch on the grass as the Park band serenaded them, and swallows soared overhead. The scene was so London and so familiar to me. The bittersweet childhood memories all came rushing back and they nearly broke my heart.

I began working to improve my voice, practicing my scales and slowly bringing my voice back. Having had surgery on my vocal chords years earlier, I was very careful but equally determined. I found myself, once again, at the Wigmore Hall taking singing lessons. Bob Bowman, a vocal coach, was a great help, and my voice began to improve dramatically.

Shortly thereafter, I recorded the CD, "The London I Love," at Advision Studios on Gosfield Street. I was overjoyed when Harrods not only stocked it, but also advertised the recording in the "The Sunday Times" and "The Daily Telegraph," and then swiftly proceeded to sell out of the CDs. Although it was successful, I had an underlying desire to return to acting.

It made me happy to know that I was still being played on the BBC as well as on many other British radio stations. During this time, many radio and television interviews across the UK had been arranged for me by my friend and manager, Derek Bolton. There were several things that I realized during the interviews: the British public still knew and remembered me as Celia Lipton and not as Celia Lipton Farris; and the contrast between my singing voice since I left London, performed on Broadway and returned, was considerably different–my voice had matured.

TONY BENNETT

SINGS
THE RODGERS & HART
COLLECTION

20 GREAT SONGS

SIDE ONE
ROCKY
CHARLIE'S ANGELS
HOTEL
CAGNEY & LACEY
HILL ST. BLUES*

SIDE TWO
QUINCY
DYNASTY*
SOAP
DALLAS
ROCKFORD FILES

Great Opera Choruses

From
AIDA
PAGLIACCI
CARMEN
BORIS GODUNOV
MADAMA BUTTERFLY
NABUCCO
TANNHAUSER
and

THE KINGSWAY
SYMPHONY
ORCHESTRA
and
CHORUS

Mantovani

The Love She

features

CELIA LIPTON

The London I Love

COLIN BUSBY'S BIG SWING BAND

Big
SWING BAND
Favourites

Features

WOODCHOPPERS BALL
SING SING SING
APRIL IN PARIS
TAKE THE A TRAIN
STRING OF PEARLS
BEGIN THE BEGUINE
1 O'CLOCK JUMP

Johnny Mercer
SONGBOOK

28 CLASSICS

Moon River
Goody Goody
Summer Wind
Something's Gotta Give
Satin Doll
You must have been a beautiful Baby
the days of Wine & Roses

Preludes
Marvellous for Words
Autumn Leaves
One for my Baby

JAN HOLLY

Sitting on top of the world

Record store promotional brochure, U.K.

Harrods

HARRODS LIMITED
KNIGHTSBRIDGE LONDON SW1X 7XL

TELEPHONE 01-730 1234 TELEX 24319 FAX 01-581 0470 REGISTERED OFFICE 87/135 BROMPTON ROAD, LONDON SW1X 7XL REGISTERED IN LONDON NO 30209

Mrs Celia Lipton Farris
60 Arlington House
Arlington Street
London SW1

29th August 1986

Dear Celia

I thought you would like to know we have just passed
the 500 unit sales of your record and cassette,
which is all very encouraging for the future.

So everyone's now awaiting your new release in the
Autumn of 1986.

Many thanks and regards.

Yours sincerely

D Mullan
Buyer
Records
AS

CELIA LIPTON ⊙ YU 102
THE LONDON I LOVE
The London I Love • Girl From Ipanema • I Go To Rio • Our
Affair • What A Difference A Day Made • When You're Smil
Tristeza • How Did He Look • I Can't Get Started • You Mak
So Young • Slow Boat To China • Come Closer To Me.

OPERA CHORUSES ⊙ YU 103
CAMARATA & KINGSWAY SYMPHONY
Verdi • Leoncavallo • Bizet • Mussorgsky • Puccini • Verdi
Wagner • Gounod.

SYDNEY THOMPSON & HIS ORCHESTRA ⊙ YU 104
20 ALL TIME PARTY FAVOURITES
Macnamara's Band (Barn Dance) • Boomps-A-Daisy • March
Mods • Yellow Submarine • Lambeth Walk • Palais Glide •
The Mood • Chestnut Tree • Knees Up Mother Brown • Roc
The Clock • St. Bernard Waltz • Charleston • Cokey Cokey
The Jack • Pied Piper (The Beeje) • Gay Gordons • I Came,
Conga'd • Zorba's Dance • Dashing White Sergeant • Popco
• Auld Lang Syne.

JAN HOLLY ⊙ YU 105
SITTING ON TOP OF THE WORLD
Too Much Too Soon • Sitting On Top Of The World (Loving
I Can Feel Your Leavin' Coming On • You're My Fantasy • W
Lonely Nights • Singing The Blues Again • No Getting Over Y
Broke Up • Wish Me Love • You Wrote The Book • Do You
Think Of Me And Amarillo.

TONY BENNETT ⊙ YU 106   🔲 CYU 106
THE MAGIC OF
Cole Porter Selection • What Is This Thing Called Love • Love For Sale
• I'm In Love Again • You'd Be So Nice To Come Home To • Easy To
Love • It's Alright By Me • Night & Day • Dream Dancing • I've Got
You Under My Skin • Get Out Of Town • Experiment • One • This
Funny World • Lost In The Stars • As Time Goes By • I Used To Be
Color Blind • Mr. Magic.

Records
THE BIG BAND & BROADWAY SOUNDS OF
CELIA LIPTON

As Advertised on Television

Foggy Day — One — Maybe This Time — Up Where We
Belong For Once in My Life — Young at Heart — Where or
When Strike Up The Band — Something Old, Something
New New York New York — I'm in the Mood For Love —
Quiet Nights

AVAILABLE EXCLUSIVELY AT

RECORD
DEPT.

Harrods

SECOND
FLOOR

Knightsbridge, London SW1X 7XL.

At first, I was nervous when speaking on the radio. I remember Derek giving me these great pep talks, encouraging me, saying "You have nothing to worry about because you are a personality, Celia!" Although his kind words made me feel less nervous, I still had to overcome the butterflies in my stomach. But, it all came back to me very quickly, especially after a good friend, not afraid to tell me the truth, said, "Celia, you have to get to the point! Answer the questions. Stop rambling on, and remember this is only a half-hour interview and not a seven-hour discussion."

BBC Radio Four featured me in a segment that contrasted the young Celia with the Celia of the day. I was delighted when David Jacobs, a famous British disk jockey from the BBC, as well as disk jockeys throughout the UK, remembered me and played my recordings. My CDs were selling in great numbers in the Midlands and in Edinburgh. Obviously, all those years of touring in the provinces in my youth were paying off.

During the radio tour of the UK, I was invited to sing with the London Philharmonic Orchestra. I was delighted by the invitation and had to evaluate my voice, and felt this was not the right time to perform.

The nostalgia I experienced being in London and the UK again was not only enhanced by working once more, but also by an interesting social life. I had a delightful lunch with Sir Emile Littler and we reminisced about the days of "Lilac Time" and "The Quaker Girl."

The Duchess of Argyll invited me to a Charity tea-tasting at the Grosvenor House, where she still lived at the time. I was also reacquainted with my good friend Jimmy Henney, the head of Chappell's Music, whom I'd known since I was 15. Jimmy was very sweet, taking me to lunch at London's trendy Langan's Restaurant that I understood Sir Michael Caine had an interest in at that time. Coincidentally, a top executive from Rogers and Cowan took me to lunch at the same restaurant where, on that occasion, I was thoroughly amused by a scene which typified classic English eccentricity. I watched in stitches as Peter Langan, the restaurant owner, burst through the swinging doors, drunk as a skunk, stumbling into the establishment. He rolled around the room pestering patrons and then was promptly thrown out by his own manager!

Enjoying an outing with the Duchess of Argyll and her escort.

Perhaps, one of my greatest joys of being in London was making a new and wonderful friend, writer Sheilah Graham. Her own life and love affair with F. Scott Fitzgerald was immortalized in her book "Beloved Infidel."

Sheilah and I spent a great deal of time together and discovered we had much in common. Like me, Sheilah had an unflinching will and would boast, "We never give up, you and I. We never give up, do we?"

Her opinion meant a great deal to me. She encouraged me to work. Sheilah also was interested in writing my life story. I resisted at first, convinced that the only life story worth telling was Victor's. Yet, I finally agreed and Sheilah interviewed me on every aspect of my life. Being interviewed and edited by Sheilah Graham was quite an experience.

I believe her own life was not the happy one that she deserved. Sheilah had terrible hip problems and suffered with great pain. Although her pain was eased by the great pleasure she enjoyed with her two children, Wendy and Rob.

Later, Sheilah visited me in Palm Beach and we enjoyed many more happy times. Tragically, we met toward the end of her life, and our time together was much too brief. But I will always remember our special friendship and the time we spent together.

After six months in London, I returned to America and discovered that my recordings were being broadcast across the nation. I gave interviews on radio stations in New York, Los Angeles, Chicago, and San Francisco, and appeared on the nationally broadcast Joe Franklin Radio Show. Joe welcomed me back saying, "Anything, Celia, anytime." I still wasn't certain as to what direction my professional future would take. I just knew I had to go forward, do whatever was offered to me, and wait and see where life would lead me. My experience in the business would prove invaluable.

I kept working with my voice and decided to continue recording. I returned to Criteria Recording Studios and worked with Mike Lewis, a brilliant musical director, and my talented pianist Bobby Swiadon. Together, we recorded several albums, including "The Best of Times" and "Timeless Magic Moments." I was elated by the success of the recordings.

I am in very good company here with two great Englishmen, Sir Roger Moore and Sir Michael Caine.

Nationally renowned musical director and arranger Mike Lewis and I in the recording studio.

I was delighted my hard work and determination brought me four Gold Records. But the most memorable highlight of my new recording career occurred when my daughters presented me with a Gold Record on my birthday, inscribed, "You will always be number 1 to us, Ce Ce and Marian."

I returned to Criteria Studios and recorded the Christmas album, "Merry Christmas from Celia Lipton." It was another hit CD to add to my recording career credits, and was broadcast worldwide. Even today, my rendition of "We Need A Little Christmas" is played at the Macy's Thanksgiving Day Parade in New York, and my recordings are still broadcast on more than 300 stations in North America, Canada, and the BBC World Service.

My recordings were being sold at the internationally-franchised Tower Records, whose UK stores were eventually bought-out by Virgin Megastores. At this time, I set my sights on a new goal: working on my own "One-Woman Show," in front of a live audience. I am, and always have been, a live performer and ready to undertake new challenges.

Regretfully, Victor and my children had never once seen me perform in front of a live audience. I was delighted that my daughters, Marian and Ce Ce, would finally have the opportunity to see me perform onstage.

A record publicity photo.

My record publicity photo printed in "The Daily Express," U.K.

Legendary comedian Pat Cooper, recently hononred by the
New York Friars' Club, opened for my "One-Woman Show."

Mike Lewis also gave me the courage to go forward with my "One-Woman Show." The talented Harry Freedman proved to be invaluable in masterminding the entire project as producer and friend, and with my experience we forged ahead.

After six months of tough work and constant rehearsals, my "One-Woman Show" was scheduled to open at a beautiful theatre in Pembroke Pines, Florida. The sold-out house was composed of 2,000 people, primarily New Yorkers—a tough audience, especially for my first time back on the stage in many years. Three days before the performance I came down with a violent flu. My doctor advised me to cancel the performance, but as they say, "The show must go on!" And it did!

The legendary comedian, Pat Cooper opened for me. The rest of the team included an incredible orchestra, a genius choreographer, and two of the most handsome and talented dancers that I could have ever hoped to work with. Nonetheless, I was incredibly nervous, but as soon as I sang the first few bars of my opening song, "A Foggy Day In in London Town," I relaxed completely, and continued to entertain the audience with 90 minutes of nonstop singing, dancing, and impersonations. The audience energized me with its applause, enthusiasm, and affection. As I sung a song from the Broadway musical "Sarah and Abraham," written by Kathy Ellis, the audience I was told became very emotional and was brought to tears. And then they applauded with resounding joy as I sang, "New York, New York."

Opening night of my "One-Woman Show."

"I Go To Rio"

Singing with my favorite dancers

"For Once in My Life"

"New York, New York"

Wonderful concept designs for my "One-Woman Show" wardrobe by fashion designer Bob Mackie

Once more, I felt the warmth of the audience and received standing ovations, but not just from the audience, from Marian and Ce Ce as well.

I left the theatre that evening and returned home to spend three weeks in bed, recovering from the flu. After the success of my sold-out "One-Woman Show," many people encouraged me to take the show on the road. Having toured before, I knew what being on the road was like; it wasn't easy. Memories of performing throughout the provinces in England as a youth flooded my mind: traveling with musicians, different lighting and sound crews at each venue, moving quickly from place to place, and countless other difficulties, and challenges. I also considered the strain of daily performances on my voice and body. One can't get sick on the road and if a performer does, "the show must go on." I loved working before a live audience and knew I could do it again, and again. Yet, these cautionary thoughts kept running through my mind as I repeatedly asked myself: "Do I really want to do this? Do I really want to travel most of the year? Leave my home? Live in hotels?" I concluded that taking my "One-Woman Show" on the road, simply, was not right for me—not at that time in my life.

Although I was still singing and recording, I knew there had to be something more—more fulfilling and life-enhancing. I had worked throughout my life to make a difference by helping others, and had remained committed to supporting several causes and charities. It was at this time that Chen Sam, the personal assistant for Elizabeth Taylor, came to see me on behalf of Elizabeth, who was wholeheartedly committed to the battle against AIDS. Chen Sam asked if I would host a benefit party in my home and donate the profits, plus a gift of my own choosing, to help in the fight against AIDS.

I had seen many reports on television and read several newspaper and magazine articles about AIDS. I knew I didn't fully understand the disease at that time and needed to acquire more information. So I talked to my daughter Ce Ce about the disease and discovered that Ce Ce had worked for an AIDS organization. She educated me about the cause.

At that time, Elizabeth was one of the few celebrities who had shown a great deal of interest in AIDS. Through her celebrity, she had working tirelessly to build awareness about AIDS and HIV, and to raise funds in the fight against the disease. I hosted a party at my home for Elizabeth Taylor in March of 1987. Four-hundred

Elizabeth and I held a press conference in my home prior to the AIDS benefit that evening.

guests attended the fundraiser; enjoying cocktails, a buffet, dancing, and the opportunity to meet Elizabeth Taylor. I was delighted to host the benefit in my home and filled the rooms with violets, the color of Elizabeth's eyes. And to think, only years before in London, I had met Elizabeth at the elegant Les Ambassadeurs with Michael Wilding.

Elizabeth was articulate, friendly, and took the time to chat with everyone at the party. She made a passionate speech to all of the guests, saying "Put your money where your mouth is," and candidly adding, "We are hoping that someone will come up with a big fat check." Elizabeth was, and still is, dedicated to raising AIDS awareness.

Elizabeth and I left the party at my home with a few guests, and went directly to the Fontainbleau in Miami. This was our second AIDS benefit in one night. I realized then how this disease could effect the entire world, and I dearly wanted to help. The event, entitled "An Extraordinary Evening with Elizabeth Taylor," was sold-out at $2,500 per ticket. As we arrived by limousine, people were picketing directly across the street—protesting AIDS. We were escorted into the Fontainbleau Hotel where Elizabeth and I gave a press conference to hundreds of news media.

Elizabeth and I at my home in Palm Beach.

Introducing Elizabeth Taylor to guests at the AIDS Benefit I hosted in her honor.

Celia Lipton Farris

requests the pleasure of your company

at a cocktail buffet reception

in honour of

Miss Elizabeth Taylor

to benefit

The American Foundation for AIDS Research

and

The Community Alliance Against AIDS

on Sunday, the thirteenth of March

nineteen hundred and eighty-eight

promptly at 6 p.m. until . . .

R.S.V.P. enclosed card   *Black Tie*

Entrance by Invitation   *Cliff Hall Orchestra*

At that press conference, I presented Elizabeth with my donation, and in a moving speech she thanked me saying, "Celia you have given this from your heart." I understand that Malcolm Forbes and I were the first two individuals to give substantial donations to support AIDS research.

Elizabeth sent me a charming note when she returned to California, with a beautiful pink, cashmere stole and a lovely decorative pillow. The party at my home had raised $2.25 million and was divided between amfAR, The American Foundation for AIDS Research, and the University of Miami School of Medicine.

My involvement in the battle against AIDS did not end after the benefits, nor will it ever as long as the disease still exists. When I discovered there was an AIDS treatment center in Belle Glade, I went to visit the facility and was horrified to find it lacked all but the most basic amenities. There was an acute shortage of supplies, including blankets, and there was no transportation for patients to and from other treatment facilities in Miami—more than an hour's drive away.

I returned home upset and determined to do something immediately. I arranged for a transportation van and dozens of blankets to be purchased at my expense and delivered to the facility the very next day. I called the University of Miami and asked that a portion of my donation be transferred to the Belle Glade AIDS treatment facility. The University of Miami agreed. Then, I made another contribution to the Belle Glade facility. Yet, I knew a donation was not the only way to help in the battle against AIDS.

Today, Elizabeth Taylor is to be congratulated for her tireless work in promoting awareness and understanding of the disease and raising funds for HIV/AIDS. She has established the Elizabeth Taylor AIDS Foundation. Sir Elton John has also admirably taken on this cause.

My charitable work to help those less fortunate continued, as did recording at Criteria Studios in Miami. Accompanied by pianist Bobby Swiadon, I recorded many songs that I had performed for Columbia Records years earlier, including "Where Or When" and "Strike Up The Band." My releases in the 1980s and 1990s included the album titles: "Love To The USA," "Love To The UK," "Canciones de Amor – Songs Of Love." The recording covered quite a range of material and styles, and included both old and new songs.

According to the National Jazz Archive in the UK, where I am listed, the musical arrangements backing my vocals, even on standards such as the song, "Sentimental Journey," are "Unexpectedly modern in style." They also noted, "While her interpretations of 'As Time Goes By,' 'A Foggy Day,' and 'I'm in the Mood for Love' are much more traditional in arrangement and performance, the album, 'The London I Love,' is amongst her very best work."

Just for fun, I recorded a two-track disco CD that featured "You've Got Your Own Life To Live" and "I've Got Your Number." To my surprise "You've Got Your Own Live To Live" reached number nineteen on the "Billboard Magazine Hot 100" chart. I was even more surprised when I received a telephone call from a journalist working for a British magazine in Singapore. He was calling all the way from Sydney, Australia, just to tell me that he'd heard my songs at a discotheque the night before.

A few of the recordings I made in the 1980s and 1990s, many are still broadcast worldwide.

259

My friend Bert Sokol and I with the amazing Sammy Cahn.

My good friend Bert Sokol was formerly the Co-owner and Managing Director of a large hotel in Pittsburgh. He booked all of the acts for the hotel, including celebrities such as Jay Leno, Gladys Knight, Natalie Cole, Wayne Newton, among others. Bert and I first met at an American Cancer Society Benefit which featured the renowned singer Al Martino. After a few moments of introductions, we soon discovered that we had a great deal in common—both of us had show business backgrounds. And it was Bert, who was so tremendous and encouraging at getting me back into the studio to record again. Over the years, he has escorted me to many charity balls and benefits, and today remains a loyal friend and steadfast confidant.

At the prompting of the legendary actor and former California Senator George Murphy (who had moved to Palm Beach)—and who had become a great friend—along with his lovely wife Betty, and Ruth (Mrs. Milton) Berle, I became involved in the production of the American Cinema Awards (ACA). Ruth had founded the ACA Benefit in Hollywood and at that time was undertaking the sixth annual show. When George asked for my help, he explained that the ACA Benefit was held to aid the Motion Picture & Television Country House and Hospital in Woodland Hills, California. The funds raised would provide homes for professional actors and

ACA Benefit photo, seated: Joseph Cotton, myself, and his wife, Patricia Medina,
standing: former Senator George Murphy, Donald O'Connor and his wife.

actresses, many of whom were in their twilight years and experiencing dire financial
and health hardships. I was deeply touched and aware that many of those in my
profession may at some time in their lives grapple with this plight.

Prior to show time, I met Joseph Cotton and his wife Patricia Medina at a
rehearsal. It was there that I also met Producer David Gest.

I thoroughly enjoyed being at the Awards Benefit. My dinner companions at
the table that night included Ruth Berle, Lucille Ball, Veronique and Gregory Peck,
Yolanda and Anthony Quinn, and Whoopi Goldberg. Lucy was an incredible woman
of great beauty, wit, and charm. When we spoke she impressed me with her warmth,
humor, and friendliness. "You are so beautiful," she said. Then, at seeing the emerald
ring I was wearing, she exclaimed, "Look at that!" and reached for my hand, exam-
ining the ring so close to her eyes that I was afraid she would poke out an eye. That
was Lucy. Whoopi and I chatted about her recent appearance in the movie "Ghost"
and the number of takes she did for the telephone-booth scene. At the table, I felt at
home amongst friends and Industry peers—everyone was perfectly wonderful.

Senator Murphy had notified me in advance that I would be speaking at the
Benefit. Knowing that some people have a tendency to be long-winded, he cautioned,

"Celia, there are 400 egos out there in that room tonight, so make your speech short, and then get your ass off." The moment had come. I stood on stage before 400 of my Hollywood peers and made my remarks short and sweet—exactly as he had advised.

Later, I took my place next to Julio Iglesias, "Performer of the Year;" Clint Eastwood, "Distinguished Film Achievement Award" winner; and one of my all-time favorite idols, Bette Davis—the woman I'd been impersonating since the age of fifteen. Standing next to the surprisingly diminutive Bette Davis, I whispered how much I admired her. Yet, I had the distinct impression that Bette was wishing I wasn't with her on stage at all. Later that evening I confided to Celeste Holm, Bette's co-star in "All About Eve," that "Bette had been rather rude to me." Rolling her eyes, Celeste remarked, "You have no idea what she was like to work with on the set." Clint Eastwood, on the other hand, made up for Bette's cool demeanor, he was very warm and kind—a true gentleman.

Over the course of the next ten years I served as the Executive Producer of the American Cinema Awards with Producer David Gest. As Executive Producer of the ACA Benefit, Producer Gest and I worked with a cast of legendary performers over the years, including Frank Sinatra, Liza Minnelli, Shirley MacLaine, Gene Kelly, Paula Abdul, Lionel Ritchie, Lauren Bacall, Tom Cruise, Bette Davis, Whoopi Goldberg, James Stewart, Buddy Ebsen, Red Buttons, Donald O'Connor, Michael Bolton, Janet Jackson, Patrick Swayze, Alexis Smith, Michael Jackson, Melanie Griffith, and countless other stars. Robert Wagner hosted several of the awards shows, and my dear friend Tristan Rogers, of the daytime drama General Hospital, was a Director.

Gest would some years later marry Liza Minnelli at New York's Collegiate Church. It was one of the most lavish, fairy-tale weddings I have had the privilege to attend. The legendary Joe Franklin of the nationally broadcast WOR-AM and the Bloomberg Radio Network later interviewed me about the Fifth Avenue nuptials and reception at the Regent Hotel, with a guest list that read like "Who's Who." Indeed, it was a beautiful and extravagant affair, later reported to be the most expensive celebrity wedding of that year.

Julio Iglesias, Bette Davis, Clint Eastwood, and I were honored at the American Cinema Awards where I served as Executive Producer for ten years with Producer David Gest.

Every year at the ACA Benefit an award was given for "Distinguished Film Achievement." Gregory Peck received the award one year, as did Elizabeth Taylor. I was greatly honored to receive the "Gloria Swanson Humanitarian Award" not once, but twice. My speech, the second time was a trifle longer, yet my words were from the heart: "I have always tried to do things that are most needed by humanity. I believe that my drive is God-given, and if I can climb a mountain for a charity or help humanity, I have an obligation to do so." Additionally, I was grateful to be the first woman to receive the annual "Joel McCrea Award" on behalf of the Motion Picture & Television Country House and Hospital, and The Actors Fund.

Senator George Murphy and I at the American Cinema Awards Benefit.

Director Lord Richard Attenborough

Friends Jack Rourke, President and Martha Moody Rourke, Editor of "Seasons" magazine graciously provided many of the Awards Benefit photos shown on the following pages.

Kirk Douglas, Lauren Bacall, Gregory Peck, myself, Elizabeth Taylor, and Robert Wagner were were honored at the American Cinema Awards where I served as Exective Producer for ten years.

Michael Jackson, Elizabeth Taylor, Gregory Pack, and I at the American Cinema Awards, Hollywood.

My talented friend Liza Minnelli

Donald O'Connor, Debbie Reynolds, and Gene Kelly   *David Gest, Sophia Loren, Ce Ce, and Michael Jackson with friends*

Gloria and James Stewart   *Kirk Douglas*

Tristan Roger directed the ACA Benefits   *Kathryn Grayson and Robert Merrill*   *Legendary Frank Sinatra*

Ted Danson, Barbara Sinatra, Liza Minnelli, Frank Sinatra, myself, Whoopi Goldberg, Jack Valenti, and Kirk Douglas

Virginia Mayo

Robert Wagner, Benefit host

Gloria De Haven and June Allyson

Melanie Griffith

Sidney and Joanna Poitier

Anne and Kirk Douglas

267

Michael Douglas, Michael Jackson, Sophia Loren, Kirk Douglas and Sylvester Stallone

Whoopi Goldberg and Brent Spiner

The American Cinema Awards

Hollywood's newest hot ticket event! The American Cinema Awards has become the most entertaining event of the year, known for its superstar line-up of stars of yesterday, today, and tomorrow. To quote Bella Shaw of CNN, "I'd have to say, in terms of star power, the American Cinema Award show is now the number one event in Hollywood...I've never seen so many stars under one roof!"

Bob Hastings and Phyllis Diller

Lisa Niemi and Patrick Swayze

Paula Abdul

Tom Cruise, Pat Medina, and Joseph Cotton

Dennis Hopper

Gregory Peck and Lauren Bacall

Mr. and Mrs. Buddy Ebsen with Executive Producer

Petula Clark and Ben Kingsley

After serving as Executive Producer of the American Cinema Awards in Hollywood, I then became the Executive Producer of the International Achievement in the Arts Awards in London with Producer David Gest. The Benefit helped raise funds for the Great Ormond Street Hospital for Children which is known for its pioneering work in children's medicine. There were approximately 100 stars at the event, including Sir Anthony Hopkins, Dame Diana Rigg, Sir John Mills, Anthony Quinn, Petula Clark, The Four Tops, and Ginger Rogers. Sadly, it was Ginger Rogers' last public appearance. After the Awards Benefit, she sent me a beautiful bouquet of Red Button Gingers and a handwritten note of thanks. She was a very kind and thoughtful person. The event received considerable media coverage and was featured on the cover of London's "What's On" magazine.

The Great Ormond Street Hospital for Children has relied on charitable contributions since it first opened in 1852. One of its most prominent supporters was playwright Sir James Barrie who left the royalties of his beloved play, "Peter Pan," to the Hospital. Paradoxically, the Awards Benefit in London brought back so many memories of when I played Peter as a youth, and visited the children at that Hospital dressed as Peter.

Alan Bates and Honoree Anthony Quinn

Barbara Eden, Jon Eicholtz, and Anne Jeffreys

Honoree Sir John and Lady Mills with Van Johnson

Sir Anthony Hopkins and Bert Sokol

Peter Graves and Tommy Steele

Arlene Dahl and Robert Merrill

The incredible Ginger Rogers

Anthony Quinn, Petula Clark, Sir Anthony Hopkins,
Douglas Fairbanks, Jr., Ann Miller, Ginger Rogers,
Michael Bolton, myself, Dame Shirley Bassey,
Sir John Mills and Robert Wagner at the International
Achievement in The Arts Awards Benefit.

Sir Anthony Hopkins was honored for "Distinguished
Achievement in Film" at the International Achievement
in the Arts Awards Benefit in London.

Ginger Rogers (seated) was honored for "Distinguished
Achievement in Film." She was joined on stage by Douglas
Fairbanks, Jr., Ann Miller, Anthony Quinn, and I.
This was Ginger's last public appearance.

271

One of the Four Tops, Dame Diana Rigg, Petula Clark, Michael Bolton, Sir Anthony Hopkins, and Jane Russell

Interviewed by Robert Wagner's daughter, Cathy

Vera and Robert Goulet

Dorothy Malone

Roddy McDowall and Gayle Hunnicut

Cliff Robertson and Bea Arthur

Leslie Caron and Gloria De Haven

The following year, I served as Executive Producer of the International Achievement in the Arts Awards in New York with Producer David Gest. The Benefit raised funds for The Michael Bolton Charities, Inc., which assists women and children at risk due to poverty and, or, abuse. It was a pleasure to work with Michael, a humanitarian who used his celebrity to improve the lives of others. The talented Whitney Houston sang at the event.

After spending twelve years producing in Hollywood, London, and New York, I had become quite adept at putting together an event. Each affair was a very interesting and challenging adventure. Initially, when I became involved with the American Cinema Awards in Beverly Hills, I envisioned staging a similar charity event in Palm Beach, and I believed if done properly it could be most successful. I had witnessed the enthusiasm of patron audiences when they saw so many well-loved stars come together in support of a charity. It created a ripple effect of interest that translated into generous charitable donations.

On February 22, 1991, I served as Chairwoman of the 33rd annual American Cancer Society Ball, "Thanks for the Memories," held at The Breakers in Palm Beach. The Ball took months of planning and organization, and two months prior to the event it was sold-out. This indicated a great fundraising success for Cancer.

Dolores and Bob Hope on the cover of Palm Beach Society magazine which has featured every major fundraising and social event on the Island and in Palm Beach County for over 53 years. The magazine's success can be credited to James Jennings Sheeran, CEO, Publisher, and Editor-in-Chief.

273

*Buddy Ebsen, Bob Hope, Senator George Murphy and Donald O'Connor dancing up
a storm at the 33rd annual American Cancer Society Ball, and yours truly above.*

Senator Murphy was the honoree for the evening. Bob Hope, so loved for all his efforts on behalf of our troops around the world, came to Palm Beach for the Ball with his lovely wife Dolores. That weekend, they also happened to be celebrating their 59th wedding anniversary. Joining the the Hopes at the "Thanks for the Memories" Ball was Phyllis Diller, Brooke Shields, Kathryn Grayson, Ann Jillian, Buddy and Dorothy Ebsen, Esther Williams, Margaret O'Brien, Glenn Ford, Penny Singleton, Janet Blair, Jane Withers, Donald O'Connor and Van Johnson. The night's entertainment was spectacular! Bob Hope, the quintessential entertainer, had the audience in stitches and Phyllis Diller almost brought the house down.

But a resounding hush filled the ballroom as Dolores Hope began to sing, soon followed by an encore of stars dancing center-stage. To this day, many still talk about that magical night. I was proud to have produced one of the most successful fundraising events ever held for the American Cancer Society. It was later reported that the Ball raised a record amount of funds, thanks to all the generous donors and stars. The Town of Palm Beach honored me for my chairmanship of the Cancer Ball with a third "Palm Beach Chamber of Commerce Award."

Taking bows at the American Cancer Society Ball: Gloria De Haven, Penny Singleton, Sen. George Murphy, Van Johnson, Ruby Keeler, Glenn Ford, Donald O'Connor, Virginia Mayo, Brooke Shields, Joan Leslie, Jane Powell, Anne Jeffreys, Jane Withers, and Phyllis Diller. (I bid farewell from the stage above.)

Mrs. Celia Lipton Farris
General Chairman

and

The Board of Trustees

cordially invite you to an evening honoring

Mr. and Mrs. Bob Hope's
59th Wedding Anniversary
and a
Nostalgic All-Star Gala

with Neal Smith's Orchestra

American Cancer Society — Palm Beach Benefit

Friday, the nineteenth of February
Nineteen hundred and ninety-three

The Breakers

Black tie   Early cocktails at seven o'clock
                             Dinner at eight o'clock

Norma Bulnes, Publisher of high-style "Selecta" magazine, and Van Johnson

Our great stars for American Cancer Society, Donald O'Connor and Bob Hope

The wonderful Tom Selleck

Brooke Shields and Ian Buchanan

Former Mayor Paul Ilyinsky and his wife, Angie

Celeste Holm and Roddy McDowall

Phyllis Diller

Honoring Sen. George Murphy on behalf of ACS

Margaret O'Brien and Jane Withers

Jane Russell

276

Buddy and Dorothy Ebsen

Petula Clark, Bob Hope, Jane Russell, June Allyson, Roddy McDowall, and Anne Jeffreys

Ann Rutherford

June Allyson, Jane Powell, and Anne Jeffreys

Lady Rainie Spencer and Judge Williams

Ann Jillian and Donald O'Connor

Tom Selleck with Dolores and Bob Hope

Esther Williams and Alexis Smith

277

Receiving the "Palm Beach Chamber of Commerce Award for my chairmanship of the Cancer Ball.

Special guest, Rex Reed at "An Extraordinary Evening with Sophia Loren" Aids Benefit.

Shortly thereafter I was asked to help with another AIDS Benefit in Miami along with the legendary, Sophia Loren. One of many planning meetings, was a luncheon at the lovely home of Sophia and her husband, Carlo Ponti, on Williams Island. As Executive Producer, with David Gest serving as Producer for the event, we gathered a glittering bill of stars including Patricia Neal, Ruby Keeler, Virginia Mayo, Kim Carnes, Donna Summer, Donald O'Connor, Rosemary Clooney, Rod Steiger, Melanie Griffith, Tippi Hedren, Connie Francis, Petula Clark, Ken Kercheval, Rex Reed, Bill Harris, and Tony Perkins. Julio Iglesias made a dramatic entrance, arriving by helicopter.

The Benefit included a silent auction in which I donated a beautiful painting of Elizabeth Taylor. It seemed a most appropriate gift because of Elizabeth's commitment to the battle against AIDS.

After the Benefit, I gave the renowned critic Rex Reed one of my recordings. He sent me a sincerely touching note that said, "Thanks for your simply wonderful CD. I now know you are more than just another rich, frivolous and gullible widow...You have an enormous heart and a big talent, too. My God, what a lovely voice and good taste to match. I love the way you sing, 'Time Heals Everything' (and it does, too, I'm told by experts). Anyway, none of this matters as long as you have a big, warm

"An Extraordinary Evening With Sophia Loren & Friends" Aids Benefit on Williams Island, where I served as Executive Producer with Producer David Gest.

heart and care so much about the human race. I was so proud and honored to be part of such a memorable evening."

I also received a fax from the famed composer, Sammy Cahn that read:

Dear CLF

The Initials as far as I'm 'Cahn-Cerned' stand for

C-aring!

L-oving!

F-abulous!

Dear Celia, Even as I'm typing this fax, I am listening to the CD and especially loving your rendition of 'Maybe It's Because I'm A Londoner.' You are a very talented lady. If I ever meet God, I am going to ask him why he gives certain people beauty and a singing voice—all he gave me was beauty!

I returned to London in 1995, where I had been asked to sing on the occasion of the 50th anniversary of VE-Day (Victory in Europe) celebrations. My performance in London's Hyde Park was in the presence of Her Majesty Queen Elizabeth, the entire Royal Family, and thousands of people. Many well-known artists including Dame Vera Lynn also performed at the celebrations.

THE NATION GIVES THANKS

Bobby Swiadon, Accompanist

Fifty years after the war ended in Europe, almost 1,000,000 people gathered in **Hyde Park** to pay tribute to those who had served and survived, and those who didn't make it, in a stirring evening of nostalgia and tribute. Fanfare filled the air as the **Queen** watched the lights go on again in a darkened London and the all-clear signal was sounded as part of the drama.

It was an inspiring moment, the climax to a day of festivities. **Dame Vera Lynn** sang the song that captured the mood of this night half-a-century ago—*When the Lights Go On Again All Over the World*. And **Celia Lipton Farris** (known as **Celia Lipton**), now a Palm Beacher, but one-time star of English theater, sang the song she made famous and which caught the mood of the crowd who had waited for hours to sing along with her—*Maybe It's Because I'm a Londoner*.

London ground to a halt as motorists and bus drivers stopped in silence to pay tribute to their fallen partners and to rejoice to the music of —*We'll Meet Again*.

For **Celia Lipton**, it was a happy/sad time. She and her family had witnessed the horrors of war and lost many friends. But, now, seeing the national spirit in a peaceful England, and the joys of her countrymen, Lipton proudly starred in several performances—(she sang five songs in an afternoon sequence for the public, and an evening presentation to **The Royal Family**) capped by her *I'm A Londoner* song before the **Queen** and the entire Royal Family.

V.I.P.
HYDE PARK
MAY 1995

HYDE PARK

THE NATION GIVES THANKS

VE·DAY 1945 V VJ·DAY 1995

Nearly 1 million people in Hyde Park rejoice as The Nation Gives Thanks. VE-Day May 1945 - May 1995; 50 years of peace.

Celia Lipton performing at "Worker's Playtime" prior to the evening performance.

Celia Lipton performing

Celia Lipton singing "Maybe It's Because I'm a Londoner."

Celia Lipton and Dame Vera Lynn who sang "The Lights Go On All Over The World."

Record crowd at Hyde Park VE-Day Celebration

Courtesy: Palm Beach Society magazine

Several years later, I was honored to receive a letter informing me that Her Majesty Queen Elizabeth had appointed me a Dame. This was a personal gift of the Sovereign, and the announcement was in the "London Gazette." Months later I received my Grant of Arms from Her Majesty's College of Arms in London.

Upon hearing the news my dear friends Diana and Llwyd Ecclestone hosted a lovely party in my honor at their home in Palm Beach, inviting my daughters and many of my friends. Diana and I came to know each while jointly working on several charity events.

*Her Majesty the Queen, Sovereign Head of the Most Venerable Order
of the Hospital of St. John of Jerusalem*

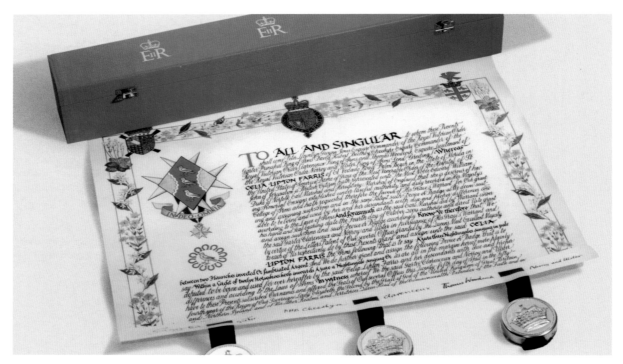

The Grant of Arms I received from Her Majesty's College of Arms in London.

Ironically, I had attended the International Red Cross Ball in Palm Beach for many years. Several years ago, my friend Ann White had served as Chairwoman of the Ball and had tried to recruit me as the next Chairwoman for some time. I continued to talk my way out of it year after year until 2000, when Diana, a friend and a great Chairwoman, asked me to serve as International Honorary Chairwoman. Over the next four years, I served as International Honorary Chairwoman of the International Red Cross Ball. Llwyd Ecclestone was tremendously supportive of Diana's work and the Ball.

He is a brilliant businessman, developer, and former owner of the PGA National Resort–one of world's most renowned golf resorts. He is also a remarkably accomplished yachtsman who has successfully competed in a number of races.

The International Red Cross Ball has been one of the most prestigious Balls in Palm Beach for almost half a century. As the most traditional Ball in Palm Beach, it has retained its red-carpet pageantry, trumpeted entrances, and stately formality over the years. Countless dignitaries from around the world attend the event and many prominent Palm Beachers generously give of their time and resources to make the Ball a success. For several years, Donald Trump has brought many Ambassadors to Palm Beach in his private plane to attend the Ball.

Courtesy: Palm Beach Society magazine

The Ambassadors of the International Red Cross Ball, 2002; Diana Ecclestone, Chairwoman; and I, Honorary Chairwoman.

Florence and Larry De George

During the time I served as
Honorary Chairwoman,
with Diana as Chairwoman,
so many members
of the community generously
supported the
International Red Cross Ball.
While too many to list here,
I would like to recognize:
Carroll Petrie
Nadine House
Ruth and Ray Perelman
Kathy and Alan Bleznak
Grace and Chris Meigher
Jean Tailer
Ellen and Bob Jaffe
The late Beverly and Barry Crown
Tom Quick
Laura and Lee Munder
Lori and Bruce Gendelman
Dorothy and Sidney Kohl
Susan and James Keenan
Robbi and Bruce Toll
Jack and Annette Friedland
Bob and Susan Tomsich
Michele and Howard Kessler
Nikki and Ira Harris
Patrick Park
Florence and Larry De George
Susan and Dom Telesco
Arlette and Bob Gordon

Forgive me, if I have left anyone out.

Ruth and Ray Perelman

My Scottish cousins Ross and Adrienne Young

Ambassador Marion Smoak

Diana and Llwyd Ecclestone

My dear friend Carroll Petrie

Patrick M. Park

Lee and Laura Munder

Jean Tailer and John Loring

Beverly and Barry Crown

Michele and Howard Kessler

Susan and Dom Telesco

Donald Trump and Actor Sylvester Stallone

As Honorary International Chairwoman of the Ball for my fourth consecutive term, I knew it was tradition that I host a luncheon at Mar-a-Lago for the Ambassadors upon their arrival from Washington. After welcoming the dignitaries and others attending the luncheon, I was honored when Chairwoman Diana Ecclestone presented me with the American Red Cross' Clara Barton Award. It was a deeply moving moment for me as I recounted singing in Red Cross Clubs to hundreds of soldiers throughout London and the UK as a young girl. And now, years later in Palm Beach I was being given the highest award the American Red Cross bestows for meritorious service over a number of years.

Donald Trump bought Mar-a-Lago from the State of Florida in 1985. Marjorie Post had originally left her palatial home to the State to be used as a museum. Sadly, Mar-a-Lago sat empty for a number of years and had fallen into great disrepair until, fortunately, Donald purchased the estate. He restored Mar-a-Lago to its original splendor and also added a magnificent ballroom which plays host to many charity balls. My dear friend Marjorie would be so proud that her home had become one of the world's greatest clubs. I was one of Donald's first Club members because of the happy memories of dinners at Mar-a-Lago with Marjorie in years past.

Donald Trump and his beautiful wife, Melania

Donald has hosted a number of concert events at the Club for members, including memorable performances by Sir Elton John, Liza Minnelli, Tony Bennett, among other great celebrities. The concerts always play to a sold-out house.

I was honored to attend Donald and Melania's wedding in 2005. The evening ceremony took place at the Bethesda-by-the Sea Episcopal Church in Palm Beach, followed by a reception at Mar-a-Lago. It was a magnificent affair. The gourmet dinner was prepared by Donald's favorite New York City chef, only to be topped by the 5-foot-high Grand Marnier chiffon wedding cake, weighing more than 200 pounds.

There were hundreds of guests in attendance, including former President Bill Clinton and Senator Hillary Clinton, Rudy Giuliani, Tina Brown, Don King, Simon Cowell, Shaquille O'Neal, Kelly Ripa, Tony Bennett, Clint Eastwood, Richard and Sessa Johnson, Mohamed Al Fayed, Barbara Walters, Katie Couric, Matt Lauer, Star Jones Reynolds, Joan Rivers, Vic and Rena, Regis Philbin, Frank and Kathie Lee Gifford, Vilda de Porro, fashion designer Dennis Basso, Donald's sisters The Honorable Maryanne Barry and Elizabeth Trump, and countless other notables.

There are countless events for charities and cultural organizations during the season in Palm Beach. It is not unusual for there to be several galas and social events

*Performing with Vic Damone at a Salvation Army
Benefit held at Mar-a-Lago*

held on the same night. Although, there are many well-deserving charitable organizations, there are a few institutions or organizations that I believe offer invaluable services to this community and the world in which we live.

Not so long ago, I attended a Benefit at the Norton Museum of Art—one of the finest museum's in the Southeastern United States. The invitation to the event noted the guest of honor as Edward Albee the renowned author and playwright. I told my secretary to pencil in the date as I couldn't miss meeting the "Who's Afraid of Virginia Woolf?" playwright. When I arrived at the Museum that evening I was introduced to Mr. Albee. He greeted me with a smile peeking out from under his groomed moustache. "How do you do Mr. Albee? I am the former British actress, Celia Lipton" I said. Through spectacles he looked me up and down, then directly into my eyes and said, "There is no such thing as a former actress." I was very happy to be put back in my place.

Betsy and George Matthews

For many years, The Renaissance Ball was one of the largest Balls in Palm Beach. It had been held to benefit our two area hospitals, Good Samaritan Medical Center and St. Mary's Medical Center. One year, I was honored to be asked to serve as Honorary Chairwoman by Betsy and George Matthews who were then Co-Chairmen of the Ball.

George is a great-grandson of Henry Flagler and is the Director of the Board of Trustees of the Flagler Museum (Whitehall). With Museum Director John Blades he has brought Whitehall into the 21st century with great care. The Whitehall Museum is one of Palm Beach's leading historical and cultural centers, and is nationally recognized for historic preservation and conservation.

Another memorable evening for which I was asked to serve as Honorary Chairwoman was for the Dreyfoos School of the Arts Foundation gala. The evening was Chaired by Dorothy Lappin, and the guest of honor was stage and television actress, Sandy Duncan who, like me, had played Peter in the play "Peter Pan." I was asked to introduce Sandy and shared with the students at the School that I had also played the part of Peter on the stage. However, they seemed a bit nonplussed to hear me, the Honorary Chairwoman, telling them about flying around the London

Theatre HALL of FAME

Honorary Chair
Dame Celia Lipton Farris

Co-Chairs
Beatrice Arthur
Rita Goldberg   George-Mariana Kaufman   Jerry Herman
Terry Allen Kramer   Lucille Lortel Foundation
Dina Merrill-Ted Hartley   Chase Mishkin   Irma Oestreicher
Martin E. Segal   Joan Sutton Straus
Dorothy Strelsin Foundation   Susan Stroman

Vice-Chair
New York Friars Club   Barbara Tober

Angels Luncheon Committee

Joanna P. Adler
Lucie Arnaz-Larry Luckinbill
David and Helen Gurley Brown
Cornelia Bregman
Marvin Hamlisch
Louise Kerz Hirschfeld
George Grizzard
Jerry and Lois Heisler
Jeffrey Eric Jenkins
William Ivey Long

Elliot and Marjorie Martin
Terrence McNally-Tom Kirdahy
Enid Nemy
Estelle Parsons
Shubert Organization, Inc.
Frances Sternhagen
Clifford Stevens
United Scenic Artists
David Zippel

*I was honored by the Theatre Hall of Fame with a permanent display at the
Gershwin Theatre in New York which contains photos of my theatrical career.*

stage in the role. Alexander Dreyfoos, for whom the School is named, and his wife
Renate looked on with great pride as students from the school performed during the
evening's festivities.

Shortly after that event I was contacted by Terry Hodge Taylor, Director of the
Theatre Hall of Fame which is located at the Gershwin Theatre in New York. Terry
explained to me that the Theatre Hall of Fame of which I am a member, along with
Carol Burnett, Tommy Tune, Lord Andrew Lloyd-Webber, Joanne Woodward, Paul
Newman, and James Earl Jones would be dedicating a permanent display featuring
photographs, scripts, music, costumes, "Playbills," and even some recordings from
my career—I was honored. The cases at the Theatre Hall of Fame are dedicated to
stage actors and actresses who have starred or are currently featured on Broadway.

For several years, I have had the great pleasure of serving as Honorary Chairwoman of the Hall of Fame Awards luncheon. The incomparable Marian Seldes,
along with her late husband Garson Kanin, were actively involved in the Theatre

HRH The Duke of Edinburgh at the Awards reception
at my home.

Hall of Fame. And to this day, Marian is still actively involved in the Hall of Fame. The talented writer and author, Enid Nemy is very generous with the Dorothy Strelsin Foundation with Theatre Hall of Fame and its annual awards. Enid wrote a story for the "New York Times," about Victor and I at our "Helicon Hall" home in Englewood, New Jersey.

Producer James M. Nederlander and his wife Elizabeth Ireland are founding members of the Theatre Hall of Fame. They spend winters in Palm Beach. In addition to being a great producer of distinguished entertainment, Mr. Nederlander is the owner of many theatres throughout the United States.

The work of the American Cancer Society remains very important to me. I have fought cancer myself, and I have done my utmost to support the organization for nearly three decades. For two years, I served as Chairwoman of the Cancer Ball, and since that time I have served as Chairman Emeritus in support of the event. When Helen Boehm was invited to Chair the Ball in 1999, she asked me to join her as Honorary Chairwoman and Chairwoman Emeritus. Helen helped build the venerable Boehm Porcelain business, which is collected by individuals around the globe, including the late Pope John Paul II.

Alicia Blodgett

Arlette and Robert Gordon

Since working with Helen in 1999, I have served as Honorary Chairwoman and Chairwoman Emeritus for the Cancer Ball. In 2000, I had the pleasure of working with Alicia Blodgett on the Cancer Ball themed "An Evening in Paris." Alicia did a wonderful job and we even brought in Can Can dancers to liven up the evening.

The following year, a long-time friend, Arlette Gordon rallied the troops for cancer research with an "Evening at El Morocco" theme. The committee under Arlette's leadership enjoyed great success raising at the time a record amount of money in one evening for the Palm Beach Cancer Ball. Brownie McLean has been my good friend for many years, and has also been a great Chairman for many important Balls in Palm Beach and New York. Brownie has worked with Arlette on an a number of projects and was helpful in developing the décor for the evening at "El Morocco."

Arlette, for two years, has Chaired the ever-popular and successful "Old Bags" luncheon, benefiting The Center For Family Services. She brought in Debbie Reynolds as the guest speaker for a very successful event. Debbie's visit was covered on the front page of the "Palm Beach Daily News" and also featured on a local television station.

Palm Beach **Society**

The Luxury Magazine 50th Year

PRSRT STD
US Postage
Paid
West Palm Beach, Fl.
Permit No. 1813

December 31, 2004-
January 6, 2005

THREE DOLLARS

THE MARDI GRAS GALA

American Cancer Society – Palm Beach Gala
Friday, February 4, 2005
The Breakers

FRENCH QUARTER CAFE
Gala Tonight

*Paula Zukov, Chairwoman; Patrick Park, Honorary Vice-Chairman;
Dame Celia Lipton Farris, Honorary Chairwoman and Chairwoman Emeritus; Tom Quick, Chairman; Jill Rau, Chairwoman (L-R)*

Courtesy: Palm Beach Society magazine

295

Edith Bliss   *Mosse Hvide and John Brogan*   *Brownie McLean*

The following year, the hard-working and beautiful Leigh Larmoyeux served as Chairwoman of the Cancer Ball with her Co-Chairwomen, Lori Gendelman, Mary Davidson, Jill Rau, and Paula Zukov dedicating the ball to Scotland. Unsurprisingly, I was enthusiastic about the Scottish theme. Leigh did an excellent job, carrying out the theme with Scottish bag-pipers and drummers who greeted guests as they arrived in the courtyard of the The Breakers Hotel. In the ballroom she used beautiful décor that simulated the Scottish countryside, hired a talented orchestra, selected a wonderful menu and even had Scottish-themed table gifts. It was a masterfully choreographed evening created by Leigh and her Co-Chairwomen.

John Brogan, my friend and a steadfast supporter of the American Cancer Society for many years, and the Chairman Emeritus of Board, announced that Leigh had raised more than $1.5 million with the Scottish Highlands Ball. My good friend and a great athlete and golfer Edith Bliss attended the event, along with Mosse Hvide and Mary Frances Turner who looked beautiful. I have known Mary Frances since she was a very young girl, growing up with my children in Palm Beach.

My dear friends Michele and Craig Millard chaired the Cancer Ball in 2004 and chose a "Winter Fantasy" theme. They assembled Patrick Park, Mary Fairbanks, Jill Rau, Paula Zukov, and Suzi Goldsmith to serve as Co-Chairmen. As Honorary Chairman and Chairman Emeritus, I was impressed with the detail in which the Millards produced the "Winter Fantasy." 600 guests entered The Breakers' Venetian Ballroom, where there were ice skaters, ice carvings, and snow. Guests were transported into a winter wonderland despite a balmy 80-degree evening in Palm Beach.

Pauline Pitt

Bob and Ellen Jaffe

Emilia & Jose Pepe Fanjul

Mary Frances Turner

Sen. George and Betty Murphy

Leigh Larmoyeux

Anka Palitz

Jane Volk

Earl of Dalkeith

Michele and Craig Millard

HRH Prince Edward, The Countess of Wessex, and Tom Quick

The Earl of Shrewsbury

Friends Bette and Mike Conrad

Richard Mineards

Patty Myura

Alex Dreyfoos

Helen Boehm

*The Hon. Yvelyne "Deedy" and her husband
Wing Commander Nigel Marix*

Renowned photographer Harry Benson

Kim and Dr. Rolla Campbell

Walter and Cathleen Ross

John and Marianne Castle

Sydell Miller and Philip Zieky

Vic and Rena Damone

Martin and Audrey Gruss

Guests at the "Winter Fantasy Ball" included Patty and Anthony Myura, Connie and Sam Frankino, Arlette and Bob Gordon, Elizabeth Bonan, John Brogan and Mosse Hvide, Helen and James Rosburg, Herme de Wyman Miro, Gloria Wolosoff, the elegant Rose Sachs, Marianne and John Castle (owners of the "Winter White House" which belonged to the Kennedy family), Kim and Dr. Rolla Campbell (Kim, sister of the late actress Kay Kendall, is a good friend and the Campbells have worked hard for the Palm Beach Zoo), the late Beverly and the late Barry Crown, Susan and Lee Gordon, Trish and Thorne Donnelly, Linda and Ed Dweck, Gail and the late Mel Nessel, Vic and Rena Damone (Vic is a great friend and tremendous singer. I sang with Vic at a Salvation Army gala which I chaired at Mar-a-Lago. Rena is a brilliant businesswoman who founded her own clothing line, "Rena Rowan."),

*Radio and television personality Dick Robinson
and his wife Sally*

Paula and Mark Cook, Talbott and Jack Maxey, Leigh and Chris Larmoyeux, Warren and Orrine Orlando, Jesse and Rand Araskog, Sydell Miller, Phil Zieky, and Betsy and James Meany. William Blodgett, Chairman of the Board of the American Cancer Society for the Town of Palm Beach, proudly announced that the Ball had raised nearly $2 million for cancer research and patient programs.

Michele and Howard Kessler served as Chairmen of the 2006 Cancer Ball, entitled "The Imperial Dynasty Ball." I was pleased to join this dynamic, hard-working couple as Honorary Chairman and Chairman Emeritus of the Ball. Michele did a spectacular job raising more than $2.2 million for the American Cancer Society. She transformed The Breakers' new Ponce de Leon Ballroom into an Asian fantasy, complete with ice sculptures, bamboo plants, and a Chinese menu.

Those attending the "The Imperial Dynasty Ball" included Phyllis and Richard Krock, Ellen and Bob Jaffe, Diana and Llwyd Ecclestone, Ruth and Ray Perelman, Dick and Sally Robinson (my dear friend Dick, a radio and television celebrity, plays my recordings on his nationally syndicated radio program "Standards by the Sea"),

Flappers Vilda B. de Porro and I with Bert Sokol and Maurice Kazzi

Jack and Helen Fealy

Sydell Miller, Patty and Anthony Myura, Nassrine and Norman Traverse, Frances and Jeff Fisher, Laura and Lee Munder (Laura is a well-known jewelry designer and her creations are as beautiful as she is), Beth Pine of Neiman Marcus, George Cloutier, Linda and Chuck Foster, Dr. Elizabeth and Colonel Charles Bowden, Judy Grubman and Sonny Castor, Darlene and Jerry Gordan, Olga Schulman, Andrea and John Stark, Katherine and Leo Vecillio, Betsy and Wally Turner, Susan and Bob Tomsich, my dear Ce Ce, Tom Quick, Lois Pope and the late Leo Albert, Shannon Donnelly (friend and the charming and eminent Society Editor for the "Palm Beach Daily News"), and many other generous supporters of the American Cancer Society.

My friend Patrick Park chaired the 2007 Cancer Ball which was held at the Mar-a-Lago Club. Patrick, truly the ultimate host, did a brilliant job for Cancer! I was pleased to serve with him as Honorary Chairwoman and Chairman Emeritus for the evening, which was a smashing success. Patrick made certain that guests would remember this evening above all others by greeting them with a 50-piece orchestra playing around the Mar-a-Lago pool. It was such a romantic way to begin the evening. Being a fine musician and pianist himself, the music for the evening was most important to Patrick. He had caviar stations and champagne strategically arranged for guests to enjoy while being serenaded by the orchestra under the twinkling stars of the night. I had the pleasure of introducing our honored guest for the evening, Julie Andrews. There were nearly 600 people attending the Ball. Patrick raised more than $2 million for the American Cancer Society.

PALM BEACH.
Society

PRESENTING SOCIETY 53RD YEAR
NEW YORK SARATOGA NEWPORT THE HAMPTONS

PRSRT STD
US Postage
PAID
West Palm Beach, FL
Permit No. 1813

December 29, 2006
thru January 4, 2007

Three Dollars

THE 49TH ANNUAL

American Cancer Society Ball

FRIDAY, FEBRUARY 2, 2007
MAR-A-LAGO CLUB, PALM BEACH

DAME CELIA LIPTON FARRIS
Honorary Chairman and
Chairman Emeritus (pictured)

MR. PATRICK M. PARK
Chairman (pictured)

MRS. DIANA ECCLESTONE
Honorary Vice Chairman

Honored Guest
DAME JULIE ANDREWS

Courtesy: Palm Beach Society magazine

Among those attending the 2007 Cancer Ball were Clo and Charles Cohen, Tiffany Spadafora and George Cloutier, Elizabeth and Jeff Bateman, Phyllis and Richard Krock, Mary and Bob Montgomery, Florence Bonsuk Seiler, Don Webster, Julie and Rob Revely, Leslie Ginn, Luciana and Joe Vittoria, Karen and Dan Swanson, Linda and Chuck Foster, Michele and Howard Kessler, Leo Albert, Marilyn Connor, Cindy and Vince Cerone, Arlette and Bob Gordon, Dr. Elizabeth and Colonel Charles Bowden, Craig and Michele Millard, Jan and Harding Willinger, Sydell Miller and Phil Zieky, Nassrine and Dr. Norman Traverse, Gita and Mark Costa, and Yvonne Lynam.

Dana-Farber Cancer Institute is one of the foremost research and cancer-treatment centers in the world. Based in Boston and affiliated with Harvard University, Dana-Farber made a number of breakthrough discoveries in the treatment and cures for certain types of cancer. Tom Quick, who originally hails from Boston and is my neighbor and friend, asked that I serve as his Honorary Chairwoman for the Institute's kick-off party for the Discovery Ball. The evening featured a Bill Blass fashion show and was held at Neiman Marcus in Palm Beach. Among those who enjoyed the evening were Ruth and Carl Shapiro, Dena and Martin Trust, Judie and Larry Schlager, Myrna and Bob Kraft, Dr. Edward Benz, Ruth Koppelman, Andrea and John Stark, James Sheeran (a friend and the owner and publisher of "Palm Beach Society–The Social Pictorial" which is a very popular publication) with the beautiful Diane Milner, John Loring the famed Tiffany Design Director, Neiman Marcus's Beth Pine, Robert Janjigian (fashion editor of the "Palm Beach Daily News"), Matt Kutcher, Karen Martins, Vicki and Arthur Loring, Sue Rapple, Michele and Howard Kessler, "Quest" magazine publishers Chris and Grace Meigher, and of course Michael Volbracht who at that time designed the Bill Blass collection. What a beautiful evening that was!

In 2007, I was again asked to serve as Honorary Chairwoman for the kick-off evening for Dana-Farber. Michele Kessler and Tom Quick were Chairwoman and Chairman for the evening and Phyllis Krock would be serving as Chairwoman for the Dana-Farber Ball to be held in February. The evening held at Neiman-Marcus began with a cocktail reception on the first floor, and invited guests including Sandy Krakoff, Bonnie and Donald Dwares, Richard Krock, Craig Miller, Dina Capehart, Sandy Heine, Howard Kessler, Ruth and Carl Shapiro, Ellen and Bob Jaffe, Nancy

Oscar de la Renta and I at the
Dana-Farber kick-off

Chairmen Michele Kessler and Tom Quick at the Dana-Farber
kick-off evening where I served as Honorary Chairwoman.

and Don Carter, Mark LaRoe and Elaine and Jerry Schuster adjourned to the second floor of the store where they were welcomed by Neiman Marcus Vice President Beth Pine. I was introduced by Michele and Tom, and then had the great pleasure and honor of introducing Oscar de la Renta, who presented his Spring Collection. It was a beautiful evening, and Oscar is not only a great designer, but also a true gentleman.

Several months later, Kathy Bleznak wrote a letter to invite me to serve as Honorary Chairwoman for a luncheon to benefit the Historical Society of Palm Beach County. The luncheon was held at Neiman Marcus. Working with Beth Pine, Neiman Marcus' most capable and talented Vice President and Kathy was a great pleasure. These are two very bright, articulate, attractive and organized women who get the job done. Nearly two-hundred women attended the luncheon which featured a panel discussion with Pamela Fiori, Editor-in-Chief of "Town & Country" Magazine and fashion designer Ralph Rucci. I had time prior to the luncheon to talk with Pamela, who I had met before on several occasions. She is a most-interesting, charming and articulate woman who has made "Town & Country" one of the foremost luxury lifestyle magazines in America. Following lunch, I was honored to introduce Pamela and Ralph Rucci to the audience as they began their program. Mr. Rucci remained after the panel discussion and previewed his beautiful women's collection for spring.

There have been so many other special moments and events that I have had the opportunity or honor to be part of.

Kathy Bleznak
Chairman, Historical
Society Luncehon

I introduced Pamela Fiori, Editor-in-Chief of "Town & Country" Magazine,
(above) and fashion designer Ralph Rucci (right) to patrons at the Historical
Society Luncheon Benefit where I served as Honorary Chairman.

I had been not only humbled but also surprised each of the three times I had been honored by the Palm Beach Chamber of Commerce with its "Outstanding Citizen Award." However, I was rendered speechless when for an unprecedented fourth time they presented me with the "One and Only" Award. This award is presented to a citizen of Palm Beach who has worked to improve the Town and the lives of its citizens.

Several weeks following that honor, I was invited to serve as Honorary Chairwoman of the Ft. Lauderdale International Film Festival. The evening honored Lord Richard Attenborough, and guests were treated to a premiere of his latest film. I introduced Lord Attenborough at the affair and we spent some time during the evening talking about his work in many films and on a number of other projects, not only in America but also around the world.

My pals "Cain and Abel" (better known as Sir Michael Caine and Sir Roger Moore) were part of the Palm Beach International Festival that particular year. It was wonderful to spend time with these two great actors and friends. They were both honored at the Festival the first year for their body of film work at that time. I served as Honorary Chairwoman of the Palm Beach International Film Festival the following year working with Janet Leigh, John Forsyth, and Tippi Hedren, on an evening that honored the work of Sir Alfred Hitchcock. Sir Alfred's daughter, Patricia Hitchcock O'Connell, attended the Festival to accept the posthumous award on behalf of her father and his brilliant career.

As Honorary Chairwoman of the Palm Beach International Film Festival I had the pleasure of working with Janet Leigh, John Forsyth, and Tippi Hedren.

I was honored myself several months following this affair by the Association of Fundraising Professionals who presented me with a prestigious award as their "Philanthropist of the Year." The Children's Home Society and their Development Director, Cora Brown had nominated me for the award.

Though doing my utmost to improve the human condition in my community and throughout the United States, I have always remained steadfast and faithful to my mother country as well, and I support a number of charities in the United Kingdom. The British Forces Foundation is very important and HRH Prince Charles is the organization's Patron. A wonderful charity "Help the Hospices" which is the Duchess of Norfolk's charity I support as well. The Duchess paints so beautifully, and sells the paintings with proceeds benefiting this worthwhile cause.

As a way to express my creativity, I returned to painting, as well. Over the course of time, I have been painting not only landscapes but also people and images of current world happenings, including 9/11. My paintings have been the subject of a number of exhibitions over these years (including Phillips Gallery on Worth Avenue) with my portion of the proceeds benefiting the Palm Beach County Chapter of the American Red Cross and the Palm Beach American Cancer Society.

In 2004, more than 1,000 people attended the opening reception for an exhibition that was held of my work at the renowned Wally Findlay Gallery on Worth

Patricia Hitchcock O'Connell   *Former New York Mayor Rudy Giuliani*

Avenue. The firm also has galleries located in New York and London. Approximately fifty paintings were on exhibition for a week-long exhibition with all proceeds of sales benefiting the American Cancer Society.

Opening night was a mob scene, with wall-to-wall people. During the course of several hours, more than twenty-six paintings were sold. A number of other paintings were sold during the remainder of the exhibition. Representatives of the gallery simply could not keep up with people asking to buy a painting on the evening of the opening, which was heartwarming but also somewhat humorous.

Here I was trying to greet everyone, looking for someone to take a check or credit card, my secretary was selling paintings, my daughter Ce Ce selling paintings and my great friend Bert Sokol selling paintings. The exhibition raised a substantial amount of money for Cancer research which made it all very worthwhile. At the opening of the evening, I surprised the patrons by donating a painting that I had done of the heroic efforts of firefighters in New York erecting the American flag at the site of the demolished World Trade Center. I also made a donation to the Town of Palm Beach Central Fire Station to assist in their fundraising campaign to build a new fire station and gave the Palm Beach Police a painting for their conference room.

Several paintings from this particular series were requested for donation to "Art for America," as well. This exhibition and auction was held in New York and included

Palm Beach firefighters at my exhibition at Wally Findlay Gallery, Palm Beach

work from other artists such as Jamie Wyeth, Cindy Sherman, Jonathan Green and Alex Katz. Proceeds from the exhibition and event benefited families of New York City firefighters and police who perished in the attacks of 9/11.

Following the Findlay exhibition, I sent a painting to Bill and Bridgett Koch for their Palm Beach home. Bill is one of the greatest art collectors in America. The painting that my late husband Victor had done was a rocket-launching. Victor and Bill had both attended Massachusetts Institute of Technology.

Palm Beach has numerous events happening throughout the season. There are celebrities, authors, and captains of business and industry coming and going all of the time.

Liz Smith, internationally syndicated columnist whom I have known for many years has hosted events for her "Literacy Partners" organization in Palm Beach and New York. She has visited Palm Beach for a number of signing events for her books, "Dishing" and "Natural Blonde."

It was a great treat to spend time with the renowned photographer and my dear friend Harry Benson and his wife Gigi who were in Palm Beach for an exhibition of his photographs at the Holden Luntz Gallery on Worth Avenue. Harry had photographed me when I played the London Palladium and at my home with Victor. That picture appeared in "Life" Magazine.

*Palm Beach resident
Rod Stewart*

*Celine Dion and I
at Mar-a-Lago*

Palm Beach is one of the unique places on earth. The Town is full of history, beauty, nature, and interesting people. I produced and hosted a program entitled "Palm Beach People & Places." The two-part documentary aired on CBS and PaxNet throughout North America and received high ratings. The documentary included interviews with a number of the Town's most recognizable residents and visitors, and included historical facts and footage and a peek at some of the events held in Palm Beach throughout the season.

309

Shirley MacLaine

Carol Channing and Mary Martin

Russell Simmons

Michael Feinstein

Julio Iglesias

Barry Gibb

Tony Bennett

Martha Stewart

The well-known columnist and author Cindy Adams has been to Palm Beach over the years as well. I especially enjoyed her book about her little dogs entitled "Living A Dog's Life: Jazzy, Juicy And Me."

Lily Pulitzer calls Palm Beach "home." The great fashion designer began her career here and has been a friend for many years. Lily comes and goes from the Island traveling around the globe to appear on behalf of the collection of clothing and home accessories that bear her name.

Stephen Yearick has designed a number of beautiful evening gowns for me. He comes to Palm Beach often to show his collection, work with clients, visit with friends, and to enjoy a weekend in the sun when it is winter in the Northeast.

David Columbia, the editor of "Quest" Magazine, along with literary agent Marianne Strong attend a number of events during the season traveling to Palm Beach from New York when their heavy schedules permit. Marianne, or Mimi as I have come to know her after all these years, has edited a number of important books on fascinating subjects. She long ago took on the responsibility of raising her nephew, Billy, who has grown into a fine, intelligent, and handsome young man.

The renowned recording artist and singer, Rod Stewart has a beautiful ocean-front estate in Palm Beach, and can be seen here from time-to-time at area shops, restaurants and even walking on the beach. The writer, Bea Cayzer divides her time between Palm Beach and Europe. Kenny Miller from the Theatre is also a regular celebrity in Palm Beach. The charming and talented artist Laurie Heinz is in Palm Beach often. My cousins Fran and Daryl Bolton visit the Island with their talented daughter Davana, for vacations.

Michele and Craig Millard chaired an event for the International Center for Missing and Exploited Children in Palm Beach and I joined them as Honorary Chairwoman. Receiving guests with the Millards and me were Queen Noor of Jordan, Marta Fox (First Lady of Mexico), the enchanting and incredibly talented Ricky Martin, John Walsh of "America's Most Wanted" and the Adam Walsh Foundation, Ambassadors from a number of countries, and Dr. Shelia Johnson (a successful businesswoman, philanthropist and member of the board of the International Center). The evening raised $1 million and drew more than 400 guests. This is a very special charity to me and has impact around the world to help locate children who have been abducted, are missing, or have fallen in harm's way.

Ricky Martin at the International Center for Missing and Exploited Children's Benefit

Marta Fox, First Lady of Mexico   *John Walsh*   *Queen Noor of Jordan*

The Preservation Foundation's annual gala is one the highlights of the Palm Beach season. Audrey Gruss chaired the evening for two years, and I was pleased to support Audrey and the Preservation Foundation as the Chairwoman. In 2006 and 2007, Pauline Pitt, whom I have known since her childhood, served as Chairwoman for the annual gala. Pauline called on Steven Stolman, to decorate the room and I served as Honorary Chairwoman for the evening. Preservation of historical architecture in Palm Beach continues to be very important to me.

My friend Jane Volk, wife of the renowned architect John Volk, has been steadfast and constant in the preservation of the Town's most important homes and landmarks. Among those supporting the Preservation Foundation and attending the gala

Ce Ce and Robert Lovey at the "Highland Ball" Benefit

Colonel Robert Spencer

were Maura and Bill Benjamin, Jean Tailer with John Loring, Ruth and Ray Perelman, Renee Wood, Betsy and Michael Kaiser, Frances Scaife, Maggie and Alan Scherer, Jesse and Rand Araskog, Ward Landrigan, Hillary and Wilbur Ross, Diana and Llwyd Ecclestone, Grace and Chris Meigher, Frayda and George Lindeman, Audrey and Martin Gruss, Thom Smith (a great columnist and social editor for the "Palm Beach Post"), Tom Quick, Bob Leidy, John Blades, Betsy and George Matthews, Jean and Will Matthews, Helene and Jesse Newman, Kathy and Alan Bleznak, Jo Carole and Ronald Lauder, Debra Koch, Iris and Carl Apfel, Frances and Jeff Fisher, and John Machek.

For the past several years, I have served as the Honorary Queen of Scots for the "Highland Ball" held annually on St. Andrew's Day at the Beach Club in Palm Beach. This very successful evening is chaired by Cathleen and Walter Ross and benefits The National Trust for Scotland of which HRH Prince Charles is Patron and my friend The Earl of Dalkeith is President. The late Princess Diana's cousin and my friend, Robert Spencer, deserves credit for starting this benefit.

The charming Brit Evelyn Harrison enjoyed the Scottish dances. The National Trust protects and promotes Scotland's national and cultural heritage for present and future generations and has more than 127 properties in its care, ranging from castles, battlefields, historic houses and gardens, to majestic mountains and lochs. I was

*The Honorable Lesly Smith,
former Mayor of Palm Beach*

*The late Paul Illyinsky, former Mayor of
Palm Beach, and his wife Angie*

pleased that my Scottish cousins who live Ft. Lauderdale, Florida, Adrienne and Ross Young and their daughters could join me for the evening.

For several years, I have served as Honorary Chairman of an event for the American Ballet Theatre of New York, which is Chaired by my friend Anka Palitz, and hosted by Julia and David Koch at their beautiful oceanfront estate in Palm Beach. Julia and David erected a tent on their lawn for the evening which included cocktails, dinner, and an incredible performance by the American Ballet Theatre.

The Honorable Lesly Smith, who was a very fine Mayor of Palm Beach for many years, was there along with Pepe Fanjul and his lovely wife Emilia and many other supporters of American Ballet Theatre and dance. Following the event, David was such a gentleman that he personally drove the Ballet dancers back to the airport for their return trip to New York.

In spite of the hurricanes that hit Palm Beach, I am still trying to conserve my historical home which was once the residence of Consuelo Vanderbilt, the Duchess of Marlborough. My home, prior to being that of the Mme. Jacques Balsan, Duchess of Marlborough, had been the estate of Audrey Emery, the former Princess Ilyinsky, widow of the Grand Duke Dmitri and mother of the late Mayor of Palm Beach and my friend, Paul Ilyinsky. Paul and his wife Angie have done wonderful things for the town. Angie is actively involved in public service and volunteers for many charities.

Florida Governor Charlie Crist

In 2005, the hurricane season started quietly. On a Saturday in August I turned on the television weather reports predicting a category-five hurricane named Katrina coming towards Florida and the Gulf states. A day later, I watched the television in horror and no one could do anything to help when Hurricane Katrina hit Mississippi and Louisiana, destroying not only homes, businesses and entire towns but also precious lives. It was heart-wrenching.

In October, weather forecasters were predicting a storm that within days would hit Florida and the entire southeastern United States. This hurricane had winds of 150 miles-per-hour. We were told to evacuate for the hurricane, but I had gone from so many hotels in Palm Beach Gardens, West Palm Beach, Ft. Lauderdale when previous hurricanes had hit. I was running from one hotel to the next like a madwoman, with two little dogs in my arms to stay ahead of the storm.

I really wanted to stay home in my own bed. If I could live through the blitz of London as a young child then surely I could get through this storm. So I did stay home when Hurricane Wilma came ashore. When the 150-mph gale-force winds hit, I carried my two little Maltese dogs, Christopher and Baby, with me into the closet. Christopher and Baby were looking up at me wondering, "What are we doing in here?" The sound of the wind was like that of a powerful train coming right through the house–everything shook. We quickly lost all electrical power, but thankfully the

My Palm Beach residence required extensive repairs after Hurricane Wilma.

emergency generator I had installed came on to power the house with electricity. The phones, on the other hand, had died. It was a frightening experience–I thought the storm would never end. My dogs were not affected by the storm at all.

After what seemed like an eternity, the storm finally passed. I eventually made my way to the bedroom window, opened the shutter and looked out. I could not believe what I saw. The surrounding area looked as though a bomb had exploded. It appeared that I had lost more than 32 shutters from the house. Most were lying in the driveway of neighbor, Tom Quick. Every sort of debris imaginable including trees, branches, leaves, and pieces from roofs lay everywhere. One year later, I still did not have any gutters and could not find anyone to repair the tiles missing from my roof or replace the gutters. Where did all the workers go?

Two years later, there were people who still had blue tarps on their roofs, looking for workmen to repair their homes. The first floor of my house was damaged by the hurricane. The driveway had to be dug up and re-engineered to keep any damage from happening again. Thank goodness for my friend and attorney Bette Conrad, who helped me get the house back in order. Each year, we are told to expect hurricanes; some years, everyone throughout the country is spared. However, one never knows living in a coastal state what will happen between the months of June and November. If you want to live in paradise, this is what you have to put up with.

And paradise, Palm Beach is! Florida has more golf courses than any other state in America and Palm Beach is home to many beautiful ones including The Breakers, Palm Beach Country Club, The Everglades Club, Palm Beach Par III and, of course, Donald Trump's Mar-a-Lago Golf Club (located just off the Island). The shops in Palm Beach on Worth Avenue are extraordinary and the equal of those of New York's Fifth and Madison Avenues, Beverly Hills' Rodeo Drive and London's Saville Row and Bond Street.

There is some irony in the fact that Worth Avenue is so named with all these glamorous stores. Wonderful dining places adjoin Worth Avenue as well. Palm Beach as an Island is a mile wide and 15-miles long and has some of the most beautiful beaches on earth. The Island is very close to the Gulf Stream which makes the water warm and beautiful, year round, with an abundance of marine life. Scuba-divers revel in the fact that there is a reef approximately 200 feet off-shore from the Island, and on some mornings and at dawn you can look out and see everything from whales to dolphins and sharks in the waters.

At the end of Worth Avenue are docks that are home from time to time to some of the most astounding and sizable yachts on earth. These homes on water, travel gracefully up and down the Intracoastal and out to sea. They are beautiful to watch as they come and go from Palm Beach. There are also a great number of yachts and sizeable boats docked at the north end of Palm Beach at the Sailfish Club, where I have been a member for many years.

I have been telling myself these past years that I must slow down, but every time I do someone comes along and asks if I can help with something. Over the past several years, I have been asked to hosts events for HRH Prince Edward, the Earl of Wessex. My next-door neighbor and friend Tom Quick and I co-hosted a lunch for the Prince in 2005. Lord and Lady Foley were guests at that event along with many others including the charming Ann Appleman. The Foleys pop into Palm Beach during the winter and Adrian Foley is an old friend, and I enjoy hearing him play the piano. He is a great pianist.

We wanted to raise funds and awareness for the Duke of Edinburgh's Award, which was founded 50 years ago to help young people all over the world. I recall hosting his father HRH Prince Philip some years earlier in my home for the Duke of Edinburgh's Award World Fellowship.

Duke of Edinburgh's Award luncheon for
HRH Prince Edward

It was a tremendous evening and among those attending were Mayor Paul and Angie Illinsky. I put a tent over the pool, with the American flag and the Union Jack side by side, there was beautiful music and what a lovely party. My only worry the entire evening was that someone would by accident fall into the swimming pool. Luckily no one did and everything went beautifully.

In January 2006, I asked Tom Quick to co-host a luncheon with me for HRH Prince Edward and his wife, Sophie, Countess of Wessex. Among those joining us for the luncheon were Jesse and Rand Araskog, Patrick Park and Mary Fairbanks, Sydell Miller, Hillary and Wilbur Ross, Elizabeth and Jeff Bateman, Polly and David Ober (David is the Vice President of Sotheby's), Yvonne Lynam and Dorie Kreidy, Eileen and Richard Ekstract (publishers of "Hampton's Cottages & Gardens" and "Palm Beach Cottages & Gardens), Ellen Jaffe, Paula and Nikita Zukov, Phyllis and Richard Krock, Ruth and Ray Perelman, Brad and Dena Martin, Renee and Carlos Morrison, Renee Wood and Frances Hayword, Bonnie Hunter, Michele and Craig Millard, Bruce Bent, Nassrine and Norman Traverse, Katy and Jeff Amling, Beth Pine, Michele and Howard Kessler, Frances Fisher, and Audrey and Martin Gruss.

It was somewhat funny that days following the luncheon a friend drew my attention to a listing on the Internet. The "net" as many call it today, is full of surprises and information. I found it funny and touching that my signature was on sale for $50 a letter. The popular web site "HistoryforSale.com" features a Playbill from the London stage production of "Point to Point" at the St. Martin's Theatre. The Playbill is signed by Nigel Bruce, Ann Todd and me. The seller says, in a description of the playbill, "Celia Lipton at a very young age was a great success on the London and Broadway stages, the BBC, American television networks including ABC, CBS, NBC and Fox, and in her own one-woman show. She enjoyed a successful recording career with over a dozen award winning CD's to her credit. Her recordings are currently played on over 200 stations in North America, Canada, South America and on the BBC. Nigel Bruce is best known as Dr Watson to close friend Basil Rathbone's 'Sherlock Holmes' in 14 films and countless radio programs. Ann Todd began her career on the London staged and went on to star in a number of films." Asking price for the program with my signature is $1,000. The seller comments that the program "Though lightly soiled" is in over-all fine condition.

Who could have guessed that people could do so well with their signature decades later? Had I known this, I would have planned ahead and would be laughing all the way to the bank! This is amazing that someone would keep this type of thing and that it would command such an amount of money. I thought it was only football and baseball players whose signatures people wanted.

Then there are the media people. Aline Franzen, of "Portrait," an American-French magazine, "The Best," headlined a feature about me, "The British Legend" and said so many kind things. BBC Breakfast Television, which goes worldwide, flew in from Washington to interview me in November 2005. The crew spent nearly two days with me interviewing me about my career.

To this day, people still ask me the question, "How do you stay so thin." Ironically, at one time in my life I was entirely too thin, and would go out of my way to put on weight. I would do everything to gain weight, and nothing worked. Yet, now, I watch my diet. People ask my secretary and me if I have a trainer. No! I train myself by walking on a treadmill inside or walking along the sea with my dogs. Walking for me is essential.

I love my children and will always be there for them. Today and always my wish for them is happiness and a great future.

There are charity events in America and the UK in gestation whose organizers need my attention. I am grateful to be able to help them.

I am grateful for the discipline that I learned through good teachers; it has helped me throughout my life. If you have God-given talent you must work at it and guard it well. The theatre, recording, performing on stage and producing has given me some of the greatest moments and memories of my life.

The body is an instrument and it must be treated with utmost respect. It gives me great pleasure to have established an Award in my name at the Royal College of Music in London, for accomplished young musicians and singers to continue in their studies.

I have a deep faith that has served me well. As I look back, I realize and share that one has to work throughout one's life to the best of one's ability, and also be kind, honest and helpful to other people and never give up. I was fortunate to have learned a great deal having lived three very different lives.

BUCKINGHAM PALACE

From: Oliver Everett MVO   8th June, 1983.

Dear Mrs Lipton Farris

    The Princess of Wales has asked me
to write and thank you for your letter and
for sending the record and tape which you
kindly enclosed.

    Her Royal Highness thought it was
so kind of you to send her these copies,
and I am to pass on to you The Princess's
sincere thanks.

Yours sincerely,

Oliver Everett

(Private Secretary)

Mrs. C. Lipton Farris.

PALACE OF HOLYROODHOUSE

3rd July, 1995.

Dear Mrs Farris,

The Queen has commanded me to thank you for your letter of 16th June, which gave Her Majesty much pleasure. The Queen well remembers listening to your singing at that memorable VE Day concert in Hyde Park, and was glad of having the opportunity of talking to you afterwards. Her Majesty was also most interested to know that you had sponsored the book "The House of Lords" and was most grateful to you for writing as you did.

Yours sincerely,

Kenneth Scott.

(KENNETH SCOTT)

Mrs. Celia Farris.

From: Brigadier Miles Hunt-Davis, C.B.E.

BUCKINGHAM PALACE

18th March, 1996.

Dear Mrs Farris,

The Duke of Edinburgh has asked me to write and convey to you his pleasure at being able to attend your wonderful party on Friday evening.

His Royal Highness appreciated the opportunity to meet so many of those present to support the worthy cause you have so generously taken to your heart.

The setting of the party in your home and garden was magnificent and made an elegant start to the whole evening.

Finally, may I say how much Sir Brian McGrath and I appreciated being included among your guests.

Yours sincerely,

Miles Hunt-Davis.

Private Secretary

Mrs. Celia Lipton Farris

BUCKINGHAM PALACE.

2nd April, 1996

Dear Mrs. Lipton Farrius,

I am very pleased to know that you have given your very generous support to the development of the Award Scheme by becoming a Fellow of The Duke of Edinburgh's Award World Fellowship.

The Award Scheme program has proved to be a great benefit to many young people growing up in a wide variety of communities and cultures. Your involvement and support will allow the program to be introduced in other parts of the world and make it possible for more young people to participate.

Yours sincerely

Philip

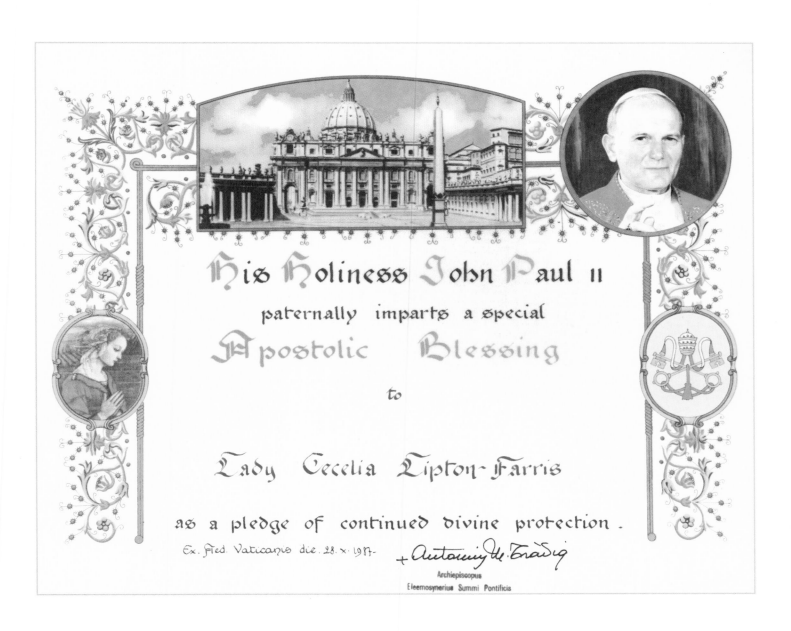

His Holiness John Paul II

paternally imparts a special

Apostolic Blessing

to

Lady Cecelia Tipton-Farris

as a pledge of continued divine protection.

Ex. Aed. Vaticanis die. 28. x. 1987.

+ Antonius M. Travia

Archiepiscopus

Eleemosynerius Summi Pontificis

EMILE LITTLER

And at
PANTOMIME HOUSE,
BIRMINGHAM. 1.
MIDLAND 6034

1st June, 1944.

Reply to
31, St. MARTIN'S LANE,
LONDON W.C. 2. (NEXT DOOR TO COLISEUM)
TEMPLE BAR 6160

KL/JB.

Mrs. Lipton,
57, Bryanston Court,
George Street,
London, W.1.

My dear Mrs. Lipton,

Thank you very much for your letter, which I much appreciate.

I am delighted with Celia and with her success, and anything I may say to her or any grumbles I may make in the future, will be because I am on your side a hundred per cent to try and preserve the simple charm of "THE QUAKER GIRL". I have great admiration for Celia because she works. All my life I have had to work and work very hard, and it is a great joy to me to find anybody else who wants success, but is willing to work for it too. What I said to your husband I really meant, and whatever Celia does, I shall have her interest at heart.

Stanley Holloway sends the following message:-

"Give her my love and tell her I think she has 'every-
"thing it takes'. Also, if she will allow an old
"Jim Crow to give her a word of advice, tell her to
"keep as she is now, talented, unaffected, honest to
"goodness little person - never to believe she has
"really 'arrived'."

NATIONAL BROADCASTING COMPANY, INC.

A SERVICE OF RADIO CORPORATION OF AMERICA

RCA Building. Radio City. New York 20. N.Y.

CIRCLE 6300

October 11, 195?

Miss Celia Lipton
146 East 46th Street
New York, New York

Dear Celia:

Many thanks for the fine job you did on the Goodyear show Sunday night. We had problems with this one, but it came off very well - by the grace of God and plenty of good hard work. You really deserve a lot of credit for all you contributed, and for bearing with us through a difficult week.

The kinescope of THE PERSONAL TOUCH will be shown on Monday, October 18th at 5:00 PM in Room 952 at NBC. I hope you can be there to see it.

Once again, thanks, and I hope we will work together again soon.

Sincerely,

Delbert Mann

BBC

BRITISH BROADCASTING CORPORATION
ARIEL HOUSE 74A CHARLOTTE STREET LONDON W1
TELEPHONE 01-580 4468 TELEX: 265781
TELEGRAMS AND CABLES: BROADCASTS LONDON TELEX
POSTAL ADDRESS BBC LONDON W1A 1AA

4th October 1984

Dear Celia,

Thank you for the album and your letter, which I found waiting for me following my visit to the United States.

You'll be pleased to know that I've included "Maybe This Time" in the programme 'Album Time', broadcast through the BBC World Service. It's scheduled to be heard at the following times, GMT.

Saturday 20th October 0630-0700.
Monday 22nd October 1130-1200.
Wednesday 24th October 2115-2145.

I trust you will be able to listen.

With best wishes.

Yours sincerely,

(Ken Evans)
Producer - Radio 2

WILLIAM O'SHAUGHNESSY

January 6, 1986

Dear Celia:

Thanks for the copy of your new album. It's just perfect for WRTN ... and we're adding many (or most) of the tunes to our permanent rotation. They're all great. And so are you.

Don't forget you have a standing invite to come by when you are in New York.

Yours,

April 11
1987

Hospers

Celia Dear: I can't tell you how much I love your two Cassettes — Superb!! I never dreamed you had such a splendid, rich voice. I loved all the songs — but some more than others — like; "You make me feel so Young" "Trötzje" "Can't get started" "Come closer to me" "Soon it's gonna rain" "I'll remember April" & "Yesterday I heard the rain" —

But all in all. They're all Terrific. I love the photos — Mon Dieu you are one Gorgeous gal!

I loved seeing you, though briefly after my performance — & Thank you for that hug when I finished — that reassured me that I was

---

FRANK SINATRA

December 2, 1992

Dear Celia,

We regret not writing sooner to express our friendship and thanks for your role as driving force and inspiration for the recent American Cinema Awards. I've been on the road traveling so much these past several months -- I'm just now getting a quiet moment before the holidays to catch up on some of the mail!

September 12 was a very special gala, and I know you were intimately involved in every aspect of its success. You are a good and true friend and Barbara and I look forward to seeing you soon.

With my warmest regards to you and yours for a happy and healthy holiday season.

All the best,

Frank Sinatra

SAMMY CAHN

Monday
Aug/22
'88.

Dear Celia -

I came home to find a lovely Christmas Gift from "our" Norman Monath, ---

I really was pleasured by your LET IT SNOW! (especially with the weather being what it is in N. Y. right now!)

I am carrying HIGH HOPES (title) that if you again do another Vhristmas Album that you will think of doing CHRISTMAS WALTZ (Sinatra recorded it THREE different times!)

Mainly there is a chance I may come to Florida with my one-man-show (plus 4!) and if and when I do I am sure we will meet and I'll express my pleasure personally, ---

Sammy.

BUDDY EBSEN ART COLLECTION
P. O. Box 2069
Palos Verdes Peninsula, CA 90274-8069
Phone: (213) 378-9223
Fax: (213) 378-8371

February 27, 1991

Dear Celia,

Dorothy and I wish to express our thanks, for the invitation to the American Cancer Society Ball, and for your peerless hospitality.

It was, as you suggested, a fabulous winter vacation, and a chance to visit old friends and make new ones.

You are indeed a hostess nonpareil, a social force, and have the further distinction, in my eyes, of being the owner of a Hunter Wood original.

With all good wishes from the Ebsens.

Sincerely
Buddy

327

REX REED

Dear Celia

Yes, I admit, purring guiltily and arching my back tardily, that I knew nothing about you when I arrived in Miami to do the AIDS benefit ... thanks to your simply wonderful tape I now know you are more than just another rich, frivolous, and gullible widow ... you have an enormous heart and a big talent, too. My god, what a lovely voice. And good taste to match. I love the way you sing "Time Heals Everything". (And it does, too, I'm told, by experts.) Anyway, none of this matters as long as you have a big, warm heart and care so much about the human race. I was so proud

THE CITY OF NEW YORK
OFFICE OF THE MAYOR
NEW YORK, N.Y. 10007

February 3, 2003

Mrs. Celia Lipton Farris
319 El Vedado Way
Palm Beach, FL 33480

Dear Celia:

Thank you for your contribution to the City of New York. We appreciate your generous response to Liz's appeal and are grateful for all the support we have received from our many friends throughout the country. Your involvement means so much, and on behalf of New York City's eight million residents, thank you again for your generosity.

All the best.

Sincerely,

Michael R. Bloomberg
Mayor

MRB:lc

cc: Ms. Liz Smith

RODDY MCDOWALL

Dear Celia
HOW KIND AND GENEROUS OF YOU

Roddy

hello to Best ∞ Happy New Year

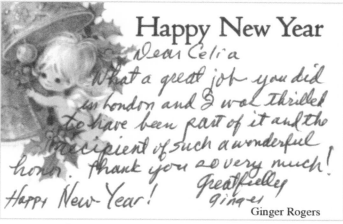

Happy New Year

Dear Celia
What a great job you did in London and I was thrilled to have been part of it and the recipient of such a wonderful honor. Thank you so very much!
Happy New Year!
Gratefully,
Ginger

Ginger Rogers

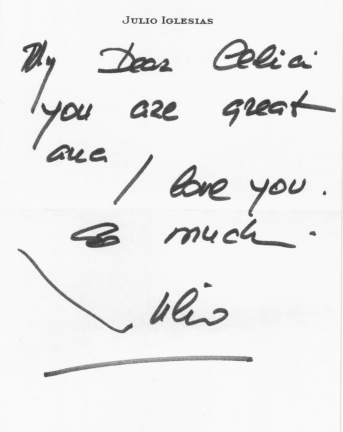

JULIO IGLESIAS

My Dear Celia you are great are / love you. So much.

Julio

Remembering Roddy McDowall who took this photo of me performing on stage

ACKNOWLEDGMENTS

Book Design
Molly Murphy, Red Letter Design Group, Lake Worth, Florida

Printing
Ellison Graphics, Jupiter, Florida

Photographs
Harry Benson
Bruno of Hollywood - Bruno Bernard
Lucien Capehart, Lucien Capehart Studios
Carrie Bradburn, Lucien Capehart Studios
Julia Hanna, Lucien Capehart Photography Studios Palm Beach
Davidoff Studios, Babe Davidoff, Bob Davidoff and The Davidoff Family
John Haynsworth
Mort and David Kaye, Mort Kaye Studios
Eston Mansfield
Keystone & Central Press
James Peltekian
Roger Karnbad
Roddy McDowall

Research, Composition, Editing, and Counsel
Martha Moody Rourke and her late husband, Jack Rourke
Publishers of "Seasons," Beverly Hills, California
Robert Smith, Smith's Peerage Limited
Michael Petry
Wendy Leigh
Harry Freedman
Bette Kester Conrad
Parker Ladd
Charles Mosley
Allison Leopold
Kyle Zimmer

Special Thanks
Gigi Benson
Richard Valvo
Shannon Donnelly, "Palm Beach Daily News"
James Jennings Sheeran, "Palm Beach Society"
Joanne Cutner, "Palm Beach Society"
Thom Smith, "Palm Beach Post"
Nora Bulnes, "Selecta Magazine"
Lise Kenny
Bert Morgan
Marianne Strong
Jack Owen
Laura Pike
Helen Fealy
Peter Wallace
Rise Jackson
Bert Sokol
Ivana Rubicondi
Maybell Lin - for her work for the Red Cross, countless charities and friendship
Jackie and Dick Cowell

Many thanks to my family
Cecile Victoria Farris (Ce Ce), Marian Farris, Stephanie, and all my grandchildren

My sincere apology if I have omitted anyone

INDEX

Here I am with the Marines coming full circle as The American Cancer Society established a National Lifetime Achievement Award in my name on February 8, 2008.

Photograph by Orlando Garcia

343